DUSK OF DAWN

Classics in Black Studies

DUSK OF DAWN

An Essay toward an Autobiography of a Race Concept

W.E. Burghardt Du Bois

With a New Introduction by
Irene Diggs

Transaction Publishers
New Brunswick (U.S.A.) and London (U.K.)

Acknowledgment is made to Harper & Brothers for permission to quote from "Heritage," one of the poems in Countee Cullen's volume, *Color*.

Fifth printing 1994
New material this edition copyright © 1984 by Transaction Publishers, New Brunswick, New Jersey 08903. Original material copyright © 1968 by Shirley Graham Du Bois, copyright © 1940 by Harcourt, Brace & World, Inc.

Library of Congress Catalog Number: 83-9142
ISBN: 0-87855-917-5 (paper)
Printed in the United States of America

Library of Congress Cataloging in Publication Data

Du Bois, W.E.B. (William Edward Burghardt), 1868-1963.
  Dusk of dawn.

  (Black classics of social science)
  Reprint. Originally published: Schocken Books, 1968.
  Includes index.
    1. Du Bois, W.E.B. (William Edward Burghardt),
  1868-1963. 2. Afro-Americans–Social conditions.
  3. United States–Race relations. 4. Afro-Americans–
  Biography. I. Title. II. Series.
  EL85.97.D73A323   1983   305.8'96073   83-9142
  ISBN 0-87855-917-5 (pbk.)

TO

KEEP THE MEMORY

OF

JOEL SPINGARN

SCHOLAR AND KNIGHT

INTRODUCTION TO THE
TRANSACTION EDITION

Irene Diggs

Du Bois dedicated books to "Nina for their Golden Wedding," to "Burghardt the Lost and Yolande the Found," to his granddaughter when she was six in the "Hope That Her Bright Eyes May One Day See Some of the Things I Dream," to Virginia Alexander whom he loved and admired, to a character of his own creation, and others. *Dusk of Dawn* is dedicated to "Keep the Memory of Joel Spingarn Scholar and Knight." Spingarn touched Du Bois "emotionally more closely" than any other White man; Du Bois was "both fascinated by his character and antagonized by some of his quick and positive judgments." Spingarn was "afraid that [he] was turning radical and dogmatic and even communistic"; Spingarn used "his power and influence in order to curb [his] acts and forestall any change of program of the Association" by Du Bois. It was at Joel Spingarn's home that the first Amenia Conference was held. Joel Spingarn was one of the speakers at the banquet honoring Du Bois's seventieth birthday. This occasion had a tremendous emotional effect upon Du Bois. He told me that he had felt he had been listening to his obituary. Afterwards he felt pressured by not having much more time to do all the things he had planned. He was aware

that biographies of him would be written, and he wished
to present his own point of view; to do so he worked
furiously on *Dusk of Dawn*.

An Essay toward an Autobiography of a Race Concept
should be read against the background of race in the
latter part of the nineteenth and first half of the twentieth centuries when throughout the dominant world,
race, color, or an ancestry of color was a badge of inferiority. This concept of race was arbitrarily defined,
bold, deep-seated, and sanctioned by science, law, religion, and public opinion. Science and distinguished scientists, with very few exceptions, supported the belief in
the intellectual, cultural, and biological inferiority of all
non-Whites. In the United States Blacks were imprisoned within the confines of segregation and discrimination where they lived, earned a living, died, and were
buried in segregated cemeteries. The theme of this
book, the history of the race concept, was the dominant
factor in Du Bois's life: race "guided, embittered, illuminated and enshrouded" his life and the lives of all
Blacks. If it had not been for racism, Du Bois probably
would have accepted the attitudes of his time and environment; he would have "been an unquestioning worshiper at the shrine of the social order and economic
development" into which he was born, including the belief that "poverty was the shadow of crime and connoted
lack of thrift and shiftlessness."

In the beginning of his fight against racism Du Bois
was provincial and narrow, thinking in terms of the relatively small group of Blacks in the United States and
not all non-Whites. At first he accused the ignorance of

the masses of men as the cause for racism. The solution was Truth: education, especially knowledge which was the result of scientific studies of Blacks using the scientific method which the intellectual world demanded and his education at Harvard and Berlin had emphasized. Later he was convinced that the problems of Blacks were not entirely due to ignorance but rather because of the determination of some Whites to discriminate and segregate, and that the actions of men not due to lack of knowledge or evil intent could be changed by influencing culture, behavior patterns, customs, and the enactment of laws. Gradually he was forced to recognize the obstacles, deliberately set by law and custom, which blocked him and thousands of others; that the rules of the game were determined by Whites. Education alone would not solve the problem: "The black world must fight for freedom. It must fight with the weapon of Truth, with the sword of the intrepid, uncompromising Spirit, with organization in boycott, propaganda and mob frenzy."

It was after Du Bois left Harvard, while at the University of Berlin, that he began to envision the race problem in the United States to include the problems of the peoples of Africa, Asia, the economics and politics of Europe. He began to see "clearly the connection of economics and politics; the fundamental influence of man's efforts to earn a living upon all his other efforts." He realized how the building of colonial empires "turned into the threat of armed competition for markets, cheap material and cheap labor." For him, economics and politics were inextricably intertwined; he perceived politics as dominant, but because most Blacks were workers and earners of wages he was fascinated by economics.

During Du Bois's lifetime there was a hierarchical arrangement of cultures and peoples into higher and lower strata: those with histories and those without. Blacks were thought of as one changeless mass; they were not considered as belonging to the homo sapiens species. As a mass they were considered incapable of modification through time or improvement in spite of "new" races constantly developing as a result of biological amalgamation and differentiation. The conviction was widespread that no person of African descent should or could become a functioning part of the mainstream of American life no matter what his capabilities were. But some Blacks were equals of Whites, some were superior to some Whites; some Blacks did get an education, live in good homes, make contributions to culture. Edward Byron Reuter, perhaps the best-known advocate of Blacks' achievements, argued in his *Mulatto in the United States* (1918) that these achievements were of those of mixed ancestry. Not only many Whites but some Blacks shared his opinion. Through the selecting, rewarding, and advancing of light-skinned rather than dark-skinned Blacks, the self-fulfilling prophecy made "mulatto superiority" appear valid. Others labeled it "mongrelization" and viewed those of mixed ancestry as inferior sterile hybrids, inferior to both Blacks and Whites, incapable of transmitting their individual characters.

Scientists sought to prove that Blacks were inferior by mortality and morbidity rates, by measuring liver size, lung capacity, brain weight, endocrine gland function, the cephalic index, respiration rate, speed of reflex action, and other physiological tests and measurements. The conclusions of these scientists reinforced the beliefs of the general White population and large numbers of Blacks. Were they not the conclusions of science? The long I.Q. road had a turn: in the army Alpha tests administered to thousands of inductees, White and Black, some southern Whites scored below some northern Blacks (and Whites).

After reasoning and observation without testing, others dressed their conclusions in medical, sociological, anthropological, and psychological clothing and helped rationalize the politics of segregation, disfranchisement, and other social policies. Howard Washington Odum published his *Social and Mental Traits of the Negro* in 1910, in which he blamed the Black family long before Daniel P. Moynihan's *The Negro Family* (1965). Sexual behavior among Blacks, it was generally argued during this period, was hopelessly unrestrained. To prove that Blacks were inferior, the age of science developed the theory of "consciousness of kind," that is, Whites had a natural antipathy toward Blacks. The instinct school of sociology, anthropology, and psychology concluded that Whites instinctively sought to have nothing to do with Blacks; that hatred of the different was inherited. Unimpressed by such catch phrases Du Bois determined to put science into sociology through scientific studies of Blacks, which resulted in the Atlanta University Publications. These widely used studies are regarded today as a historical point of departure.

The theory of the "survival of the fittest" was thought to provide a ray of hope; insurance actuaries and Frederick Ludwig Hoffman in his *Race Traits and Tendencies of the American Negro* (1896) authoritatively predicted the extinction of Blacks; disease and death would solve the race problem. The fact is that during Du Bois's life Blacks not only survived in one of the world's most competitive cultures but increased in number without the benefit of large immigration.

Characterics that were considered good traits for Whites, such as being cheerful, forgiving, happy, and content were indicators of inferiority when possessed by Blacks. Did they not smile, laugh, sing, and dance at all times? Regardless of treatment, would not a Black when shown the least kindness forget and forgive? In areas where Blacks were considered equal or superior, the equality and superiority were explained away, rationalized: Blacks excelled Whites only in those areas that really did not matter; they were good dancers but not classical or ballet; good singers and musicians but not classical or opera. Blacks were superior in rote memory, making rhymes; Whites were better in the aesthetic and abstract, in observation, reading, motor and emotional control, logical memory, use of words, resistance to suggestion.

During Du Bois's life what was assumed as true for Whites had to be proven beyond a shadow of doubt if it related to Blacks and other non-Whites. One had to insist without ceasing that Blacks were normal human beings. In the case of no other group of people was so narrow a description of physical characteristics applied: the spectacular made the universal; the exceptional—

the representative. A White might be of any color, size, or facial conformation and have an endless variety of cranial measurement and physical characteristics. The image of Blacks as a group, manufactured and but partly based on fact, was transferred to the individual Black whether or not that individual had the sup-posed-to-be-inherited characteristic.

During his ninety-five years, Du Bois witnessed the zenith of Reconstruction voting and office holding by Blacks and poor Whites in the South after the Civil War; the overthrow of Reconstruction; the driving of Blacks and poor Whites from power. During the nadir around the turn of the century, Blacks were strung up, riddled with bullets, shot down, starved, roasted alive. Schools and churches for Blacks were burned; land was often stolen from Blacks after having been paid for more than once; sharecropping cheated Blacks; stringent laws were enacted segregating Blacks and Whites from the cradle to the grave. The defense of Black women in law and custom against the aggression of White men or the aggression of White women against Black men was dif-ficult. During much of Du Bois's life, Blacks were to a large extent without civil and political rights as well as judicial self-defense. The most ignorant, the most prej-udiced often performed jury duties; wide discretion as to punishment was in the hands of juries and petty offi-cials; peonage and debt slavery were common methods of securing cheap labor. Punishment involving the con-vict lease system was more often a technique for en-hancing city and state revenues rather than the rehabil-itation of offenders.

During Du Bois's lifetime the United States Supreme

Court turned its back on the enforcement of the Fourteenth and Fifteenth Amendments. The 1896 Decision
of *Plessy vs. Ferguson* established the validity of separate but equal which Du Bois characterized as a legal
caste system based on race and color openly grafted on
the Constitution of the United States. Blacks, especially
in the South, were oppressed so hard at times that there
were those who were willing to migrate or to be half
men with half a loaf. It became increasingly difficult for
Du Bois to remain detached and calm. He lived during
"years of cosmic significance" and turbulent times in a
culture of which he was "integrally a part" but one of the
"rejected parts." The problem of race was "the central
problem of the greatest of the world's democracies and
so the Problem of the future world." Du Bois's life was a
mirror of the problem of race as it existed from 1868 to
1940.

Du Bois was born in 1868 in Great Barrington, Massachusetts, the son of parents who were poor but without the culture of poverty. In less than a year after he
finished high school in 1884 at the age of sixteen, he was
an orphan, living with his aunt, responsible for his own
welfare. He assumed very early that most people, later
most Americans, were not interested in knowing him
personally; that it was best to protect one's self from as
much pain and as many hurts as possible for one's "own
peace and quiet." To earn all his spending change and
supplement the family income, he did various chores
after school and on Saturdays—sold newspapers, distributed tea, was local correspondent of the *Springfield
Republican*. Aware of his potential, his high-school prin-

cipal suggested that he take the college preparatory course and the mother of one of his playmates purchased the necessary books. He worked for a year as a timekeeper before going to Fisk University. In the fall of 1885 he entered Fisk University in Nashville on a scholarship provided by four Connecticut churches. He was glad to go there and his love of and interest in Fisk never wavered, but he considered Fisk as a short detour on his way to Harvard. While at Fisk he spent his summers teaching in the rural districts of Tennessee.

During the summer, after graduation from Fisk, he was business manager of the Fisk Glee Club at a resort on Lake Minnetonka, Minnesota, where he also worked as a bus boy. He made few tips because he was unwilling to learn and practice the necessary servility and had difficulty getting enough to eat because the servants were not systematically fed but expected to forage in devious ways for food. He became "critical of religion and resentful of its practice . . . first by the heresy trials, particularly the one which expelled Briggs from the Presbyterian Church"; and later because of the "insistence by the local church at Fisk University that dancing was a sin."

Throughout his life his concern and interest was the problem of race: how non-Whites might be openly and effectively admitted into the freedom of democracy. Seldom in his long life did he write on any subject without indicating its significance to Blacks. His high school oration was on Wendell Phillips, the antislavery agitator. His speech at Fisk was on Bismarck, which to him indicated "the kind of thing that American Negroes must do, marching forth with strength and determination under trained leadership." His Harvard commencement speech was originally titled "Jefferson Davis and the African." Between 1888 and 1894 he attended Harvard University and the University of Berlin. His *Suppression of the Slave-Trade* is the first volume of the Harvard Historical Studies, published in 1896. While at the University of Berlin he wrote a paper on American agriculture. Du Bois was happy at Harvard when he accepted racial segregation. He was rejected when he attempted to join student organizations; he was very active in the Black communities of Boston and its environs. As a member of a group of Black students, Aristophanes' *The Birds* was presented in a Black church.

While being a teacher from 1894 to 1910, he was struggling to find a way of applying science to the problems of race and color. The results were *The Philadelphia Negro* (1899) and the series of Atlanta University Publications. When *The Souls of Black Folk* with its chapter "Of Booker T. Washington and Others" appeared in 1903, Du Bois's future career was fairly well determined. His presence at Atlanta University interfered with its support and the support of the Atlanta University Publications which received unusual recognition from the scientific world and were used in America, Europe, Asia, and Africa for information on Blacks. With all their imperfections these publications were widely distributed in the libraries of the world and used by scholars. Between 1896 and 1920 there was no study made of the race problem in America which did not depend in some degree upon the investigations made at Atlanta University; the series was widely quoted and commended. Atlanta University was the only institution in the world carrying on a systematic study of Blacks and publishing the results in a form available for scholars. In addition, articles by Du Bois appeared in the major journals of the day.

Because of the reception of the Publications series it was difficult for Du Bois to convince himself that his program for solving the problem of race and color by scientific investigation was not working. But when scholarly research failed to budge the prejudices of White Americans, when Du Bois became convinced that the difficulties of Blacks were not due "to ignorance but rather difficulties due to the determination of certain people to suppress and mistreat the darker race"; "that this evil group formed a minority and a small minority of the nation and of all civilized peoples," he stepped down from his "ivory tower of statistics and investigation." For some time he had been convinced that a critical periodical was necessary, and together with others had published *The Moon*, beginning in 1906, and the *Horizon*, from 1907 to 1910. When the National Association for the Advancement of Colored People was formed in 1909, he readily accepted the position of director of publications and research and the opportunity to edit a magazine. When he arrived in New York he found his office bare and the treasurer, Oswald Garrison Villard, told him frankly, "I don't know who is going to pay your salary; I have no money." Undaunted he considered his first job was to get *The Crisis* started and allay the fears of "a generally critical, if not hostile, public," who feared he would launch a frontal attack on Booker T. Washington. In 1910 to discuss the race

problem was to discuss Washington. The first issue of
The Crisis appeared in November 1910. From time to
time Du Bois did attack the theories of Washington but
he did not attack Washington's work at Tuskegee. Few
Blacks would agree today with much of what Washington advocated; perhaps most of them would agree with
most of what Du Bois pleaded and struggled for.

Du Bois lived in what he called "The White World," a
world in which he was not an American, a world in
which he "was not a man," in which he was by "daily reminder, a colored man in a white world; and that white
world often existed primarily, so far as [he] was concerned, to see with sleepless vigilance that [he] was kept
within bounds." He felt he "could not stir, [he] could not
act, [he] could not live, without taking into careful daily
account the reaction of [his] white environing world." A
minority of Whites not only subordinated the majority
of Whites but sought the subordination of all non-
Whites. This was what the struggle was all about; this
was what democracy, socialism, communism were all
about: how to bring about individual equality. Du Bois's
impact on this White minority was extraordinary.

Du Bois's cultural and economic solutions to the
problem of race and color maintained that "the progress
of the White world" should "cease to rest upon the poverty and the ignorance of its own proletariat and of the
colored world"; the minority should "listen to the complaint of those human beings today who are suffering
most from white attitudes, from white habits, from the
conscious and unconscious wrongs which white folk are
today inflicting on their victims."

"The Colored World Within" was also a part of Du

Bois's environment. With understanding of the reasons Du Bois recognized the fact that the mass of non-Whites in Asia, Africa, North and South America, and the islands of the seas "are in the mass ignorant, diseased, and inefficient; that the governments which they have evolved, even allowing for the interested interference of the white world, have seldom reached the degree of efficiency of modern European governments"; but he was quick to add "there is no reason to doubt, that whatever white folk have accomplished, black, brown and yellow folk might have done possibly in differing ways with different results." The reaction of the educated, ambitious, and financially better off of any group to the condition of the masses is the same: "None have more pitilessly castigated Jews than the Jewish prophets, ancient and modern. It is the Irish themselves who rail at 'dirty Irish tricks.' Nothing could exceed the self-abasement of the Germans during *Sturm und Drang.*" Self-criticism by Blacks is no different. The culture of the upper-class White is often considered typical of all Whites while Blacks are usually considered "as one undifferentiated low-class mass" and the culture of the lowest-class Black is considered typical of all Blacks. Neither Blacks nor Whites are a homogeneous group.

Du Bois joined the New York Local No. 1 of the Socialist Party in 1911 and resigned in 1912 in order to avoid discipline for not voting the Socialist ticket because he supported Woodrow Wilson. Many of his statements may be interpreted as socialist statements, especially statements having to do with Black and White laborers but specifically when discussing Blacks as an exploited class of cheap laborers. Fortunately in various of his writings, specifically in his 1 October 1961 application for admission to membership, Du Bois gives the history of his decision to join the Communist Party of the United States.

That Du Bois was in agreement with the aims of socialism and communism there can be no doubt: "Capitalism cannot reform itself; it is doomed to self-destruction. No universal selfishness can bring social good to all." "Communism—the effort to give all men what they need and to ask of each the best they can contribute—this is the only way of human life. It is a difficult and hard end to reach—it has and will make mistakes, but today it marches triumphantly on in education and science, in home and food, with increased freedom of thought and deliverance from dogma. In the end communism will triumph. I want to help to bring that day." He listed the aims of socialism and communism many times and added: "These aims are not crimes. They are practiced increasingly over the world. No nation can call itself free which does not allow its citizens to work for these ends."

Du Bois's enthusiasm for the USSR and communism did not always extend to American Communists whom he described as "young jackasses" who mouthed Marxist clichés without understanding American conditions. The judgment was reciprocated: the Communists labeled Du Bois an imperialist follower of Booker T. Washington, a "betrayer of the Negro people" and a spokesman for "Negro bourgeois reformism." In an article in the *Journal of Negro Education* (5, January 1936) Du Bois writes: "I must, nevertheless, ask myself seriously; how far can American Negroes forward this eventual end? ... that eventually land, machines, and materials must belong to the state; that private profit must be abolished; that the system of exploiting labor must disappear; that people who work must have essentially equal income; and that in their hands the political rulership of the state must eventually rest. . . ." He continues: "My answer has long been clear. There is no automatic power in socialism to override and suppress race prejudice. . . . One of the worst things that Negroes could do today [1936] would be to join the American Communist Party or any of its many branches."

Of Norman Thomas, Du Bois wrote: "The Socialist, as represented by Norman Thomas... invites the Negro as a worker to vote for the Socialist Party as the party of the workers. He offers the Negro no panacea for prejudice and caste but assumes that the uplift of the white worker will automatically emancipate the yellow, brown and black" (*Crisis* 38, September 1931: 313). "The American Socialist party is out to emancipate the white worker and if this does not automatically free the colored man, he can continue in slavery. The only time that so fine a man and so logical a reasoner as Norman Thomas becomes vague and incoherent is when he touches the black man, and consequently he touches him as seldom as possible."

It was and still is the shame of sociologists then and now that Du Bois is not only not given the recognition he deserves as a sociologist but recognition as the pioneer scientific sociologist. True, he spent most of his sociological career at Atlanta University, in the South, away from those institutions where sociology was becoming recognized. True also, the distinguished University of Pennsylvania recognized him to the extent of hiring him as an assistant instructor in sociology in 1896, where he not only made his monumental sociological study *The Philadelphia Negro* but presented in public session in 1897 before the American Academy of Political and Social Sciences, affiliated with the University of Pennsylvania, a broad program of systematic and continuous sociological study of Blacks, "The Study of the Negro Problems," and appealed to Harvard, Columbia, and Pennsylvania to help. The same racism that motivated the University of Pennsylvania to hire Du Bois—one of the best educated men of his day—as an assistant instructor whose name never appeared in the catalogue; an instructor who never instructed nor came in contact with other instructors, explains the attitude of early sociologists toward Du Bois. The University of Pennsylvania hired Du Bois because they were convinced that he was the best prepared to "prove" by facts and figures their theory that the city of Philadelphia was going to the dogs because of the crime and venality of Blacks centered in the slum at the lower end of the Seventh Ward.

It is not difficult to explain and understand why Du Bois never joined the American Sociological Society although he joined the American Association for the Advancement of Science in 1900 and was made a Fellow in 1904. One has only to remember he could not stay in the hotels where they were meeting, attend their luncheons and banquets, and when they met in the South, he could not even enter their meetings through the front door.

Not to publish in journals of sociology was not voluntary then for Du Bois nor is it for Blacks now. Try and get an article by a Black person published in any professional journal today. It is still difficult, if not impossible, for Blacks to get published unless their point of view is compatible with that of Whites—and often not even then.

Du Bois may not have built a "Du Bois School," but the Black intelligentsia were in his camp versus Booker T. Washington's, and he was mentor for most Black sociologists, historians, artists, poets, musicians, etc. of his day. Du Bois critically examined the most sacred tenets of the White world. For this reason he has been deliberately ignored by American scholarship. By any standard Du Bois's contributions rate him high even when his errors are taken into consideration. Of course he made errors, serious errors; but his achievements far outweigh the errors.

Maybe I have forgotten his shortcomings or at least minimized them, but even so I feel I have a right to articulate a personal remembrance: When belief in the inherent inferiority of Blacks was rampant and segregation and discrimination were the order of the day, he was fearlessly outspoken. From 1910 to 1930 he "was a main factor in revolutionizing the attitude of the American Negro toward caste." His "stinging hammer blows made Negroes aware of themselves, confident of their possibilities and determined in self-assertion. So much so that today common slogans among Black people are taken bodily from the words of "his mouth." He had absolute confidence in the future of Blacks; there was never a doubt in any of his writings. Hope may be Du Bois's most valuable legacy to Blacks. Hope, without the slightest doubt, at a time when he had every reason and right to be utterly hopeless. When Blacks were afraid to say they believed in social equality, which in the minds of many was equated with "mixing of the races," he wrote articles on intermarriage. Under his leadership many rallied for civil rights, social justice, human dignity. His dedication and confidence in the outcome of the struggle inspired thousands here and around the world. His determination strengthened women and men everywhere. His first strategy—information based on scientific investigation—was based on the belief that the behavior of the enemy was based on ignorance. When that solution did not work he proposed other plans and programs.

When in the latter years of his life he advocated what he designated as *changes in emphases* and others label *contradictions and paradoxes*, these did not represent a sudden break from his former solutions but rather place special stress on what he had advocated all his life. He remained convinced of the soundness of his judgment in the "Close Ranks" article. He did not abandon his theories of the "talented tenth" and the "submerged tenth." He was certain of the ultimate triumph of his emphases in later life; that his economic plans of action would "permit the full development of the capacities and aspirations of blacks"; that his economic plans were fundamental; that self-imposed segregation would work for instead of against Blacks. Self-segregation would "obtain admission of the colored group to cooperation and incorporation into the White group on the best possible terms"; that by using the planned and deliberate self-segregation technique Blacks could be industrially emancipated; that Blacks would approach economic equality much more nearly as an organized consumer than as a producer. Complete economic segregation was not possible so he advocated segregation sufficient to "wield so much power that its influence upon the total economy of Negroes and the total industrial organization of the United States would be decisive for the great ends toward which the Negro moves." Were he living today, Du Bois would have probably offered a program for the future that would rekindle hope that peoples everywhere would turn from the horrors of war and live together in peace.

The history of race in the United States is a history of sustained and violent catastrophe for Blacks. The road has been long and winding for non-Whites in their continuing confrontation with prejudice and segregation not only in the United States but around the world. Most of the problems faced by Blacks continue in greater or lesser degree. Many of Du Bois's analyses and interpretations of the attitudes and demands of non-Whites are as meaningful now as then. His statements, resolutions, credos, and appeals, his political and economic programs are basic documents for the definitive history of the civil rights movement.

Du Bois possessed an inner strength, uncurbed by fear, which served him well as a haven of survival under crippling conditions of life in an exasperating and destructive environment. His inner world helped contain

the outer. His tireless quest of ideals; his struggle to free
Black folk in the United States and the non-White peoples of the world in order that they might function
normally and effectively everywhere as men and
women; his historical insight, his *Autobiography of a Race
Concept* are still meaningful as guides along the path to
that "inevitable and logical democracy" for which he
struggled a lifetime. Ardently he believed that, "Surely
there shall yet dawn some mighty morning to lift the
Veil and set the prisoned free. Not for me,—I shall die
in my bonds." And he did on the Eve of the March on
Washington, 11:40 p.m., 27 August 1963, Ghana time.

CONTENTS

APOLOGY

I HAVE essayed in a half century three sets of thought centering around the hurts and hesitancies that hem the black man in America. The first of these, "The Souls of Black Folk," written thirty-seven years ago, was a cry at midnight thick within the veil, when none rightly knew the coming day. The second, "Darkwater," now twenty years old, was an exposition and militant challenge, defiant with dogged hope. This the third book started to record dimly but consciously that subtle sense of coming day which one feels of early mornings even when mist and murk hang low. But midway in its writing, it changed its object and pattern, because of the revelation of a seventieth birthday and the unawaited remarks and comments thereon. It threatened thereupon to become mere autobiography. But in my own experience, autobiographies have had little lure; repeatedly they assume too much or too little: too much in dreaming that one's own life has greatly influenced the world; too little in the reticences, repressions and distortions which come because men do not dare to be absolutely frank. My life had its significance and its only deep significance because it was part of a Problem; but that problem was, as I continue to think, the central problem of the greatest of the world's democracies and so the Problem of the future world. The problem of the future world is the charting, by means of intelligent reason, of a path not simply through the resistances of physical force, but through the vaster and far more intricate jungle of ideas conditioned on unconscious and subconscious reflexes of living things; on blind unreason and often irresistible urges of sensitive matter; of which the concept of race is today one of the most unyielding and threatening. I seem to see a way of elucidating the inner meaning and significance of that race problem by explaining it in terms of the one human life that I know best.

I have written then what is meant to be not so much my autobiography as the autobiography of a concept of race, elucidated, magnified and doubtless distorted in the thoughts and deeds which were mine. If the first two books were written in tears and blood, this is set down no less determinedly but yet with wider hope in some more benign fluid. Wherefore I have not hesitated in calling it "Dusk of Dawn."

DUSK OF DAWN

CHAPTER 1. THE PLOT

FROM 1868 to 1940 stretch seventy-two mighty years, which are incidentally the years of my own life but more especially years of cosmic significance, when one remembers that they rush from the American Civil War to the reign of the second Roosevelt; from Victoria to the Sixth George; from the Franco-Prussian to the two World Wars. They contain the rise and fall of the Hohenzollerns, the shadowy emergence, magnificence and miracle of Russia; the turmoil of Asia in China, India and Japan, and the world-wide domination of white Europe.

In the folds of this European civilization I was born and shall die, imprisoned, conditioned, depressed, exalted and inspired. Integrally a part of it and yet, much more significant, one of its rejected parts; one who expressed in life and action and made vocal to many, a single whirlpool of social entanglement and inner psychological paradox, which always seem to me more significant for the meaning of the world today than other similar and related problems.

Little indeed did I do, or could I conceivably have done, to make this problem or to loose it. Crucified on the vast wheel of time, I flew round and round with the Zeitgeist, waving my pen and lifting faint voices to ex-

3

plain, expound and exhort; to see, foresee and prophesy, to the few who could or would listen. Thus very evidently to me and to others I did little to create my day or greatly change it; but I did exemplify it and thus for all time my life is significant for all lives of men.

What now was this particular social problem which, through the chances of birth and existence, became so peculiarly mine? At bottom and in essence it was as old as human life. Yet in its revelation, through the nineteenth century, it was significantly and fatally new: the differences between men; differences in their appearance, in their physique, in their thoughts and customs; differences so great and so impelling that always from the beginning of time, they thrust themselves forward upon the consciousness of all living things. Culture among human beings came to be and had to be built upon knowledge and recognition of these differences.

But after the scientific method had been conceived in the seventeenth century it came toward the end of the eighteenth century to be applied to man and to man as he appeared then, with no wide or intensive inquiry into what he had been or how he had lived in the past. In the nineteenth century however came the revolution of conceiving the world not as permanent structure but as changing growth and then the study of man as changing and developing physical and social entity had to begin.

But the mind clung desperately to the idea that basic racial differences between human beings had suffered no change; and it clung to this idea not simply from inertia and unconscious action but from the fact that because of the modern African slave trade a tremendous economic structure and eventually an industrial revolution had been based upon racial differences between men; and this racial difference had now been rationalized into a difference mainly of skin color. Thus in the latter part of the nineteenth century when I was born and grew to manhood, color had become an abiding unchangeable fact chiefly because a mass of self-conscious instincts and unconscious prejudices had arranged themselves rank on rank in its defense. Government, work, religion and education became based upon and determined by the color line. The future of mankind was implicit in the race and color of men.

Already in my boyhood this matter of color loomed significantly. My skin was darker than that of my schoolmates. My family confined itself not entirely but largely to people of this same darker hue. Even when in fact the color was lighter, this was an unimportant variation from the norm. As I grew older, and saw the peoples of the land and of the world, the problem changed from a simple thing of color, to a broader, deeper matter of social condition: to millions of folk born of dark slaves, with the slave heritage in mind and home; millions of people spawned in compulsory ignorance; to a whole problem of the uplift of the lowly who formed the darker races.

This social condition pictured itself gradually in my mind as a matter of education, as a matter of knowledge; as a matter of scientific procedure in a world which had become scientific in concept. Later, however, all this frame of concept became blurred and distorted. There was evidently evil and hindrance blocking the way of life. Not science alone could settle this matter, but force must come to its aid. The black world must fight for freedom. It must fight with the weapons of Truth, with the sword of the intrepid, uncompromising Spirit, with organization in boycott, propaganda and mob frenzy. Upon this state of mind after a few years of conspicuous progress fell the horror of World War—of ultimate agitation, propaganda and murder.

The lesson of fighting was unforgettable; it was eternal loss and cost in victory or defeat. And again my problem of human difference, of the color line, of social degradation, of the fight for freedom became transformed. First and natural to the emergence of colder and more mature manhood from hot youth, I saw that the color bar could not be broken by a series of brilliant immediate assaults. Secondly, I saw defending this bar not simply ignorance and ill will; these to be sure; but also certain more powerful motives less open to reason or appeal. There were economic motives, urges to build wealth on the backs of black slaves and colored serfs; there followed those unconscious acts and irrational reactions, unpierced by reason, whose current form depended on the long history of relation and contact between thought and idea. In this case not sudden assault but long siege was indicated; careful planning and subtle campaign with the education of growing generations and propaganda.

For all this, time was needed to move the resistance in vast areas of unreason and especially in the minds of men where conscious present motive had been built on false rationalization. Meantime the immediate problem of the Negro was the question of securing existence, of labor and income, of food and home, of spiritual independence and democratic control of the industrial process. It would not do to concenter all effort on economic well-being and forget freedom and manhood and equality. Rather Negroes must live and eat and strive, and still hold unfaltering commerce with the stars.

Finally, I could see that the scientific task of the twentieth century would be to explore and measure the scope of chance and unreason in human action, which does not yield to argument but changes slowly and with difficulty after long study and careful development.

My intent in this book is to set forth the interaction of this stream and change of my thought, on my work and in relation to what has been going on in the world since my birth. Not so much its causal relation, for that in sheer limitation of opportunity was small; but rather of its intellectual relations, of its psychological interactions, and of the consequent results of these for me and many millions, who with me have had their lives shaped and directed by this course of events.

CHAPTER 2. A NEW ENGLAND
BOY AND RECONSTRUCTION

AS I have written elsewhere, "I was born by a golden river and in the shadow of two great hills." My birthplace was Great Barrington, a little town in western Massachusetts in the valley of the Housatonic, flanked by the Berkshire hills. Physically and socially our community belonged to the Dutch valley of the Hudson rather than to Puritan New England, and travel went south to New York more often and more easily than east to Boston. But my birthplace was less important than my birth-time. The Civil War had closed but three years earlier and 1868 was the year in which the freedmen of the South were enfranchised and for the first time as a mass took part in government. Conventions with black delegates voted new constitutions all over the South; and two groups of laborers —freed slaves and poor whites—dominated the former slave states. It was an extraordinary experiment in democracy. Thaddeus Stevens, the clearest-headed leader of this attempt at industrial democracy, made his last speech impeaching Andrew Johnson on February sixteenth and on February twenty-third I was born.

Less than a month after my birth Andrew Johnson passed from the scene and Ulysses Grant became President of the United States. The Fifteenth Amendment en-

8

franchising the Negro as a race became law and the work of abolishing slavery and making Negroes men was accomplished, so far as law could do it. Meanwhile elsewhere in the world there were stirring and change which were to mean much in my life: in Japan the Meiji Emperors rose to power the year I was born; in China the intrepid Empress Dowager was fighting strangulation by England and France; Prussia had fought with Austria and France, and the German Empire arose in 1871. In England, Victoria opened her eighth parliament; the duel of Disraeli and Gladstone began; while in Africa came the Abyssinian expedition and opening of the Suez Canal, so fateful for all my people.

My town was shut in by its mountains and provincialism; but it was a beautiful place, a little New England town nestled shyly in its valley with something of Dutch cleanliness and English reticence. The Housatonic yellowed by the paper mills, rolled slowly through its center; while Green River, clear and beautiful, joined in to the south. Main Street was lined with ancient elms; the hills held white pines and orchards and then faded up to magnificent rocks and caves which shut out the neighboring world. The people were mainly of English descent with much Dutch blood and with a large migration of Irish and German workers to the mills as laborers.

The social classes of the town were built partly on landholding farmers and more especially on manufacturers and merchants, whose prosperity was due in no little degree to the new and high tariff. The rich people of the town were not very rich nor many in number. The middle class were farmers, merchants and artisans; and beneath these was a small proletariat of Irish and German mill workers. They lived in slums near the woolen mills and across the river clustering about the Catholic Church. The number of colored people in the town and county was small. They were all, save directly after the war, old families, well-known to the old settlers among the whites. The color line was manifest and yet not absolutely drawn. I remember a cousin of mine who brought home a white wife. The chief objection was that he was not able to support her and nobody knew about her family; and knowledge of family history was counted as highly important. Most of the colored people had some white blood from unions several generations past. That they congregated together in their own social life was natural because that was the rule in the town: there were little social knots of people, but not much that today would be called social life, save that which centered about the churches; and there the colored folk often took part. My grandmother was Episcopalian and my mother, Congregational. I grew up in the Congregational Sunday school.

In Great Barrington there were perhaps twenty-five, certainly not more than fifty, colored folk in a population of five thousand. My family was among the oldest inhabitants of the valley. The family had spread slowly through the county intermarrying among cousins and other black folk with some but limited infiltration of white blood. Other dark families had come in and there was some intermingling with local Indians. In one or two cases there were groups of apparently later black immigrants, near Sheffield for instance. There survives there even to this day an isolated group of black folk whose origin is obscure.

We knew little of them but felt above them because of our education and economic status.

The economic status was not high. The early members of the family supported themselves on little farms of a few acres; then drifted to town as laborers and servants, but did not go into the mills. Most of them rented homes, but some owned little homes and pieces of land; a few had very pleasant and well-furnished homes, but none had anything like wealth.

My immediate family, which I remember as a young child, consisted of a very dark grandfather, Othello Burghardt, sitting beside the fireplace in a high chair, because of an injured hip. He was good-natured but not energetic. The energy was in my grandmother, Sally, a thin, tall, yellow and hawk-faced woman, certainly beautiful in her youth, and efficient and managing in her age. My mother, Mary Sylvina, was born at Great Barrington, January 14, 1831, and died there in 1885 at the age of fifty-four years. She had at the age of thirty a son, Idelbert, born of her and her cousin, John Burghardt. The circumstances of this romance I never knew. No one talked of it in the family. Perhaps there was an actual marriage. If so, it was not recorded in the family Bible. Perhaps the mating was broken up on account of the consanguinity of the cousins by a family tradition which had a New England strictness in its sex morals. So far as I ever knew there was only one illegitimate child throughout the family in my grandfather's and the two succeeding generations. My mother was brown and rather small with smooth skin and lovely eyes, and hair that curled and crinkled down each side her forehead from the part in the middle. She was rather

silent but very determined and very patient. My father, a
light mulatto, died in my infancy so that I do not remember him. I shall later speak more intimately of him.

I was born in a rather nice little cottage which belonged to a black South Carolinian, whose own house
stood next, at the lower end of one of the pleasant streets
of the town. Then for a time I lived in the country at
the house of my grandfather, Othello, one of three farming brothers. It was sturdy, small and old-fashioned.
Later we moved back to town and lived in quarters over
the woodshed of one of the town's better mansions. After
that we lived awhile over a store by the railway and
during my high school years in a little four-room tenement
house on the same street where I was born, but farther
up, down a lane and in the rear of a home owned by the
widow of a New York physician. None of these homes
had modern conveniences but they were weatherproof,
fairly warm in winter and furnished with some comfort.

For several generations my people had attended schools
for longer or shorter periods so most of them could read
and write. I was brought up from earliest years with the
idea of regular attendance at school. This was partly because the schools of Great Barrington were near at hand,
simple but good, well-taught, and truant laws were enforced. I started on one school ground, which I remember
vividly, at the age of five or six years, and continued there
in school until I was graduated from high school at sixteen. I was seldom absent or tardy, and the school ran
regularly ten months in the year with a few vacations. The
curriculum was simple: reading, writing, spelling and
arithmetic; grammar, geography and history. We learned

the alphabet; we were drilled rigorously on the multiplication tables and we drew accurate maps. We could spell correctly and read clearly.

By the time I neared the high school, economic problems and questions of the future began to loom. These were partly settled by my own activities. My mother was then a widow with limited resources of income through boarding the barber, my uncle; supplemented infrequently by day's work, and by some kindly but unobtrusive charity. But I was keen and eager to eke out this income by various jobs: splitting kindling, mowing lawns, doing chores. My first regular wage began as I entered the high school: I went early of mornings and filled with coal one or two of the new so-called "base-burning" stoves in the millinery shop of Madame L'Hommedieu. From then on, all through my high school course, I worked after school and on Saturdays; I sold papers, distributed tea from the new A & P stores in New York; and for a few months, through the good will of Johnny Morgan, actually rose to be local correspondent of the *Springfield Republican*.

Meantime the town and its surroundings were a boy's paradise: there were mountains to climb and rivers to wade and swim; lakes to freeze and hills for coasting. There were orchards and caves and wide green fields; and all of it was apparently property of the children of the town. My earlier contacts with playmates and other human beings were normal and pleasant. Sometimes there was a dearth of available playmates but that was peculiar to the conventions of the town where families were small and children must go to bed early and not loaf on the streets or congregate in miscellaneous crowds. Later, in the high school, there came some rather puzzling distinctions which I can see now were social and racial; but the racial angle was more clearly defined against the Irish than against me. It was a matter of income and ancestry more than color. I have written elsewhere of the case of exchanging visiting cards where one girl, a stranger, did not seem to want mine to my vast surprise.

I presume I was saved evidences of a good deal of actual discrimination by my own keen sensitiveness. My companions did not have a chance to refuse me invitations; they must seek me out and urge me to come as indeed they often did. When my presence was not wanted they had only to refrain from asking. But in the ordinary social affairs of the village—the Sunday school with its picnics and festivals; the temporary skating rink in the town hall; the coasting in crowds on all the hills—in all these, I took part with no thought of discrimination on the part of my fellows, for that I would have been the first to notice.

Later, I was protected in part by the fact that there was little social activity in the high school; there were no fraternities; there were no school dances; there were no honor societies. Whatever of racial feeling gradually crept into my life, its effect upon me in these earlier days was rather one of exaltation and high disdain. They were the losers who did not ardently court me and not I, which seemed to be proven by the fact that I had no difficulty in outdoing them in nearly all competition, especially intellectual. In athletics I was not outstanding. I was only moderately good at baseball and football; but at running, exploring, story-telling and planning of intricate games, I was often if not always the leader. This made discrimination all the more difficult.

When, however, during my high school course the matter of my future career began to loom, there were difficulties. The colored population of the town had been increased a little by "contrabands," who on the whole were well received by the colored group; although the older group held some of its social distinctions and the newcomers astonished us by forming a little Negro Methodist Zion Church, which we sometimes attended. The work open to colored folk was limited. There was day labor; there was farming; there was house-service, particularly work in summer hotels; but for a young, educated and ambitious colored man, what were the possibilities? And the practical answer to this inquiry was: Why encourage a young colored man toward such higher training? I imagine this matter was discussed considerably among my friends, white and black, and in a way it was settled partially before I realized it.

My high school principal was Frank Hosmer, afterward president of Oahu College, Hawaii. He suggested, quite as a matter of fact, that I ought to take the college preparatory course which involved algebra, geometry, Latin and Greek. If Hosmer had been another sort of man, with definite ideas as to a Negro's "place," and had recommended agricultural "science" or domestic economy, I would doubtless have followed his advice, had such "courses" been available. I did not then realize that Hosmer was quietly opening college doors to me, for in those days they were barred with ancient tongues. This meant a considerable expenditure for books which were not free in those days—more than my folk could afford; but the wife of one of the mill-owners, or rather I ought to describe her as the mother of one of my playmates, after some hesitation offered to furnish all the necessary school books. I became therefore a high school student preparing for college and thus occupying an unusual position in the town even among whites, although there had been one or two other colored boys in the past who had gotten at least part of a high school education. In this way I was thrown with the upper rather than the lower social classes and protected in many ways. I came in touch with rich folk, summer boarders, who made yearly incursions from New York. Their beautiful clothes impressed me tremendously but otherwise I found them quite ordinary. The children did not have much sense or training; they were not very strong and rather too well dressed to have a good time playing.

I had little contact with crime and degradation. The slums in the town were not bad and repelled me, partly because they were inhabited by the foreign-born. There was one house among colored folk, where I now realize there must have been a good deal of gambling, drinking and other looseness. The inmates were pleasant to me but I was never asked to enter and of course had no desire. In the whole town, colored and white, there was not much crime. The one excess was drunkenness and there my mother quietly took a firm stand. I was never to enter a liquor saloon. I never did. I donned a Murphy "blue ribbon." And yet perhaps, as I now see, the one solace that this pleasant but spiritually rather drab little town had against the monotony of life was liquor; and rich and poor got drunk more or less regularly. I have seen one of the mill owners staggering home, and my very respectable uncle used to come home now and then walking exceedingly straight.

I was born in a community which conceived itself as having helped put down a wicked rebellion for the purpose of freeing four million slaves. All respectable people belonged to the Republican Party, but Democrats were tolerated, although regarded with some surprise and hint of motive. Most of the older men had been soldiers, including members of my own family. The town approached in politics a pure democracy with annual town meeting and elections of well-known and fairly qualified officials. We were placidly religious. The bulk of the well-to-do people belonged to the Episcopal and Congregational churches, a small number of farmers and artisans to the Methodist Church and the Irish workers to the Catholic Church across the river. The marriage laws and family relations were fairly firm. The chief delinquency was drunkenness and the major social problem of the better classes was the status of women who had little or no opportunity to marry.

My ideas of property and work during my boyhood were vague. They did not present themselves to me as problems. As a family we owned little property and our income was always small. Spending money for me came first as small gifts of pennies or a nickel from relatives; once I received a silver dollar, a huge fortune. Later I earned all my spending funds. I can see now that my mother must have struggled pretty desperately on very

narrow resources and that the problem of shoes and
clothes for me must have been at times staggering. But
these matters seldom bothered me because they were not
brought to my attention. My general attitude toward
property and income was that all who were willing to
work could easily earn a living; that those who had property had earned it and deserved it and could use it as they
wished; that poverty was the shadow of crime and connoted lack of thrift and shiftlessness. These were the current patterns of economic thought of the town in my
boyhood.

In Great Barrington the first glimpse of the outer and
wider world I got, was through Johnny Morgan's news
shop which occupied the front end of the post office.
There newspapers and books were on display and I remember very early seeing pictures of "U. S." Grant, and
of "Bill" Tweed who was beginning his extraordinary
career in New York City; and later I saw pictures of
Hayes and of the smooth and rather cruel face of Tilden.
Of the great things happening in the United States at that
time, we were actually touched only by the Panic of 1873.
When my uncle came home from a little town east of us
where he was the leading barber, he brought me, I remember, a silver dollar which was an extraordinary thing: up
to that time I had seen nothing but paper money. I was
six when Charles Sumner died and the Freedmen's Bank
closed; and when I was eight there came the revolution
of 1876 in the South, and Victoria of England became
Empress of India; but I did not know the meaning of
these events until long after.

In general thought and conduct I became quite thor-

oughly New England. It was not good form in Great
Barrington to express one's thought volubly, or to give
way to excessive emotion. We were even sparing in our
daily greetings. I am quite sure that in a less restrained
and conventional atmosphere I should have easily learned
to express my emotions with far greater and more unrestrained intensity; but as it was I had the social heritage
not only of a New England clan but Dutch taciturnity.
This was later reinforced and strengthened by inner with-
drawals in the face of real and imagined discriminations.
The result was that I was early thrown in upon myself. I
found it difficult and even unnecessary to approach other
people and by that same token my own inner life perhaps
grew the richer; but the habit of repression often returned
to plague me in after years, for so early a habit could not
easily be unlearned. The Negroes in the South, when I
came to know them, could never understand why I did
not naturally greet everyone I passed on the street or
slap my friends on the back.

During my high school career I had a chance for the
first time to step beyond the shadow of the hills which
hemmed in my little valley. My father's father was living
in New Bedford and his third wife who had greatly loved
my own father wanted my grandfather to know and recognize me. The grandfather, a short thick-set man, "colored"
but quite white in appearance, with austere face, was hard
and set in his ways, proud and bitter. My father and
grandfather had not been able to get along together. Of
them, I shall speak more intimately later. I went to New
Bedford in 1883 at the age of fifteen. On the way I saw
Hartford and Providence. I called on my uncle in Amherst

and received a new navy-blue suit. Grandfather was a
gentleman in manner, precise and formal. He looked at
me coolly, but in the end he was not unpleasant. I went
down across the water to Martha's Vineyard and saw
what was then "Cottage City" and came home by way of
Springfield and Albany where I was a guest of my older
half-brother and saw my first electric street light blink
and sputter.

I was graduated from high school in 1884 and was of
course the only colored student. Once during my course
another young dark man had attended the school for a
short time but I was very much ashamed of him because
he did not excel the whites as I was quite used to doing.
All thirteen of us had orations and mine was on "Wendell
Phillips." The great anti-slavery agitator had just died in
February and I presume that some of my teachers must
have suggested the subject, although it is quite possible
that I chose it myself. But I was fascinated by his life
and his work and took a long step toward a wider conception of what I was going to do. I spoke in June and
then came face to face with the problem of my future life.

My mother lived proudly to see me graduate but died
in the fall and I went to live with an aunt. I was strongly
advised that I was too young to enter college. Williams
had been suggested, because most of our few high school
graduates who went to college had attended there; but
my heart was set on Harvard. It was the greatest and
oldest college and I therefore quite naturally thought it
was the one I must attend. Of course I did not realize
the difficulties: some difficulties in entrance examinations
because our high school was not quite up to the Harvard

standard; but a major difficulty of money. There must have been in my family and among my friends a good deal of anxious discussion as to my future but finally it was temporarily postponed when I was offered a job and promised that the next fall I should begin my college work.

The job brought me in unexpected touch with the world. There had been a great-uncle of mine, Tom Burghardt, whose tombstone I had seen often in the town graveyard. My family used to say in undertones that the money of Tom Burghardt helped to build the Pacific Railroad and that this came about in this wise: nearly all his life Tom Burghardt had been a servant in the Kellogg family, only the family usually forgot to pay him; but finally they did give him a handsome burial. Then Mark Hopkins, a son or relative of the great Mark, appeared on the scene and married a daughter of the Kelloggs. He became one of the Huntington-Stanford-Crocker Pacific Associates who built, manipulated and cornered the Pacific railroads and with the help of the Kellogg nest-egg, Hopkins made nineteen million dollars in the West by methods not to be inquired into. His widow came back to Great Barrington in the eighties and planned a mansion out of the beautiful blue granite which formed our hills. A host of workmen, masons, stone-cutters and carpenters were assembled, and in the summer of 1884 I was made time-keeper for the contractors who carried on this job. I received the fabulous wage of a dollar a day. It was a most interesting experience and had new and intriguing bits of reality and romance. As time-keeper and the obviously young and inexperienced agent of superiors, I was the one who handed the discharged workers their last wage envelopes. I talked with contractors and saw the problems of employers. I pored over the plans and specifications and even came in contact with the elegant English architect Searles who finally came to direct the work.

The widow had a steward, a fine, young educated colored fellow who had come to be her right-hand man; but the architect supplanted him. He had the glamour of an English gentleman. The steward was gradually pushed aside and down into his place. The architect eventually married the widow and her wealth and the steward killed himself. So the Hopkins millions passed strangely into foreign hands and gave me my first problem of inheritance. But in the meantime the fabrication and growth of this marvelous palace, beautiful beyond anything that Great Barrington had seen, went slowly and majestically on, and always I could sit and watch it grow.

Finally in the fall of 1885, the difficulty of my future education was solved. The whole subtlety of the plan was clear neither to me nor my relatives at the time. Merely I was offered through the Reverend C. C. Painter, once excellent Federal Indian Agent, a scholarship to attend Fisk University in Nashville, Tennessee; the funds were to be furnished by four Connecticut churches which Mr. Painter had formerly pastored. Disappointed though I was at not being able to go to Harvard, I merely regarded this as a temporary change of plan; I would of course go to Harvard in the end. But here and immediately was adventure. I was going into the South; the South of slavery, rebellion and black folk; and above all I was going to meet colored people of my own age and education, of my own ambitions. Once or twice already I had had swift glimpses of the colored world: at Rocky Point on Narragansett Bay, I had attended an annual picnic beside the sea, and had seen in open-mouthed astonishment the whole gorgeous color gamut of the American Negro world; the swaggering men, the beautiful girls, the laughter and gaiety, the unhampered self-expression. I was astonished and inspired. I became aware, once a chance to go to a group of such young people was opened up for me, of the spiritual isolation in which I was living. I heard too in these days for the first time the Negro folk songs. A Hampton Quartet had sung them in the Congregational Church. I was thrilled and moved to tears and seemed to recognize something inherently and deeply my own. I was glad to go to Fisk.

On the other hand my people had undoubtedly a more discriminating and unromantic view of the situation. They said frankly that it was a shame to send me South. I was Northern born and bred and instead of preparing me for work and giving me an opportunity right there in my own town and state, they were bundling me off to the South. This was undoubtedly true. The educated young white folk of Great Barrington became clerks in stores, bookkeepers and teachers, while a few went into professions. Great Barrington was not able to conceive of me in such local position. It was not so much that they were opposed to it, but it did not occur to them as a possibility.

On the other hand there was the call of the black South; teachers were needed. The crusade of the New England schoolmarm was in full swing. The freed slaves, if properly led, had a great future. Temporarily deprived of their full voting privileges, this was but a passing set-back. Black folk were bound in time to dominate the South. They needed trained leadership. I was sent to help furnish it.

I started out and went into Tennessee at the age of seventeen to be a sophomore at Fisk University. It was to me an extraordinary experience. I was thrilled to be for the first time among so many people of my own color or rather of such various and such extraordinary colors, which I had only glimpsed before, but who it seemed were bound to me by new and exciting and eternal ties. Never before had I seen young men so self-assured and who gave themselves such airs, and colored men at that; and above all for the first time I saw beautiful girls. At my home among my white school mates there were a few pretty girls; but either they were not entrancing or because I had known them all my life I did not notice them; but at Fisk at the first dinner I saw opposite me a girl of whom I have often said, no human being could possibly have been as beautiful as she seemed to my young eyes that far-off September night of 1885.

CHAPTER 3. EDUCATION
IN THE LAST DECADES
OF THE NINETEENTH CENTURY

TODAY both youth and age look upon a world whose foundations seem to be tottering. They are not sure what the morrow will bring; perhaps the complete overthrow of European civilization, of that great enveloping mass of culture into which they were born. Everything in their environment is a meet subject for criticism. They can dispassionately evaluate the past and speculate upon the future. It is a day of fundamental change. On the other hand when I was a young man, so far as I conceived, the foundations of present culture were laid, the way was charted, the progress toward certain great goals was undoubted and inevitable. There was room for argument concerning details and methods and possible detours in the onsweep of civilization; but the fundamental facts were clear, unquestioned and unquestionable.

Between the years 1885 and 1894 I received my education at Fisk University, Harvard College and the University of Berlin. It was difficult for me at the time to form any critical estimate of any meaning of the world which differed from the conventional unanimity about me. Apparently one consideration alone saved me from complete conformity with the thoughts and confusions of then current social trends; and that was the problems

of racial and cultural contacts. Otherwise I might easily
have been simply the current product of my day. Even
as it was, the struggle for which I was preparing and the
situations which I was trying to conceive and study, related themselves primarily to the plight of the comparatively small group of American Negroes with which I was
identified, and theoretically to the larger Negro race. I did
not face the general plight and conditions of all humankind. That I took for granted, and in the unanimity of
thought and development of that day, this was scarcely
to be wondered at.

It was a day of Progress with a capital P. Population
in all the culture lands was increasing, doubling and
more; cities everywhere were growing and expanding and
making themselves the centers and almost the only centers
of civilization; transportation by land and sea was drawing
the nations near and making the lands of the earth increasingly accessible. Invention and technique were a per-
petual marvel and their accomplishment infinite in possibility; commerce was madly seeking markets all around
the earth; colonies were being seized and countries integrated in Asia, Africa, South America and the islands.

Above all science was becoming religion; psychology
was reducing metaphysics to experiment and a sociology
of human action was planned. Fighting the vast concept
of evolution, religion went into its heresy trials, its
struggle with "higher criticism," its discomfort at the
"revised version" of the New Testament which was published the year I entered college. Wealth was God. Everywhere men sought wealth and especially in America there
was extravagant living; everywhere the poor planned to

be rich and the rich planned to be richer; everywhere wider, bigger, higher, better things were set down as inevitable.

All this, of course, dominated education; especially the economic order determined what the next generation should learn and know. On the whole, looking at the marvelous industrial expansion of America, seeing the rise of the western farmer and the wages of the eastern mechanic, all was well; or if not, if there were ominous protests and upheavals, these were but the friction necessary to all advance. "God's in His heaven; All's right with the world," Browning was singing—that colored Robert Browning, who died just after I received my first bachelor's degree.

Had it not been for the race problem early thrust upon me and enveloping me, I should have probably been an unquestioning worshiper at the shrine of the social order and economic development into which I was born. But just that part of that order which seemed to most of my fellows nearest perfection, seemed to me most inequitable and wrong; and starting from that critique, I gradually, as the years went by, found other things to question in my environment. At first, however, my criticism was confined to the relation of my people to the world movement. I was not questioning the world movement in itself. What the white world was doing, its goals and ideals, I had not doubted were quite right. What was wrong was that I and people like me and thousands of others who might have my ability and aspiration, were refused permission to be a part of this world. It was as though moving on a rushing express, my main thought

was as to the relations I had to other passengers on the
express, and not to its rate of speed and its destination.
In the day of my formal education, my interest was con-
centered upon the race struggle. The fight on the moving
car had to do with my relations to the car and its folk;
but on the whole, nothing to do with the car's own movement. My attention from the first was focused on democracy and democratic development and upon the problem
of the admission of my people into the freedom of democracy. This my school training touched but obliquely. We
studied history and politics almost exclusively from the
point of view of ancient German freedom, English and
New England democracy, and the development of the
United States.

Here, however, I could bring criticism from what I
knew and saw touching the Negro. I was brought up in
the primary democracy of a New England village. I attended the town meeting every spring and in the upper
room in that little red brick town hall, fronted by a
Roman "Victory" commemorating the Civil War, I listened
to the citizens discuss things about which I knew and had
opinions: streets and bridges and schools, and particularly
the high school. Baretown Beebee, a dirty, ragged old
hermit, used regularly to come down from his rocks and
woods and denounce high school education and expense.
Regularly the responsible citizens of the town sat and
listened and then quietly voted the usual appropriation.
That one recurring incident was a splendid part of my
education.

The rest of my early political knowledge came largely
from newspapers which I read outside my curriculum. I

read of the contests of the Democratic and Republican parties, from the first seating of Hayes, through the administrations of Garfield and Arthur, Cleveland, Harrison, Cleveland again, and McKinley in 1895. All this complied with the conventional theory of party government, and while the issues were not as clear cut and the motives as unmixed as they ought to have been, nevertheless the increasing triumph of democratic government was in my mind unquestioned. The Populists as a third party movement beginning during this time, did not impress me.

The year before I entered college, England killed the arbitrary power of the Justice of the Peace and the County Squire, doubled the number of its voters and was forced into a struggle to yield Ireland home rule; eventually Japan attempted a constitution with elective representatives; Brazil became a republic while I was at Harvard, and during that time France fought successfully to curtail the political power of the Catholic Church.

My problem then was how, into the inevitable and logical democracy which was spreading over the world, could black folk in America and particularly in the South be openly and effectively admitted; and the colored people of the world allowed their own self-government? I therefore watched, outside my textbooks and without reference to my teachers, the race developments throughout the world. The difficulty here, however, was securing any real and exhaustive knowledge of facts. I could not get any clear picture of the current change in Africa and Asia.

Lynching was a continuing and recurrent horror during my college days: from 1885 through 1894, seventeen hundred Negroes were lynched in America. Each death was a scar upon my soul, and led me on to conceive the plight of other minority groups; for in my college days Italians were lynched in New Orleans, forcing the Federal government to pay $25,000 in indemnity, and the anti-Chinese riots in the West culminated in the Chinese Exclusion Act of 1892. Some echoes of Jewish segregation and pogroms in Russia came through the magazines; I followed the Dreyfus case; and I began to see something of the struggle between East and West in the Sino-Japanese War.

The three years at Fisk were years of growth and development. I learned new things about the world. My knowledge of the race problem became more definite. I saw discrimination in ways of which I had never dreamed; the separation of passengers on the railways of the South was just beginning; the race separation in living quarters throughout the cities and towns was manifest; the public disdain and even insult in race contact on the street continually took my breath; I came in contact for the first time with a sort of violence that I had never realized in New England; I remember going down and looking wide-eyed at the door of a public building, filled with buck-shot, where the editor of the leading daily paper had been publicly murdered the day before. I was astonished to find many of my fellow students carrying fire-arms and to hear their stories of adventure. On the other hand my personal contact with my teachers was inspiring and beneficial as indeed I suppose all personal contacts between human beings must be. Adam Spence of Fisk first taught me to know what the Greek language meant. In a funny little basement room crowded with apparatus,

Frederick Chase gave me insight into natural science and talked with me about future study. I knew the President, Erastus Cravath, to be honest and sincere.

I determined to know something of the Negro in the country districts; to go out and teach during the summer vacation. I was not compelled to do this, for my scholarship was sufficient to support me, but that was not the point. I had heard about the country in the South as the real seat of slavery. I wanted to know it. I walked out into east Tennessee ten or more miles a day until at last in a little valley near Alexandria I found a place where there had been a Negro public school only once since the Civil War; and there for two successive terms during the summer I taught at $28 and $30 a month. It was an enthralling experience. I met new and intricate and unconscious discrimination. I was pleasantly surprised when the white school superintendent, on whom I had made a business call, invited me to stay for dinner; and he would have been astonished if he had dreamed that I expected to eat at the table with him and not after he was through. All the appointments of my school were primitive: a windowless log cabin; hastily manufactured benches; no blackboard; almost no books; long, long distances to walk. And on the other hand, I heard the sorrow songs sung with primitive beauty and grandeur. I saw the hard, ugly drudgery of country life and the writhing of landless, ignorant peasants. I saw the race problem at nearly its lowest terms.

At Fisk I began my writing and public speaking. I edited the *Fisk Herald*. I became an impassioned orator and developed a belligerent attitude toward the color

bar. I was determined to make a scientific conquest of
my environment, which would render the emancipation
of the Negro race easier and quicker. The persistence
which I had learned in New England stood me now in
good stead. Because my first college choice had been
Harvard, to Harvard I was still resolved to go. When I
heard that Harvard, seeking to shed something of its New
England provincialism, was offering scholarships in various parts of the country, I immediately wrote, and to the
astonishment of teachers and fellow students, not to mention myself, received Price Greenlead Aid of $300.

I was graduated from Fisk in 1888 and took as my subject "Bismarck." This choice in itself showed the abyss between my education and the truth in the world. Bismarck
was my hero. He had made a nation out of a mass of
bickering peoples. He had dominated the whole development with his strength until he crowned an emperor at
Versailles. This foreshadowed in my mind the kind of
thing that American Negroes must do, marching forth
with strength and determination under trained leadership.
On the other hand, I did not understand at all, nor had
my history courses led me to understand, anything of
current European intrigue, of the expansion of European
power into Africa, of the Industrial Revolution built on
slave trade and now turning into Colonial Imperialism;
of the fierce rivalry among white nations for controlling
the profits from colonial raw material and labor—of all
this I had no clear conception. I was blithely European
and imperialist in outlook; democratic as democracy was
conceived in America.

So far my formal education had touched politics and

religion, but on the whole had avoided economics. At Fisk a very definite attempt was made to see that we did not lose or question our Christian orthodoxy. At first the effort seemed to me entirely superfluous, since I had never questioned my religious upbringing. Its theory had presented no particular difficulties: God ruled the world, Christ loved it, and men did right, or tried to; otherwise they were rightly punished. But the book on "Christian Evidences" which we were compelled to read, affronted my logic. It was to my mind, then and since, a cheap piece of special pleading. Our course in general philosophy under the serious and entirely lovable president was different. It opened vistas. It made me determine to go further in this probing for truth. Eventually it landed me squarely in the arms of William James of Harvard, for which God be praised.

I became critical of religion and resentful of its practice for two reasons: first the heresy trials, particularly the one which expelled Briggs from the Presbyterian Church; and especially the insistence of the local church at Fisk University that dancing was a "sin." I was astonished to find that anybody could possibly think this; as a boy I had attended with my mother little parlor dances; as a youth at Fisk I danced gaily and happily. I was reminded by a smug old hypocrite of the horrible effects my example might have even if my own conscience was clear. I searched my soul with the Pauline text: "If meat maketh my brother to offend," etc. I have never had much respect for Paul since.

After graduation, the members of the Fisk Glee Club went to Lake Minnetonka, a resort in Minnesota, for the summer of 1888, with the idea of working in the dining room and giving concerts. I was to act as their business manager. During college I had developed rather as the executive and planner, the natural secretary of affairs rather than ornamental president and chairman. The only difficulty about the Minnesota excursion was that I had never worked in a hotel in my life; I could not wait on table and therefore became one of the bus boys. It was so unusual a pageant to watch the dining room that I made no tips and for a long time had difficulty in getting enough to eat, not realizing that in that day servants in great hotels were not systematically fed but foraged for food in devious ways. I saw the Americans, rich and near-rich, at play; it was not inspiring. The servility necessary for the successful waiter I could not or would not learn. After the season, I went on ahead and succeeded in making engagements for a respectable number of concerts for the students who followed me down all the way to Chicago; while I went on to Harvard to enter the junior class.

I was happy at Harvard, but for unusual reasons. One of these unusual circumstances was my acceptance of racial segregation. Had I gone from Great Barrington high school directly to Harvard I would have sought companionship with my white fellows and been disappointed and embittered by a discovery of social limitations to which I had not been used. But I came by way of Fisk and the South and there I had accepted and embraced eagerly the companionship of those of my own color. It was, of course, no final end. Eventually with them and in mass assault, led by culture, we were going to break down the boundaries of race; but at present we were banded together in a great crusade and happily so. Indeed, I suspect that the joy of full human intercourse without reservations and annoying distinctions, made me all too willing to consort with mine own and to disdain and forget as far as was possible that outer, whiter world.

Naturally it could not be entirely forgotten, so that now and then I plunged into it, joined its currents and rose or fell with it. The joining was sometimes a matter of social contact. I escorted colored girls, and as pretty ones as I could find, to the vesper exercises and the class day and commencement social functions. Naturally we attracted attention and sometimes the shadow of insult as when in one case a lady seemed determined to mistake me for a waiter. A few times I attempted to enter student organizations, but was not greatly disappointed when the expected refusals came. My voice, for instance, was better than the average. The glee club listened to it but I was not chosen a member. It posed the later recurring problem of a "nigger" on the team.

In general, I asked nothing of Harvard but the tutelage of teachers and the freedom of the library. I was quite voluntarily and willingly outside its social life. I knew nothing of and cared nothing for fraternities and clubs. Most of those which dominated the Harvard life of my day were unknown to me even by name. I asked no fellowship of my fellow students. I found friends and most interesting and inspiring friends among the colored folk of Boston and surrounding places. With them I carried on lively social intercourse, but one which involved little expenditure of money. I called at their homes and ate at their tables. We danced at private parties. We went on excursions down the Bay. Once, with a group of colored students gathered from surrounding institutions, we gave Aristophanes' "The Birds" in a colored church.

So that of the general social intercourse on the campus I consciously missed nothing. Some white students made themselves known to me and a few, a very few, became life-long friends. Most of them, even of my own more than three hundred classmates, I knew neither by sight nor name. Among my Harvard classmates many made their mark in life: Norman Hapgood, Robert Herrick, Herbert Croly, George A. Dorsey, Homer Folks, Augustus Hand, James Brown Scott, and others. I knew practically none of these. For the most part I do not doubt that I was voted a somewhat selfish and self-centered "grind" with a chip on my shoulder and a sharp tongue.

Something of a certain inferiority complex was possibly present: I was desperately afraid of not being wanted; of intruding without invitation; of appearing to desire the company of those who had no desire for me. I should have been pleased if most of my fellow students had desired to associate with me; if I had been popular and envied. But the absence of this made me neither unhappy nor morose. I had my "island within" and it was a fair country.

Only once or twice did I come to the surface of college life. First, by careful calculation, I found that I needed the cash of one of the Boylston prizes to piece out my year's expenses. I got it through winning a second oratorical prize. The occasion was noteworthy by the fact that the first prize went to a black classmate of mine, Clement Morgan. He and I became fast friends and spent a summer giving readings along the North Shore to help our college costs. Later Morgan became the center of a revolt within the college. By unwritten rule, all of the honorary offices of the class went to Bostonians of Back Bay. No Westerner, Southerner, Jew, nor Irishman, much less a Negro, had thought of aspiring to the honor of being class day official. But in 1890, after the oratorical contest, the students of the class staged an unexpected revolt and elected Morgan as class orator. There was national surprise and discussion and later several smaller Northern colleges elected colored class orators.

This cutting of myself off from my fellows did not mean unhappiness nor resentment. I was in my early young manhood, unusually full of high spirits and humor. I thoroughly enjoyed life. I was conscious of understanding and power, and conceited enough still to think, as in high school, that they who did not know me were the losers, not I. On the other hand, I do not think that my classmates found in me anything personally objectionable. I was clean, not well-dressed but decently clothed. Manners I regarded as more or less superfluous and deliberately cultivated a certain brusquerie. Personal adornment I regarded as pleasing but not important. I was in Harvard but not of it and realized all the irony of "Fair Harvard." I sang it because I liked the music.

The Harvard of 1888 was an extraordinary aggregation of great men. Not often since that day have so many distinguished teachers been together in one place and at one time in America. There were William James, the psychologist; Palmer in ethics; Royce and Santayana in philosophy; Shaler in geology and Hart in history. There were Francis Child, Charles Eliot Norton, Justin Winsor, and John

Trowbridge; Goodwin, Taussig and Kittredge. The president was the cold, precise but exceedingly just and efficient Charles William Eliot, while Oliver Wendell Holmes and James Russell Lowell were still alive and emeriti.

By good fortune, I was thrown into direct contact with many of these men. I was repeatedly a guest in the house of William James; he was my friend and guide to clear thinking; I was a member of the Philosophical Club and talked with Royce and Palmer; I sat in an upper room and read Kant's Critique with Santayana; Shaler invited a Southerner, who objected to sitting by me, out of his class; I became one of Hart's favorite pupils and was afterwards guided by him through my graduate course and started on my work in Germany.

It was a great opportunity for a young man and a young American Negro, and I realized it. I formed habits of work rather different from those of most of the other students. I burned no midnight oil. I did my studying in the daytime and had my day parceled out almost to the minute. I spent a great deal of time in the library and did my assignments with thoroughness and with prevision of the kind of work I wanted to do later. I have before me a theme which I wrote October 3, 1890, for Barrett Wendell, then the great pundit of Harvard English. I said: "Spurred by my circumstances, I have always been given to systematically planning my future, not indeed without many mistakes and frequent alterations, but always with what I now conceive to have been a strangely early and deep appreciation of the fact that to live is a serious thing. I determined while in the high school to go to college—partly because other men went, partly because

I foresaw that such discipline would best fit me for life.
. . . I believe foolishly perhaps, but sincerely, that I have
something to say to the world, and I have taken English 12
in order to say it well." Barrett Wendell rather liked that
last sentence. He read it out to the class.

It was at Harvard that my education, turning from
philosophy, centered in history and then gradually in economics and social problems. Today my course of study
would have been called sociology; but in that day Harvard
did not recognize any such science. I had taken in high
school and at Fisk the old classical course with Latin and
Greek, philosophy and some history. At Harvard I started
in with philosophy and then turned toward United States
history and social problems. The turning was due to
William James. He said to me, "If you must study philosophy you will; but if you can turn aside into something
else, do so. It is hard to earn a living with philosophy."

So I turned toward history and social science. But there
the way was difficult. Harvard had in the social sciences
no such leadership of thought and breadth of learning as
in philosophy, literature, and physical science. She was
then groping and is still groping toward a scientific treatment of human action. She was facing at the end of the
century a tremendous economic era. In the United States,
finance was succeeding in monopolizing transportation,
and raw materials like sugar, coal and oil. The power of
the trust and combine was so great that the Sherman Act
was passed in 1890. On the other hand, the tariff at the
demand of manufacturers continued to rise in height from
the McKinley to the indefensible Wilson tariff of 1894. A
financial crisis shook the land in 1893 and popular discon-

tent showed itself in the Populist movement and Coxey's Army. The whole question of the burden of taxation began to be discussed and England barred an income tax in 1894.

These things we discussed with some clearness and factual understanding at Harvard. The tendency was toward English free trade and against the American tariff policy. We reverenced Ricardo and wasted long hours on the "Wages-fund." The trusts and monopolies were viewed frankly as dangerous enemies of democracies, but at the same time as inevitable methods of industry. We were strong for the gold standard and fearful of silver. On the other hand, the attitude of Harvard toward labor was on the whole contemptuous and condemnatory. Strikes like that of the anarchists in Chicago, the railway strikes of 1886; the terrible Homestead strike of 1892 and Coxey's Army of 1894 were pictured as ignorant lawlessness, lurching against conditions largely inevitable. Karl Marx was hardly mentioned and Henry George given but tolerant notice. The anarchists of Spain, the Nihilists of Russia, the British miners—all these were viewed not as part of the political development and the tremendous economic organization but as sporadic evil. This was natural. Harvard was the child of its era. The intellectual freedom and flowering of the late eighteenth and early nineteenth centuries were yielding to the deadening economic pressure which made Harvard rich but reactionary. This defender of wealth and capital, already half ashamed of Sumner and Phillips, was willing finally to replace an Eliot with a Lowell. The social community that mobbed Garrison, easily hanged Sacco and Vanzetti.

It was not until I was long out of college and had finished the first phase of my teaching career that I began to see clearly the connection of economics and politics; the fundamental influence of man's efforts to earn a living upon all his other efforts. The politics which we studied in college were conventional, especially when it came to describing and elucidating the current scene in Europe. The Queen's Jubilee in June, 1887, while I was still at Fisk, set the pattern of our thinking. The little old woman of Windsor became a magnificent symbol of Empire. Here was England with her flag draped around the world, ruling more black folk than white and leading the colored peoples of the earth to Christian baptism, civilization and eventual self-rule. Only two years before, in 1885, Stanley, the traveling reporter, became a hero and symbol of white world leadership in Africa. The wild, fierce fight of the Mahdi and the driving of the English out of the Sudan for sixteen years did not reveal its inner truth to me. I heard only of the martyrdom of the drunken Bible-reader and freebooter, Gordon.

The Congo Free State was established and the Berlin Conference of 1885 was reported to be an act of civilization against the slave trade and liquor. French, English and Germans pushed on in Africa, but I did not question the interpretation which pictured this as the advance of civilization and the benevolent tutelage of barbarians. I read of the confirmation of the Triple Alliance in 1891. Later I saw the celebration of the renewed Triple Alliance on the Tempelhofer Feld, with the new young Emperor Wilhelm II, who, fresh from his dismissal of Bismarck, led the splendid pageantry; and finally the year

I left Germany, Nicholas II became Czar of all the Russias. In all this I had not yet linked the political development of Europe with the race problem in America.

In 1890, I took my bachelor's degree from Harvard and was one of the six commencement speakers, taking as my subject "Jefferson Davis." This was a better subject than Bismarck for Davis was no hero of mine; yet the New York *Nation* said, July 3, 1890, that I handled my subject "with absolute good taste, great moderation, and almost contemptuous fairness." I was graduated just at the beginning of the term of President Harrison, when the trusts were dominating industry and the McKinley tariff making that domination easier. The understanding between the Industrial North and the New South was being perfected and in 1890 the series of disfranchising laws began to be enacted by the Southern states destined in the next sixteen years to make voting by Southern Negroes practically impossible.

Already I had received more education than most young white men, having been almost continuously in school from the age of six to the age of twenty-two. But I did not yet feel prepared. I felt that to cope with the new and extraordinary situations then developing in the United States and the world, I needed to go further and that as a matter of fact I had just well begun my training in knowledge of social conditions. On the other hand, I had no resources in wealth nor friends. I applied for a fellowship in the graduate school of Harvard and was appointed Henry Bromsfield Rogers fellow for a year and later the appointment was renewed; so that from 1890 to 1892 I was a fellow in Harvard University, studying in history and political science and what would have been sociology if Harvard had yet recognized such a field. I worked on my thesis, "The Suppression of the Slave Trade," taking my master's degree in 1891 and hoping to get my doctor's degree in another two years.

Then came one of these tricks of fortune which always seem partly due to chance: in 1882, the Slater Fund for the education of Negroes had been established and the board in 1890 was headed by ex-President R. B. Hayes. President Hayes went down to Johns Hopkins University and talked frankly about the plans of the fund. The *Boston Herald* of November 2, 1890, quoted him as saying: "If there is any young colored man in the South whom we find to have a talent for art or literature or any special aptitude for study, we are willing to give him money from the education funds to send him to Europe or give him an advanced education." He added that so far they had been able to find only "orators." This seemed to me a nasty fling at my black classmate, Morgan, who had been Harvard class orator a few months earlier, and indirectly at me.

The Hayes statement was brought to my attention at a card party one evening; it not only made me good and angry but inspired me to write President Hayes and ask for a scholarship. I received a pleasant reply saying that the newspaper quotation was incorrect; that his board had had some such program in the past but had no present plans for such scholarships. I proceeded to collect letters from every person I knew in the Harvard Yard and places outside, and literally deluged the unfortunate chairman of the Slater Fund, intimating that his change of plan did not seem to me fair or honest. He wrote again in

apologetic mood and said that he was sorry the plan had
been given up; that he recognized that I was a candidate
who might otherwise have been given attention.

I sat down and wrote Mr. Hayes a letter that could
be described as nothing less than impudent and flatly
accused him of bad faith. He was undoubtedly stirred. He
apologized again, re-asserted his good faith, and further
promised to take up the matter the next year with the
board. Thereupon, the next year I proceeded to write the
board: "At the close of the last academic year at Harvard,
I received the degree of Master of Arts, and was re-
appointed to my fellowship for the year 1891-92. I have
spent most of the year in the preparation of my doctor's
thesis on the suppression of the slave trade in America.
I prepared a preliminary paper on this subject and read
it before the American Historical Association at its annual
meeting at Washington during the Christmas holidays.
. . . Properly to finish my education, careful training in
an European university for at least a year is, in my mind
and the minds of my professors, absolutely indispensable."
I thereupon asked respectfully "aid to study at least a
year abroad under the direction of the graduate department of Harvard or other reputable auspices" and if this
was not practicable, "that the board loan me a sufficient
sum for this purpose." I did not of course believe that
this would get me an appointment, but I did think that
possibly through the influence of people who thus came
to know about my work, I might somehow borrow or beg
enough to get to Europe. To my surprise, I was given a
fellowship of seven hundred and fifty dollars, half grant
and half repayable loan, to study abroad; with the promise

that it might possibly be renewed for a second year. I remember rushing down to New York and talking with President Hayes in the old Astor House, and then going out walking on air. I saw an especially delectable shirt in a shop window. I went in and asked about it. It cost three dollars, which was about four times as much as I had ever paid for a shirt in my life; but I bought it.

I sailed in the summer of 1892 on a Dutch boat, the old "Amsterdam," landing in Holland. I wrote gaily, "Holland is an extremely neat and well-ordered mud-puddle, situated at the confluence of the English, French, and German languages." My first memory of it is inextricably interwoven with the smell of clover and the sight of black and white cows.

Europe modified profoundly my outlook on life and my thought and feeling toward it, even though I was there but two short years with my contacts limited and my friends few. But something of the possible beauty and elegance of life permeated my soul; I gained a respect for manners. I had been before, above all, in a hurry. I wanted a world, hard, smooth and swift, and had no time for rounded corners and ornament, for unhurried thought and slow contemplation. Now at times I sat still. I came to know Beethoven's symphonies and Wagner's Ring. I looked long at the colors of Rembrandt and Titian. I saw in arch and stone and steeple the history and striving of men and also their taste and expression. Form, color, and words took new combinations and meanings.

My introduction to Europe had some characteristic incidents. In my journey up the Rhine I found myself with a Dutch family: a lady, two daughters about my own age or a little younger, and a girl of ten or twelve. They were white and I therefore avoided them; when they strolled to one end of the deck I strolled to the other; but at last they approached and introduced themselves. They spoke both English and German, and I ended by having a delightful trip and by feeling more at home with cultured white folk than I had before in my life. This experience was continued when I spent a summer with Oberpfarrer Dr. Marbach in Eisenach. There were other boarders, German, French, and English, boys and girls; we had a delightful time. There was only one false note, when an American husband and wife from the West came, and were so alarmed about my social relations with German girls that they solemnly warned the Marbach family against racial intermarriage. The warning was quite unnecessary. I had already told the daughter, Dora, with whom I was most frequently coupled, that it would not be fair to marry her and bring her to America. She said she would come "gleich!" but I assured her that she would not be happy; and besides, I had work to do.

In the fall I went up to Berlin and registered in the university. In groups of one hundred we went into a large room with a high ceiling ornamented with busts of Berlin's famous professors. The year's Rector Magnificus was the widely famous Rudolf Virchow. He was a meek and calm little man, white-haired and white-bearded, with kindly face and pleasant voice. I had again at Berlin as at Harvard unusual opportunity. Although a foreigner, I was admitted my first semester to two seminars under Schmoller and Wagner, both of them at the time the most distinguished men in their line; I received eventually from both of them pleasant testimony on my work. That work was in economics, history, and sociology. I sat under the voice of the fire-eating Pan-German, von Treitschke; I heard Sering and Weber; I wrote on American agriculture for Schmoller and discussed social conditions in Europe with teachers and students. Under these teachers and in this social setting, I began to see the race problem in America, the problem of the peoples of Africa and Asia, and the political development of Europe as one. I began to unite my economics and politics; but I still assumed that in these groups of activities and forces, the political realm was dominant.

But more especially, I traveled; living cheaply, I saved good sums for the numerous vacations. I went to the Hansa cities; I made the celebrated Harzreise up to the Brocken in the spring. One Christmas vacation I spent in making a trip through south Germany along with a German-American and an Englishman. We visited Weimar, Frankfort, Heidelberg and Mannheim. Over Christmas Day and New Year's we stopped in a little German "Dorf" in the Rheinpfalz, where I had an excellent opportunity to study the peasant life closely and compare it with country life in the South. We visited perhaps twenty different families, talked, ate and drank with them; listened to their gossip, attended their assemblies, etc. We then went to Strassburg, Stuttgart, Ulm, München, Nürnberg, Prague and Dresden. In those places we stayed from one to five days following our Baedekers closely and paying much attention to the München and Dresden art galleries. The whole trip cost about eighty dollars. Later I went down to Italy; to Genoa, Rome and Naples, and over to Venice

and Vienna and Budapest; up to Krakau, where the father
of a fellow-student was the head of a Polish library. From
this friend, Stanislaus von Estreicher, I learned of the race
problems of the Poles. Then by Breslau I came back to
Berlin. In 1940, von Estreicher died in a German concentration camp, after he had refused to be one of Germany's
puppet rulers of Poland.

I received a renewal of my fellowship and spent a second
year in Germany. By that time I knew my Germany well
and spoke its tongue. I had associated with some of the
lower nobility, many of the "Gelehrten," artists, business
men, and members of the Social Democracy.

I returned to the United States by way of Paris where
I stayed as long as possible and then, having reduced myself almost to the last cent, took passage to the United
States in steerage. It was by no means a pleasant trip, but
perhaps it was good introduction to the new life; because
now at last at twenty-six years of age and after twenty
years of study I was coming home to look for a job and
begin work.

I need not dwell on the difficulties of finding that
job. It was a disturbed world in which I landed; 1892 saw
the high tide of lynching in the United States; Cleveland
had entered his second term in 1893 and the Chicago Exposition had taken place. The Dreyfus case had opened
in France with his conviction and imprisonment, and he
was destined for twelve years to suffer martyrdom. The
war between China and Japan broke out the year of my
return. I had rejoiced in the million dollar gift of Daniel
Hand for education in my graduation year but recognized
clearly the blow that democracy received when Congress

repealed the so-called Force bills in 1894, refusing longer even to try to protect the legal citizenship rights of Negroes. But on the other hand, I did not at all understand the implications of the Matabele War in 1893. I did not see how the gold and diamonds of South Africa and later the copper, ivory, cocoa, tin and vegetable oils of other parts of Africa and especially black labor force were determining and conditioning the political action of Europe.

I received eventually three offers of work. On August 17, the chair of "classics" at Wilberforce University, Ohio, with a salary of $800 was offered, which I immediately accepted with gratitude. A little later there came an offer of a position at Lincoln Institute in Missouri at $1050; but I stuck to my previous promise; and finally, August 25, I received this telegram: "Can give mathematics if terms suit. Will you accept. Booker T. Washington." It would be interesting to speculate just what would have happened, if I had accepted the last offer of Tuskegee instead of that of Wilberforce.

CHAPTER 4. SCIENCE AND EMPIRE

FROM the fall of 1894 to the spring of 1910, for sixteen years, I was a teacher. For two years I remained at Wilberforce; for something over a year, at the University of Pennsylvania; and for thirteen years at Atlanta University in Georgia. I sought in these years to teach youth the meaning and way of the world. What did I know about the world and how could I teach my knowledge?

The main result of my schooling had been to emphasize science and the scientific attitude. I got some insight into the laws of the physical world at Fisk and in the chemical laboratory and class in geology at Harvard. I was interested in evolution, geology, and the new psychology. I began to conceive of the world as a continuing growth rather than a finished product. In Germany I turned still further from religious dogma and began to grasp the idea of a world of human beings whose actions, like those of the physical world, were subject to law. The triumphs of the scientific world thrilled me: the X-ray and radium came during my teaching term, the airplane and the wireless. The machine increased in technical efficiency and the North and South Poles were invaded.

On the other hand the difficulties of applying scientific law and discovering cause and effect in the social world were still great. Social thinkers were engaged in vague statements and were seeking to lay down the methods by which, in some not too distant future, social law analogous to physical law would be discovered. Herbert Spencer finished his ten volumes of Synthetic Philosophy in 1896. The biological analogy, the vast generalizations, were striking, but actual scientific accomplishment lagged. For me an opportunity seemed to present itself. I could not lull my mind to hypnosis by regarding a phrase like "consciousness of kind" as a scientific law. But turning my gaze from fruitless word-twisting and facing the facts of my own social situation and racial world, I determined to put science into sociology through a study of the condition and problems of my own group.

I was going to study the facts, any and all facts, concerning the American Negro and his plight, and by measurement and comparison and research, work up to any valid generalization which I could. I entered this primarily with the utilitarian object of reform and uplift; but nevertheless, I wanted to do the work with scientific accuracy. Thus, in my own sociology, because of firm belief in a changing racial group, I easily grasped the idea of a changing developing society rather than a fixed social structure.

The decade and a half in which I taught, was riotous with happenings in the world of social development; with economic expansion, with political control, with racial difficulties. Above all, it was the era of empire and while I had some equipment to deal with a scientific approach to social studies, I did not have any clear conception or grasp of the meaning of that industrial imperialism which was beginning to grip the world. My only approach to meanings and helpful study there again was through my interest in race contact.

That interest began to clear my vision and interpret the whirl of events which swept the world on. Japan was rising to national status and through the Chinese War and the Russian War, despite rivalry with Germany, Russia and Great Britain, she achieved a new and nearly equal status in the world, which only the United States refused to recognize. But all this, I began to realize, was but a result of the expansion of Europe into Africa where a fierce fight was precipitated for the labor, gold, and diamonds of South Africa; for domination of the Nile Valley; for the gold, cocoa, raw materials, and labor of West Africa; and for the exploitation of the Belgian Congo. Europe was determined to dominate China and all but succeeded in dividing it between the chief white nations, when Japan stopped the process. After sixteen years, stirred by the triumph of the Abyssinians at Adowa, and pushing forward of the French in North Africa, England returned to the Egyptian Sudan.

The Queen's Jubilee then, I knew, was not merely a sentimental outburst; it was a triumph of English economic aggression around the world and it aroused the cupidity and fear of Germany who proceeded to double her navy, expand into Asia, and consolidate her European position. Germany challenged France and England at Algeciras, prelude to the World War. Imperialism, despite Cleveland's opposition, spread to America, and the Hawaiian sugar fields were annexed. The Spanish war brought Cuban sugar under control and annexed Puerto Rico and the Philippines. The Panama Canal brought the

Pacific nearer the Atlantic and we protected capital invest-ment in San Domingo and South America.

All this might have been interpreted as history and pol-itics. Mainly I did so interpret it; but continually I was forced to consider the economic aspects of world move-ments as they were developing at the time. Chiefly this was because the group in which I was interested were workers, earners of wages, owners of small bits of land, servants. The labor strikes interested and puzzled me. They were for the most part strikes of workers led by organizations to which Negroes were not admitted. There was the great steel strike; the railway strikes, actual and threatened; the team-sters' strike in Chicago; the long strike in Leadville, Col-orado. Only in the coal strike were Negroes involved. But there was a difference. During my school days, strikes were regarded as futile and ill-advised struggles against eco-nomic laws; and when the government intervened, it was to cow the strikers as law-breakers. But during my teaching period, the plight of the worker began to sift through into the consciousness of the average citizen. Public opinion not only allowed but forced Theodore Roosevelt to inter-vention in the coal strike, and the steel strikers had wide-spread sympathy.

Then there were the tariff agitations, the continual rais-ing and shifting and manipulation of tariff rates, always in the end for the purpose of subsidizing the manufacturer and making the consumer pay. The political power of the great organizations of capital in coal, oil and sugar, the extraordinary immunities of the corporations, made the President openly attack the trusts as a kind of super-gov-ernment and we began to see more and more clearly the outlines of economic battle. The Supreme Court stood staunchly behind capital. It outlawed the labor boycott, it denied the right of the states to make railway rates. It declared the income tax unconstitutional.

With all that, and the memory of the Panic of 1873 not forgotten, came the Panic of 1893 and the financial upheaval of 1907. Into this economic turmoil, politics had to intrude. The older role of free, individual enterprise, with little or no government interference, had to be surrendered and the whole political agitation during these days took on a distinct economic tinge and object. The impassioned plea of Bryan in 1896 that labor be not "crucified upon a cross of gold" could not be wholly ridiculed to silence. The Populist Movement which swept over the West and South, I began now to believe, was a third party movement of deep significance and it was kept from political power on the one hand by the established election frauds of the South, of which I knew, and by the fabulous election fund which made McKinley President of the United States. With this went the diversion of the Spanish war with its sordid scandals of rotten beef, cheating and stealing, fever and death from neglect. Politics and economics thus in those days of my teaching became but two aspects of a united body of action and effort.

I tried to isolate myself in the ivory tower of race. I wanted to explain the difficulties of race and the ways in which these difficulties caused political and economic troubles. It was this concentration of thought and action and effort that really, in the end, saved my scientific accuracy and search for truth. But first came a period of three years when I was casting about to find a way of applying science to the race problem. In these years I was torn with excitement of quick-moving events. Lynching, for instance, was still a continuing horror in the United States at the time of my entrance upon a teaching career. It reached a climax in 1892, when 235 persons were publicly murdered, and in the sixteen years of my teaching nearly two thousand persons were publicly killed by mobs, and not a single one of the murderers punished. The partition, domination and exploitation of Africa gradually centered my thought as part of my problem of race. I saw in Asia and the West Indies the results of race discrimination while right here in America came the wild foray of the exasperated Negro soldiers at Brownsville and the political-economic riot at Atlanta.

One happening in America linked in my mind the race problem with the general economic development and that was the speech of Booker T. Washington in Atlanta in 1895. When many colored papers condemned the proposition of compromise with the white South, which Washington proposed, I wrote to the *New York Age* suggesting that here might be the basis of a real settlement between whites and blacks in the South, if the South opened to the Negroes the doors of economic opportunity and the Negroes co-operated with the white South in political sympathy. But this offer was frustrated by the fact that between 1895 and 1909 the whole South disfranchised its Negro voters by unfair and illegal restrictions and passed a series of "Jim Crow" laws which made the Negro citizen a subordinate caste.

As a possible offset to this came the endowment of the General Education Board and the Sage Foundation; but they did not to my mind plan clearly to attack the Negro problem; the Sage Foundation ignored us, and the General Education Board in its first years gave its main attention to the education of whites and to black industrial schools. Finally the riot and lynching at Springfield, the birthplace of Abraham Lincoln, one hundred years after his birth, sounded a knell which in the end stopped my teaching career. This, then, was the general setting when I returned to America for work.

Wilberforce was a small colored denominational college, married to a state normal school. The church was too poor to run the college; the State tolerated the normal school so as to keep Negroes out of other state schools. Consequently, there were enormous difficulties in both church and state politics. Into this situation I landed with the cane and gloves of my German student days; with my rather inflated ideas of what a "university" ought to be and with a terrible plainness of speech that was continually getting me into difficulty; when, for instance, the student leader of a prayer meeting into which I had wandered casually to look local religion over, suddenly and without warning announced that "Professor Du Bois would lead us in prayer," I simply answered, "No, he won't," and as a result nearly lost my job. It took a great deal of explaining to the board of bishops why a professor in Wilberforce should not be able at all times and sundry to address God in extemporaneous prayer. I was saved only by the fact that my coming to Wilberforce had been widely advertised and I was so willing to do endless work when the work seemed to me worth doing.

My program for the day at Wilberforce looked almost

as long as a week's program now. I taught Latin, Greek, German, and English, and wanted to add sociology. I had charge of some of the most unpleasant duties of discipline and had outside work in investigation. But I met and made many friends: Charles Young, not long graduated from West Point, was one; Charles Burroughs, a gifted reader, was a student in my classes; Paul Laurence Dunbar came over from Dayton and read to us. I had known his work but was astonished to find that he was a Negro. And not least, I met the slender, quiet, and dark-eyed girl who became Mrs. Du Bois in 1896. Her father was chef in the leading hotel of Cedar Rapids, Iowa, and her dead mother a native of Alsace.

We younger teachers had a hard team fight, and after a two years' struggle I knew I was whipped and that it was impossible to stay at Wilberforce. It had a fine tradition, a strategic position, and a large constituency; but its religion was narrow dogma; its finances cramped; its policies too intertwined with intrigue and worse; and its future in grave doubt. When, therefore, a temporary appointment came from the University of Pennsylvania for one year as "assistant instructor" at $600, I accepted forthwith in the fall of 1896; that year Abyssinia overthrew Italy and England, suddenly seeing two black nations threatening her Cape to Cairo plans, threw her army back into the Sudan and re-captured Khartoum. The next year, the free silver controversy of Bryan and McKinley flamed.

The two years at Wilberforce was my uneasy apprenticeship, and with my advent into the University of Pennsylvania, I began a more clearly planned career which had an unusual measure of success, but was in the end pushed aside by forces which, if not entirely beyond my control, were yet of great weight.

The opportunity opened at the University of Pennsylvania seemed just what I wanted. I had offered to teach social science at Wilberforce outside of my overloaded program, but I was not allowed. My vision was becoming clearer. The Negro problem was in my mind a matter of systematic investigation and intelligent understanding. The world was thinking wrong about race, because it did not know. The ultimate evil was stupidity. The cure for it was knowledge based on scientific investigation. At the University of Pennsylvania I ignored the pitiful stipend. It made no difference to me that I was put down as an "assistant instructor" and even at that, that my name never actually got into the catalogue; it goes without saying that I did no instructing save once to pilot a pack of idiots through the Negro slums.

The fact was that the city of Philadelphia at that time had a theory; and that theory was that this great, rich, and famous municipality was going to the dogs because of the crime and venality of its Negro citizens, who lived largely centered in the slum at the lower end of the seventh ward. Philadelphia wanted to prove this by figures and I was the man to do it. Of this theory back of the plan, I neither knew nor cared. I saw only here a chance to study an historical group of black folk and to show exactly what their place was in the community.

I did it despite extraordinary difficulties both within and without the group. Whites said, Why study the obvious? Blacks said, Are we animals to be dissected and by an unknown Negro at that? Yet, I made a study of the

Philadelphia Negro so thorough that it has withstood the criticism of forty years. It was as complete a scientific study and answer as could have then been given, with defective facts and statistics, one lone worker and little money. It revealed the Negro group as a symptom, not a cause; as a striving, palpitating group, and not an inert, sick body of crime; as a long historic development and not a transient occurrence.

Of the methods of my research, I wrote:

"The best available methods of sociological research are at present so liable to inaccuracies that the careful student discloses the results of individual research with diffidence; he knows that they are liable to error from the seemingly ineradicable faults of the statistical method; to even greater error from the methods of general observation; and, above all, he must ever tremble lest some personal bias, some moral conviction or some unconscious trend of thought due to previous training, has to a degree distorted the picture in his view. Convictions on all great matters of human interest one must have to a greater or less degree, and they will enter to some extent into the most cold-blooded scientific research as a disturbing factor.

"Nevertheless, here are some social problems before us demanding careful study, questions awaiting satisfactory answers. We must study, we must investigate, we must attempt to solve; and the utmost that the world can demand is, not lack of human interest and moral conviction, but rather the heart-quality of fairness, and an earnest desire for the truth despite its possible unpleasantness."

At the end of that study, I announced with a certain pride my plan of studying the complete Negro problem in

the United States. I spoke at the forty-second meeting of
the American Academy of Political and Social Sciences
in Philadelphia, November 19, 1897, and my subject was
"The Study of the Negro Problems." I began by asserting
that in the development of sociological study there was at
least one positive answer which years of research and speculation had been able to return, and that was: "The phenomena of society are worth the most careful and systematic study, and whether or not this study may
eventually lead to a systematic body of knowledge deserving the name of science, it cannot in any case fail to give
the world a mass of truth worth the knowing." I then defined and tried to follow the development of the Negro
problem not as one problem, but "rather a plexus of social
problems, some new, some old, some simple, some complex; and these problems have their one bond of unity
in the fact that they group themselves about those Africans
whom two centuries of slave-trading brought into the
land."

I insisted on the necessity of carefully studying these
problems and said: "The American Negro deserves study
for the great end of advancing the cause of science in
general. No such opportunity to watch and measure the
history and development of a great race of men ever presented itself to the scholars of a modern nation. If they
miss this opportunity—if they do the work in a slip-shod,
unsystematic manner—if they dally with the truth to
humor the whims of the day, they do far more than hurt
the good name of the American people; they hurt the
cause of scientific truth the world over, they voluntarily
decrease human knowledge of a universe of which we are

ignorant enough, and they degrade the high end of truth-
seeking in a day when they need more and more to dwell
upon its sanctity."

Finally I tried to lay down a plan for the study, postulat-
ing only: that the Negro "is a member of the human race,
and as one who, in the light of history and experience, is
capable to a degree of improvement and culture, is en-
titled to have his interests considered according to his numbers in all conclusions as to the common weal."

Dividing the prospective scientific study of the Negro
into two parts: the social group and his peculiar social
environment, I proposed to study the social group by
historical investigation, statistical measurement, anthropological measurement and sociological interpretation. Particularly with regard to anthropology I said:

"That there are differences between the white and black
races is certain, but just what those differences are is
known to none with an approach to accuracy. Yet here in
America is the most remarkable opportunity ever offered
of studying these differences, of noting influences of climate and physical environment, and particularly of studying the effect of amalgamating two of the most diverse
races in the world—another subject which rests under a
cloud of ignorance."

In concluding, I said:

"It is to the credit of the University of Pennsylvania
that she has been the first to recognize her duty in this respect and in so far as restricted means and opportunity
allowed, has attempted to study the Negro problems in a
single definite locality. This work needs to be extended
to other groups, and carried out with larger system; and

here it would seem is the opportunity of the Southern
Negro college. We hear much of higher Negro education,
and yet all candid people know there does not exist today
in the center of Negro population a single first-class fully
equipped institution, devoted to the higher education of
Negroes; not more than three Negro institutions in the
South deserve the name of 'college' at all; and yet what is
a Negro college but a vast college settlement for the study
of a particular set of peculiarly baffling problems? What
more effective or suitable agency could be found in which
to focus the scientific efforts of the great universities of
the North and East, than an institution situated in the
very heart of these social problems, and made the center
of careful historical and statistical research? Without doubt
the first effective step toward the solving of the Negro
question will be the endowment of a Negro college which
is not merely a teaching body, but a center of sociological
research, in close connection and co-operation with Harvard, Columbia, Johns Hopkins, and the University of
Pennsylvania.

"Finally the necessity must again be emphasized of keeping clearly before students the object of all science, amid
the turmoil and intense feeling that clouds the discussion
of a burning social question. We live in a day when in
spite of the brilliant accomplishments of a remarkable
century, there is current much flippant criticism of scientific work; when the truth-seeker is too often pictured as
devoid of human sympathy, and careless of human ideals.
We are still prone in spite of all our culture to sneer at
the heroism of the laboratory while we cheer the swagger
of the street broil. At such times true lovers of humanity

can only hold higher the pure ideals of science, and continue to insist that if we would solve a problem we must study it, and there is but one coward on earth, and that is the coward that dare not know."

I had, at this time, already been approached by President Horace Bumstead of Atlanta University and asked to come there and take charge of the work in sociology, and of the new conferences which they were inaugurating on the Negro problem. With this program in mind, I eagerly accepted the invitation, although at the last moment there came a curious reminiscence of Wilberforce in a little hitch based on that old matter of extemporaneous public prayer. Dr. Bumstead and I compromised on my promise to use the Episcopal prayer book; later I used to add certain prayers of my own composing. I am not sure that they were orthodox or reached heaven, but they certainly reached my audience.

Without thought or consultation I rather peremptorily changed the plans of the first two Atlanta Conferences. They had been conceived as conferences limited to city problems, contrasting with the increasingly popular conferences on rural problems held at Tuskegee. But I was not thinking of mere conferences. I was thinking of a comprehensive plan for studying a human group and if I could have carried it out as completely as I conceived it, the American Negro would have contributed to the development of social science in this country an unforgettable body of work.

Annually our reports carried this statement of aims: "This study is a further carrying out of a plan of social study by means of recurring decennial inquiries into the same general set of human problems. The object of these studies is primarily scientific—a careful search for truth conducted as thoroughly, broadly, and honestly as the material resources and mental equipment at command will allow; but this is not our sole object; we wish not only to make the Truth clear but to present it in such shape as will encourage and help social reform. Our financial resources are unfortunately meager: Atlanta University is primarily a school and most of its funds and energy go to teaching. It is, however, also a seat of learning and as such it has endeavored to advance knowledge, particularly in matters of racial contact and development which seemed obviously its nearest field. In this work it has received unusual encouragement from the scientific world, and the published results of these studies are used in America, Europe, Asia, and Africa."

Social scientists were then still thinking in terms of theory and vast and eternal laws, but I had a concrete group of living beings artificially set off by themselves and capable of almost laboratory experiment. I laid down an ambitious program for a hundred years of study. I proposed to take up annually in each decade the main aspects of the group life of Negroes with as thorough study and measurement as possible, and repeat the same program in the succeeding decade with additions, changes and better methods. In this way, I proposed gradually to broaden and intensify the study, sharpen the tools of investigation and perfect our methods of work, so that we would have an increasing body of scientifically ascertained fact, instead of the vague mass of the so-called Negro problems. And through this laboratory experiment I hoped to make the laws of social living clearer, surer, and more definite.

Some of this was accomplished, but of course only an approximation of the idea. For thirteen years we poured forth a series of studies; limited, incomplete, only partially conclusive, and yet so much better done than any other attempt of the sort in the nation that they gained attention throughout the world. We studied during the first decade Negro mortality, urbanization, the effort of Negroes for their own social betterment, Negroes in business, college-bred Negroes, the Negro common school, the Negro artisan, the Negro church, and Negro crime. We ended the decade by a general review of the methods and results of this ten year study and a bibliography of the Negro. Taking new breath in 1906 I planned a more logical division of subjects but was not able to carry it out quite as I wished, because of lack of funds. We took up health and physique of American Negroes, economic co-operation and the Negro American family. We made a second study of the efforts for social betterment, the college-bred Negro, the Negro common school, the Negro artisan, and added a study of morals and manners among Negroes instead of further study of the church. In all we published a total of 2,172 pages which formed a current encyclopaedia on the American Negro problems.

These studies with all their imperfections were widely distributed in the libraries of the world and used by scholars. It may be said without undue boasting that between 1896 and 1920 there was no study of the race problem in America made which did not depend in some degree upon the investigations made at Atlanta University; often they were widely quoted and commended.

It must be remembered that the significance of these studies lay not so much in what they were actually able to accomplish, as in the fact that at the time of their publication Atlanta University was the only institution in the world carrying on a systematic study of the Negro and his development, and putting the result in a form available for the scholars of the world.

In addition to the publications, we did something toward bringing together annually at Atlanta University persons and authorities interested in the problems of the South. Among these were Booker T. Washington, Frank Sanborn, Franz Boas, Jane Addams and Walter Wilcox. We were asked from time to time to co-operate in current studies. I wrote a number of studies for the Bureau of Labor in Washington. I co-operated in the taking of the Twelfth Census and wrote one of the monographs. I not only published the Atlanta Conference reports, but wrote magazine articles in the *World's Work* and in the *Atlantic Monthly* where I joined in a symposium and one of my fellow contributors was Woodrow Wilson. At the same time I joined with the Negro leaders of Georgia in efforts to better local conditions; to stop discrimination in the distribution of school funds; to keep the legislature from making further discriminations in railway travel. I prepared an exhibit showing the condition of the Negro for the Paris Exposition which gained a Grand Prize. I became a member of the American Association for the Advancement of Science in 1900 and was made a fellow in 1904.

I testified before Congressional Commissions in Washington and appeared on the lecture platform with Walter Page, afterwards war ambassador to England; I did a considerable amount of lecturing throughout the United States. I had wide correspondence with men of prominence in America and Europe: Lyman Abbott of the *Outlook;* E. D. Morel, the English expert on Africa; Max Weber of Heidelberg; Professor Wilcox of Cornell; Bliss Perry of the *Atlantic Monthly;* Horace Traubel, the great protagonist for Walt Whitman; Charles Eliot Norton and Talcott Williams. I began to be regarded by many groups and audiences as having definite information on the Negro to which they might listen with profit.

At the very time when my studies were most successful, there cut across this plan which I had as a scientist, a red ray which could not be ignored. I remember when it first, as it were, startled me to my feet: a poor Negro in central Georgia, Sam Hose, had killed his landlord's wife. I wrote out a careful and reasoned statement concerning the evident facts and started down to the Atlanta *Constitution* office, carrying in my pocket a letter of introduction to Joel Chandler Harris. I did not get there. On the way news met me: Sam Hose had been lynched, and they said that his knuckles were on exhibition at a grocery store farther down on Mitchell Street, along which I was walking. I turned back to the University. I began to turn aside from my work. I did not meet Joel Chandler Harris nor the editor of the *Constitution.*

Two considerations thereafter broke in upon my work and eventually disrupted it: first, one could not be a calm, cool, and detached scientist while Negroes were lynched, murdered and starved; and secondly, there was no such definite demand for scientific work of the sort that I was doing, as I had confidently assumed would be easily forth-

coming. I regarded it as axiomatic that the world wanted
to learn the truth and if the truth was sought with even
approximate accuracy and painstaking devotion, the world
would gladly support the effort. This was, of course, but
a young man's idealism, not by any means false, but also
never universally true. The work of the conference for
thirteen years including my own salary and small office
force did not average five thousand dollars a year. Probably with some effort and sacrifice Atlanta University
might have continued to raise this amount if it had not
been for the controversy with Booker T. Washington that
arose in 1903 and increased in virulence until 1908.

There were, of course, other considerations which made
Atlanta University vulnerable to attack at this time. The
university from the beginning had taken a strong and
unbending attitude toward Negro prejudice and discrimination; white teachers and black students ate together in
the same dining room and lived in the same dormitories.
The charter of the institution opened the doors of Atlanta
University to any student who applied, of any race or
color; and when the state in 1887 objected to the presence
of a few white students, all children of teachers and professors, the institution gave up the small appropriation
from the State rather than repudiate its principles. In fact,
this appropriation represented not State funds, but the
Negroes' share of the sum received from the Federal government for education. When later there came an attempt
on the part of the Southern Education Board and afterwards of the General Education Board to form a working
program between educated Negroes and forward-looking
whites in the South, it gradually became an understood

principle of action that colored teachers should be encouraged in colored schools; that the races in the schools should be separated socially; that colored schools should be chiefly industrial; and that every effort should be made to conciliate Southern white public opinion. Schools which were successfully carrying out this program could look for further help from organized philanthropy. Other schools, and this included Atlanta University, could not.

Even this would not necessarily have excluded Atlanta University from consideration at the hands of the philanthropists. The university had done and was doing excellent and thorough work. Even industrial training in the South was often in the hands of Atlanta graduates. Tuskegee had always been largely manned by graduates of Atlanta and some of the best school systems of the South were directed by persons trained at Atlanta University. The college department was recognized as perhaps the largest and best in the South at the time. But unfortunately, at this time, there came a controversy between myself and Booker Washington, which became more personal and bitter than I had ever dreamed and which necessarily dragged in the University.

It was no controversy of my seeking; quite the contrary. I was in my imagination a scientist, and neither a leader nor an agitator; I had nothing but the greatest admiration for Mr. Washington and Tuskegee, and I had applied at both Tuskegee and Hampton for work. If Mr. Washington's telegram had reached me before the Wilberforce bid, I should have doubtless gone to Tuskegee. Certainly I knew no less about mathematics than I did about Latin and Greek.

Since the controversy between myself and Mr. Washington has become historic, it deserves more careful statement than it has had hitherto, both as to the matters and the motives involved. There was first of all the ideological controversy. I believed in the higher education of a Talented Tenth who through their knowledge of modern culture could guide the American Negro into a higher civilization. I knew that without this the Negro would have to accept white leadership, and that such leadership could not always be trusted to guide this group into self-realization and to its highest cultural possibilities. Mr. Washington, on the other hand, believed that the Negro as an efficient worker could gain wealth and that eventually through his ownership of capital he would be able to achieve a recognized place in American culture and could then educate his children as he might wish and develop his possibilities. For this reason he proposed to put the emphasis at present upon training in the skilled trades and encouragement in industry and common labor.

These two theories of Negro progress were not absolutely contradictory. I recognized the importance of the Negro gaining a foothold in trades and his encouragement in industry and common labor. Mr. Washington was not absolutely opposed to college training, and sent his own children to college. But he did minimize its importance, and discouraged the philanthropic support of higher education; while I openly and repeatedly criticized what seemed to me the poor work and small accomplishment of the Negro industrial school. Moreover, it was characteristic of the Washington statesmanship that whatever he or anybody believed or wanted must be subordinated to dominant public opinion and that opinion deferred to and cajoled until it allowed a deviation toward better ways. This is no new thing in the world, but it is always dangerous.

But beyond this difference of ideal lay another and more bitter and insistent controversy. This started with the rise at Tuskegee Institute, and centering around Booker T. Washington, of what I may call the Tuskegee Machine. Of its existence and work, little has ever been said and almost nothing written. The years from 1899 to 1905 marked the culmination of the career of Booker T. Washington. In 1899 Mr. Washington, Paul Laurence Dunbar, and myself spoke on the same platform at the Hollis Street Theatre, Boston, before a distinguished audience. Mr. Washington was not at his best and friends immediately raised a fund which sent him to Europe for a three months' rest. He was received with extraordinary honors: he had tea with the aged Queen Victoria, but two years before her death; he was entertained by two dukes and other members of the aristocracy; he met James Bryce and Henry M. Stanley; he was received at the Peace Conference at The Hague and was greeted by many distinguished Americans, like ex-President Harrison, Archbishop Ireland and two justices of the Supreme Court. Only a few years before he had received an honorary degree from Harvard; in 1901, he received a LL.D. from Dartmouth and that same year he dined with President Roosevelt to the consternation of the white South.

Returning to America he became during the administrations of Theodore Roosevelt and William Taft, from 1901 to 1912, the political referee in all Federal appointments or action taken with reference to the Negro and in many regarding the white South. In 1903 Andrew Carnegie made the future of Tuskegee certain by a gift of $600,000. There was no question of Booker T. Washington's undisputed leadership of the ten million Negroes in America, a leadership recognized gladly by the whites and conceded by most of the Negroes.

But there were discrepancies and paradoxes in this leadership. It did not seem fair, for instance, that on the one hand Mr. Washington should decry political activities among Negroes, and on the other hand dictate Negro political objectives from Tuskegee. At a time when Negro civil rights called for organized and aggressive defense, he broke down that defense by advising acquiescence or at least no open agitation. During the period when laws disfranchising the Negro were being passed in all the Southern states, between 1890 and 1909, and when these were being supplemented by "Jim Crow" travel laws and other enactments making color caste legal, his public speeches, while they did not entirely ignore this development, tended continually to excuse it, to emphasize the shortcomings of the Negro, and were interpreted widely as putting the chief onus for his condition upon the Negro himself.

All this naturally aroused increasing opposition among Negroes and especially among the younger classes of educated Negroes, who were beginning to emerge here and there, especially from Northern institutions. This opposition began to become vocal in 1901 when two men, Monroe Trotter, Harvard 1895, and George Forbes, Amherst 1895, began the publication of the Boston *Guardian*.

The *Guardian* was bitter, satirical, and personal; but it was well-edited, it was earnest, and it published facts. It attracted wide attention among colored people; it circulated among them all over the country; it was quoted and discussed. I did not wholly agree with the *Guardian,* and indeed only a few Negroes did, but nearly all read it and were influenced by it.

This beginning of organized opposition, together with other events, led to the growth at Tuskegee of what I have called the Tuskegee Machine. It arose first quite naturally. Not only did presidents of the United States consult Booker Washington, but governors and congressmen; philanthropists conferred with him, scholars wrote to him. Tuskegee became a vast information bureau and center of advice. It was not merely passive in these matters but, guided by a young unobtrusive minor official who was also intelligent, suave and far-seeing, active efforts were made to concentrate influence at Tuskegee. After a time almost no Negro institution could collect funds without the recommendation or acquiescence of Mr. Washington. Few political appointments were made anywhere in the United States without his consent. Even the careers of rising young colored men were very often determined by his advice and certainly his opposition was fatal. How much Mr. Washington knew of this work of the Tuskegee Machine and was directly responsible, one cannot say, but of its general activity and scope he must have been aware.

Moreover, it must not be forgotten that this Tuskegee Machine was not solely the idea and activity of black folk at Tuskegee. It was largely encouraged and given financial aid through certain white groups and individuals in the

North. This Northern group had clear objectives. They
were capitalists and employers and yet in most cases sons,
relatives, or friends of the abolitionists who had sent teachers into the new Negro South after the war. These younger
men believed that the Negro problem could not remain a
matter of philanthropy. It must be a matter of business.
These Negroes were not to be encouraged as voters in the
new democracy, nor were they to be left at the mercy of
the reactionary South. They were good laborers and they
might be better. They could become a strong labor force
and properly guided they would restrain the unbridled
demands of white labor, born of the Northern labor
unions and now spreading to the South.

One danger must be avoided and that was to allow the
silly idealism of Negroes, half-trained in Southern missionary "colleges," to mislead the mass of laborers and keep
them stirred-up by ambitions incapable of realization. To
this school of thought, the philosophy of Booker Washington came as a godsend and it proposed by building up
his prestige and power to control the Negro group. The
control was to be drastic. The Negro intelligentsia was to
be suppressed and hammered into conformity. The process
involved some cruelty and disappointment, but that was
inevitable. This was the real force back of the Tuskegee
Machine. It had money and it had opportunity, and it
found in Tuskegee tools to do its bidding.

There were some rather pitiful results in thwarted ambition and curtailed opportunity. I remember one case
which always stands in my memory as typical. There was
a young colored man, one of the most beautiful human
beings I have ever seen, with smooth brown skin, velvet

eyes of intelligence, and raven hair. He was educated and well-to-do. He proposed to use his father's Alabama farm and fortune to build a Negro town and independent economic unit in the South. He furnished a part of the capital but soon needed more and he came North to get it. He struggled for more than a decade; philanthropists and capitalists were fascinated by his personality and story; and when, according to current custom, they appealed to Tuskegee for confirmation, there was silence. Mr. Washington would not say a word in favor of the project. He simply kept still. Will Benson struggled on with ups and downs, but always balked by a whispering galley of suspicion, because his plan was never endorsed by Tuskegee. In the midst of what seemed to us who looked on the beginnings of certain success, Benson died of overwork, worry, and a broken heart.

From facts like this, one may gauge the bitterness of the fight of young Negroes against Mr. Washington and Tuskegee. Contrary to most opinion, the controversy as it developed was not entirely against Mr. Washington's ideas, but became the insistence upon the right of other Negroes to have and express their ideas. Things came to such a pass that when any Negro complained or advocated a course of action, he was silenced with the remark that Mr. Washington did not agree with this. Naturally the bumptious, irritated, young black intelligentsia of the day declared, "I don't care a damn what Booker Washington thinks! This is what I think, and *I have a right to think.*"

It was this point, and not merely disagreement with Mr. Washington's plans, that brought eventually violent outbreak. It was more than opposition to a program of education. It was opposition to a system and that system was part of the economic development of the United States at the time. The fight cut deep: it went into social relations; it divided friends; it made bitter enemies. I can remember that years later, when I went to live in New York and was once invited to a social gathering among Brooklyn colored people, one of the most prominent Negroes of the city refused to be present because of my former attitude toward Mr. Washington.

When the *Guardian* began to increase in influence, determined effort was made to build up a Negro press for Tuskegee. Already Tuskegee filled the horizon so far as national magazines and the great newspapers were concerned. In 1901 the *Outlook,* then the leading weekly, chose two distinguished Americans for autobiographies. Mr. Washington's "Up from Slavery" was so popular that it was soon published and circulated all over the earth. Thereafter, every magazine editor sought articles with his signature and publishing houses continued to ask for books. A number of talented "ghost writers," black and white, took service under Tuskegee, and books and articles poured out of the institution. An annual letter "To My People" went out from Tuskegee to the press. Tuskegee became the capital of the Negro nation. Negro newspapers were influenced and finally the oldest and largest was bought by white friends of Tuskegee. Most of the other papers found it to their advantage certainly not to oppose Mr. Washington, even if they did not wholly agree with him. Negroes who sought high positions groveled for his favor.

I was greatly disturbed at this time, not because I was

in absolute opposition to the things that Mr. Washington was advocating, but because I was strongly in favor of more open agitation against wrongs and above all I resented the practical buying up of the Negro press and choking off of even mild and reasonable opposition to Mr. Washington in both the Negro press and the white.

Then, too, during these years there came a series of influences that were brought to bear upon me personally, which increased my discomfort and resentment. I had tried to keep in touch with Hampton and Tuskegee, for I regarded them as great institutions. I attended the conferences which for a long time were held at Hampton, and at one of them I was approached by a committee. It consisted of Walter Hines Page, editor of the *Atlantic Monthly;* William McVickar, Episcopal bishop of Rhode Island; and Dr. Frissel, principal of Hampton. They asked me about the possibilities of my editing a periodical to be published at Hampton. I told them of my dreams and plans, and afterwards wrote them in detail. But one query came by mail: that was concerning the editorial direction. I replied firmly that editorial decisions were to be in my hands, if I edited the magazine. This was undiplomatic and too sweeping; and yet, it brought to head the one real matter in controversy: would such a magazine be dominated by and subservient to the Tuskegee philosophy, or would it have freedom of thought and discussion? Perhaps if I had been more experienced, the question could have been discussed and some reasonable outcome obtained; but I doubt it. I think any such magazine launched at the time would have been seriously curtailed in its freedom of speech. At any rate, the project was dropped.

Beginning in 1902 considerable pressure was put upon me to give up my work at Atlanta University and go to Tuskegee. There again I was not at first adverse in principle to Tuskegee, except that I wanted to continue what I had begun and if my work was worth support, it was worth support at Atlanta University. Moreover, I was unable to be assured that my studies would be continued at Tuskegee, and that I would not sink to the level of a "ghost writer." I remember a letter came from Wallace Buttrick late in 1902, asking that I attend a private conference in New York with Felix Adler, William H. Baldwin, Jr., George Foster Peabody, and Robert Ogden. The object of the conference was ostensibly the condition of the Negro in New York City. I went to the conference and I did not like it. Most of the more distinguished persons named were not present. The conference itself amounted to little, but I was whisked over to William H. Baldwin's beautiful Long Island home and there what seemed to me to be the real object of my coming was disclosed. Mr. Baldwin was at that time president of the Long Island Railroad and slated to be president of the Pennsylvania. He was the rising industrial leader of America; also he was a prime mover of the Tuskegee board of trustees. Both he and his wife insisted that my place was at Tuskegee; that Tuskegee was not yet a good school, and needed the kind of development that I had been trained to promote.

This was followed by two interviews with Mr. Washington himself. I was elated at the opportunity and we met twice in New York City. The results to me were disappointing. Booker T. Washington was not an easy person to know. He was wary and silent. He never expressed himself frankly or clearly until he knew exactly to whom he was talking and just what their wishes and desires were. He did not know me, and I think he was suspicious. On the other hand, I was quick, fast-speaking and voluble. I found at the end of the first interview that I had done practically all the talking and that no clear and definite offer or explanation of my proposed work at Tuskegee had been made. In fact, Mr. Washington had said about as near nothing as was possible.

The next interview did not go so well because I myself said little. Finally, we resorted to correspondence. Even then I could get no clear understanding of just what I was going to do at Tuskegee if I went. I was given to understand that the salary and accommodations would be satisfactory. In fact, I was invited to name my price. Later in the year I went to Bar Harbor for a series of speeches in behalf of Atlanta University, and while there met Jacob Schiff, the Schieffelins and Merriam of Webster's dictionary. I had dinner with the Schieffelins and again was urged to go to Tuskegee.

Early in the next year I received an invitation to join Mr. Washington and certain prominent white and colored friends in a conference to be held in New York. The conference was designed to talk over a common program for the American Negro and evidently it was hoped that the growing division of opinion and opposition to Mr. Washington within the ranks of Negroes would thus be overcome. I was enthusiastic over the idea. It seemed to me just what was needed to clear the air.

There was difficulty, however, in deciding what persons ought to be invited to the conference, how far it should

include Mr. Washington's extreme opponents, or how far
it should be composed principally of his friends. There
ensued a long delay and during this time it seemed to me
that I ought to make my own position clearer than I had
hitherto. I was increasingly uncomfortable under the statements of Mr. Washington's position: his depreciation of
the value of the vote; his evident dislike of Negro colleges;
and his general attitude which seemed to place the onus of
blame for the status of Negroes upon the Negroes themselves rather than upon the whites. And above all, I resented the Tuskegee Machine.

I had been asked sometime before by A. C. McClurg
and Company of Chicago if I did not have some material
for a book; I planned a social study which should be perhaps a summing up of the work of the Atlanta Conferences, or at any rate, a scientific investigation. They asked,
however, if I did not have some essays that they might put
together and issue immediately, mentioning my articles
in the *Atlantic Monthly* and other places. I demurred because books of essays almost always fall so flat. Nevertheless, I got together a number of my fugitive pieces. I then
added a chapter, "Of Mr. Booker T. Washington and
Others," in which I sought to make a frank evaluation
of Booker T. Washington. I left out the more controversial
matter: the bitter resentment which young Negroes felt
at the continued and increasing activity of the Tuskegee
Machine. I concentrated my thought and argument on
Mr. Washington's general philosophy. As I read that statement now, a generation later, I am satisfied with it. I see
no word that I would change. The "Souls of Black Folk"
was published in 1903 and is still selling today.

My book settled pretty definitely any further question of my going to Tuskegee as an employee. But it also drew pretty hard and fast lines about my future career. Meantime, the matter of the conference in New York dragged on until finally in October, 1903, a circular letter was sent out setting January, 1904, as the date of meeting. The conference took place accordingly in Carnegie Hall, New York. About fifty persons were present, most of them colored and including many well-known persons. There was considerable plain speaking but the whole purpose of the conference seemed revealed by the invited guests and the tone of their message. Several white persons of high distinction came to speak to us, including Andrew Carnegie and Lyman Abbott. Their words were lyric, almost fulsome in praise of Mr. Washington and his work, and in support of his ideas. Even if all they said had been true, it was a wrong note to strike in a conference of conciliation. The conferences ended with two speeches by Mr. Washington and myself, and the appointment of a Committee of Twelve in which we were also included.

The Committee of Twelve which was thus instituted was unable to do any effective work as a steering committee for the Negro race in America. First of all, it was financed, through Mr. Washington, probably by Mr. Carnegie. This put effective control of the committee in Mr. Washington's hands. It was organized during my absence and laid down a plan of work which seemed to me of some value but of no lasting importance and having little to do with the larger questions and issues. I, therefore, soon resigned so as not to be responsible for work and pronouncements over which I would have little influence. My friends and others accused me of refusing to play the game after I had assented to a program of co-operation. I still think, however, that my action was wise.

Meantime, the task of raising money for Atlanta University and my work became increasingly difficult. In the fall of 1904 the printing of our conference report was postponed by the trustees until special funds could be secured. I did not at the time see the handwriting on the wall. I did not realize how strong the forces were back of Tuskegee and how they might interfere with my scientific study of the Negro. My continuing thought was that we must have a vehicle for both opinion and fact which would help me carry on my scientific work and at the same time be a forum less radical than the *Guardian*, and yet more rational than the rank and file of Negro papers now so largely arrayed with Tuskegee. With this in mind, as early as 1904, I helped one of the Atlanta University graduates, who was a good printer, to set up a job office in Memphis.

In 1905 I wrote to Jacob Schiff, reminding him of having met him in Bar Harbor in 1903: "I want to lay before you a plan which I have and ask you if it is of sufficient interest to you for you to be willing to hear more of it and possibly to assist in its realization. The Negro race in America is today in a critical condition. Only united concerted effort will save us from being crushed. This union must come as a matter of education and long continued effort. To this end there is needed a high class of journal to circulate among the intelligent Negroes, tell them of the deeds of themselves and their neighbors, interpret the news of the world to them, and inspire them toward definite ideals. Now we have many small weekly papers and one or two monthlies, and none of them fill the great need I have outlined. I want to establish, therefore, for the nine million American Negroes and eventually for the whole Negro world, a monthly journal. To this end I have already in Memphis a printing establishment which has been running successfully at job work a year under a competent printer—self-sacrificing educated young man. Together we shall have about $2,000 invested in this plant by April 15."

Mr. Schiff wrote back courteously, saying: "Your plans to establish a high class journal to circulate among the intelligent Negroes is in itself interesting, and on its face has my sympathy. But before I could decide whether I can become of advantage in carrying your plans into effect, I would wish to advise with men whose opinion in such a matter I consider of much value." Nothing ever came of this, because, as I might have known, most of Mr. Schiff's friends were strong and sincere advocates of Tuskegee.

It was with difficulty that I came fully to realize the situation that was thus developing: first of all, I could not persuade myself that my program of solving the Negro problem by scientific investigation was wrong, or that it could possibly fail of eventual support when once it was undertaken; that it was understood in widening circles of readers and thinkers, I was convinced, because of the reception accorded the Atlanta University Studies. When, however, in spite of that, the revenue of the University continued to fall off, and no special support came for my particular part of its work, I tried several times by personal effort to see if funds could not be raised.

In 1906 I made two appeals: first and boldly, I outlined the work of the Atlanta Conference to Andrew Carnegie, reminding him that I had been presented to him and Carl Schurz some years before. I hoped that despite his deep friendship for Mr. Washington and the Tuskegee idea, he would see the use and value of my efforts at Atlanta. The response was indirect. At the time a white Mississippi planter, Alfred W. Stone, was popular in the North. He had grave doubts about the future of the Negro race, widely criticized black labor, and once tried to substitute Italians on his own plantations, until they became too handy with the knife. To his direction, Mr. Carnegie and others entrusted a fund for certain studies among Negroes. Why they selected him and neglected an established center like Atlanta University, I cannot imagine; but at any rate, Stone turned to me and offered to give the University a thousand dollars to help finance a special study of the history of economic co-operation among Negroes. I had planned that year, 1907, to study the Negro in politics, but here was needed support and I turned aside and made the study asked for.

About the same time, I approached the United States Commissioner of Labor. For several years I had been able to do now and then certain small studies for the Bureau of Labor, which had been accepted and paid for. It began with a proposal to Carroll D. Wright for a study of the Negro in a Virginia town in 1898, which Mr. Wright authorized me to make on my own responsibility, promising only to print it if he liked it. He did like it. This was followed by a study of the Negro in the Black Belt in 1899 and among Negroes in Georgia in 1901, and I now approached the Bureau with a new proposal.

I asked United States Commissioner of Labor Neill, in 1906, to authorize a study of a Black Belt community. I wanted to take Lownes County, Alabama, in a former slave state with a large majority of Negroes, and make a social and economic study from the earliest times where documents were available, down to the present; supplemented by studies of official records and a house to house canvas. I plied Commissioner Neill with plans and specifications until at last he authorized the study. Helped by Monroe Work, now at Tuskegee Institute, and R. R. Wright, now a bishop of the A. M. E. Church, and a dozen or more local employees, I settled at the Calhoun School and began the study.

It was carried on with all sorts of difficulties, including financing which was finally arranged by loans from the University, and with the greeting of some of my agents with shotguns in certain parts of the county; but it was eventually finished. The difficult schedules were tabulated and I made chronological maps of the division of the land; I considered the distribution of labor; the relation of landlord and tenant; the political organization and the family life and distribution of the population. The report went to Washington and I spent some weeks there in person, revising and perfecting it. It was accepted by the government, and $2,000 paid for it, most of which went back to the University in repayment of funds which they had kindly furnished me to carry on the work. But the study was not published. I knew the symptoms of this sort of treatment: in 1898, S. S. McClure had sent me to south

Georgia to make a study of social situations there. He paid for the report but never published the manuscript and afterward did the same thing in the case of Sir Harry Johnston.

I finally approached the bureau and tried to find out when it would be published and was told that the bureau had decided not to publish the manuscript, since it "touched on political matters." I was astonished and disappointed, but after a year went back to them again and asked if they would allow me to have the manuscript published since they were not going to use it. They told me it had been destroyed. And while I was down in Lownes County finishing this study, there came the news of the Atlanta riot. I took the next train for Atlanta and my family. On the way, I wrote the "Litany of Atlanta."

By this time I was pretty thoroughly disillusioned. It did not seem possible for me to occupy middle ground and try to appease the *Guardian* on the one hand and the Hampton-Tuskegee idea on the other. I began to feel the strength and implacability of the Tuskegee Machine; the Negro newspapers were definitely showing their reaction and publishing jibes and innuendoes at my expense. Filled with increasing indignation, I published in the *Guardian* a statement concerning the venality of certain Negro papers which I charged had sold out to Mr. Washington. It was a charge difficult of factual proof without an expenditure of time and funds not at my disposal. I was really at last openly tilting against the Tuskegee Machine and its methods. These methods have become common enough in our day for all sorts of purposes: the distribution of advertising and favors, the sending out of special correspondence, veiled and open attacks upon recalcitrants, the narrowing of opportunities for employment and promotion. All this is a common method of procedure today, but in 1904 it seemed to me monstrous and dishonest, and I resented it. On the other hand, the public expression of this resentment greatly exercised and annoyed Mr. Washington's friends. Some knew little about these activities at Tuskegee; others knew and approved. The New York *Evening Post* challenged me to present proof of my extraordinary statements and refused to regard my answer as sufficient, which was of course true.

Then came a new and surprising turn to the whole situation which in the end quite changed my life. In the early summer of 1905, Mr. Washington went to Boston and arranged to speak in a colored church to colored people—a thing which he did not often do in the North. Trotter and Forbes, editors of the *Guardian,* determined to heckle him and make him answer publicly certain questions with regard to his attitude toward voting and education. William H. Lewis, a colored lawyer whom I myself had introduced to Mr. Washington, had charge of the meeting, and the result was a disturbance magnified by the newspapers into a riot, which resulted in the arrest of Mr. Trotter. Eventually he served a term in jail.

With this incident I had no direct connection whatsoever. I did not know beforehand of the meeting in Boston, nor of the projected plan to heckle Mr. Washington. But when Trotter went to jail, my indignation overflowed. I did not always agree with Trotter then or later. But he was an honest, brilliant, unselfish man, and to treat as a crime that which was at worst mistaken judgment was

an outrage. I sent out from Atlanta in June, 1905, a call to
a few selected persons "for organized determination and
aggressive action on the part of men who believe in Negro
freedom and growth." I proposed a conference during the
summer "to oppose firmly present methods of strangling
honest criticism; to organize intelligent and honest
Negroes; and to support organs of news and public opinion."

Fifty-nine colored men from seventeen different states
signed a call for a meeting near Buffalo, New York, during
the week of July 9, 1905. I went to Buffalo and hired a
little hotel on the Canada side of the river at Fort Erie,
and waited for the men to attend the meeting. If sufficient
men had not come to pay for the hotel, I should certainly
have been in bankruptcy and perhaps in jail; but as a
matter of fact, twenty-nine men, representing fourteen
states, came. The "Niagara Movement" was organized
January 31, 1906, and was incorporated in the District of
Columbia.

Its particular business and objects are to advocate and
promote the following principles:

1. Freedom of speech and criticism.
2. Unfettered and unsubsidized press.
3. Manhood suffrage.
4. The abolition of all caste distinctions based simply
   on race and color.
5. The recognition of the principles of human
   brotherhood as a practical present creed.
6. The recognition of the highest and best human
   training as the monopoly of no class or race.

7. A belief in the dignity of labor.
8. United effort to realize these ideals under wise and courageous leadership.

The Niagara Movement raised a furor of the most disconcerting criticism. I was accused of acting from motives of envy of a great leader and being ashamed of the fact that I was a member of the Negro race. The leading weekly of the land, the New York *Outlook,* pilloried me with scathing articles. But the movement went on. The next year, 1906, instead of meeting in secret, we met openly at Harper's Ferry, the scene of John Brown's raid, and had in significance if not numbers one of the greatest meetings that American Negroes have ever held. We made pilgrimage at dawn bare-footed to the scene of Brown's martyrdom and we talked some of the plainest English that has been given voice to by black men in America. The resolutions which I wrote expressed with tumult of emotion my creed of 1905:

"The men of the Niagara Movement, coming from the toil of the year's hard work, and pausing a moment from the earning of their daily bread, turn toward the nation and again ask in the name of ten million the privilege of a hearing. In the past year the work of the Negro hater has flourished in the land. Step by step the defenders of the rights of American citizens have retreated. The work of stealing the black man's ballot has progressed and the fifty and more representatives of stolen votes still sit in the nation's capital. Discrimination in travel and public accommodation has so spread that some of our weaker brethren are actually afraid to thunder against color discrimination as such and are simply whispering for ordinary decencies.

"Against this the Niagara Movement eternally protests. We will not be satisfied to take one jot or title less than our full manhood rights. We claim for ourselves every single right that belongs to a freeborn American, political, civil, and social; and until we get these rights we will never cease to protest and assail the ears of America. The battle we wage is not for ourselves alone, but for all true Americans. It is a fight for ideals, lest this, our common fatherland, false to its founding, become in truth the land of the Thief and the home of the Slave—a by-word and a hissing among the nations for its sounding pretensions and pitiful accomplishment.

"Never before in the modern age has a great and civilized folk threatened to adopt so cowardly a creed in the treatment of its fellow-citizens, born and bred on its soil. Stripped of verbiage and subterfuge and in its naked nastiness, the new American creed says: fear to let black men even try to rise lest they become the equals of the white. And this is the land that professes to follow Jesus Christ. The blasphemy of such a course is only matched by its cowardice.

"In detail our demands are clear and unequivocal. First, we would vote; with the right to vote goes everything: freedom, manhood, the honor of your wives, the chastity of your daughters, the right to work, and the chance to rise, and let no man listen to those who deny this.

"We want full manhood suffrage, and we want it now, henceforth and forever.

"Second. We want discrimination in public accommodation to cease. Separation in railway and street cars, based simply on race and color, is un-American, undemocratic, and silly. We protest against all such discrimination.

"Third. We claim the right of freemen to walk, talk, and be with them that wish to be with us. No man has a right to choose another man's friends, and to attempt to do so is an impudent interference with the most fundamental human privilege.

"Fourth. We want the laws enforced against rich as well as poor; against Capitalist as well as Laborer; against white as well as black. We are not more lawless than the white race, we are more often arrested, convicted and mobbed. We want justice even for criminals and outlaws. We want the Constitution of the country enforced. We want Congress to take charge of the Congressional elections. We want the Fourteenth Amendment carried out to the letter and every State disfranchised in Congress which attempts to disfranchise its rightful voters. We want the Fifteenth Amendment enforced and no State allowed to base its franchise simply on color.

"The failure of the Republican Party in Congress at the session just closed to redeem its pledge of 1904 with reference to suffrage conditions at the South seems a plain, deliberate, and premeditated breach of promise, and stamps that party as guilty of obtaining votes under false pretense.

"Fifth. We want our children educated. The school system in the country districts of the South is a disgrace and in few towns and cities are the Negro schools what they ought to be. We want the national government to step in and wipe out illiteracy in the South. Either the

United States will destroy ignorance, or ignorance will destroy the United States.

"And when we call for education, we mean real education. We believe in work. We ourselves are workers, but work is not necessarily education. Education is the development of power and ideal. We want our children trained as intelligent human beings should be, and we will fight for all time against any proposal to educate black boys and girls simply as servants and underlings, or simply for the use of other people. They have a right to know, to think, to aspire.

"These are some of the chief things which we want. How shall we get them? By voting where we may vote; by persistent, unceasing agitation; by hammering at the truth; by sacrifice and work.

"We do not believe in violence, neither in the despised violence of the raid nor the lauded violence of the soldier, nor the barbarous violence of the mob; but we do believe in John Brown, in that incarnate spirit of justice, that hatred of a lie, that willingness to sacrifice money, reputation, and life itself on the altar of right. And here on the scene of John Brown's martyrdom, we reconsecrate ourselves, our honor, our property to the final emancipation of the race which John Brown died to make free."

Meantime, I refused to give up the idea that a critical periodical for the American Negro might be founded. I had started in Memphis with the help of two graduates of Atlanta University the little printing shop that I have already mentioned, and from this was published weekly a paper called *The Moon* beginning in 1906. *The Moon* was in some sort precursor of *The Crisis*. It was published for a year in Memphis and then the printing office given up and in 1907 in conjunction with two friends in Washington there was issued a miniature monthly called the *Horizon*. The *Horizon* was published from 1907 to 1910, and in the fall of 1910 *The Crisis* was born.

Gradually I began to realize that the difficulty about support for my work in Atlanta University was personal; that on account of my attitude toward Mr. Washington I had become *persona non grata* to powerful interests, and that Atlanta University would not be able to get support for its general work or for its study of the Negro problem so long as I remained at the institution. No one ever said this to me openly, but I sensed it in the worries which encompassed the new young President Ware who had succeeded Dr. Bumstead. I began to realize that I would better look out for work elsewhere.

About this time an offer came from the city of Washington. The merging of the white and colored school systems into one, had thrown colored folk into uproar lest their control of their own schools be eliminated. The new and rather eccentric W. C. Chancellor, superintendent of schools, wanted an assistant superintendent to put in charge of the Negro schools. To my great surprise he offered the position to me, while I was on a chance visit to the city. I asked for time to consider it. My reaction was to refuse even though the salary was twice what I was getting; for I doubted my fitness for such a job; but when I thought the matter over further and my position of Atlanta University, I began to wonder if I should not accept.

I was not called upon to decide, for forces started

moving in Washington. The Tuskegee Machine was definitely against me and local interests in the Negro group were opposed. A prominent colored official took the matter straight to President Theodore Roosevelt and emphasized the "danger" of my appointment. He never forgot the "danger" of my personality as later events proved. The offer was never actually withdrawn, but it was not pressed, and I finally realized that it probably would not have gone through even if I had indicated my acceptance.

Still my eventual withdrawal from Atlanta University seemed wise. Young President Ware had received almost categorical promise that under certain circumstances increased contributions from the General Education Board and other sources might be expected, which would make the University secure, and perhaps even permit the continuance of my studies. I was sure that I was at least one of these "circumstances," and so my work in Atlanta and my dream of the settlement of the Negro problem by science faded. I began to be acutely conscious of the difficulty which my attitudes and beliefs were making for Atlanta University.

My career as a scientist was to be swallowed up in my role as master of propaganda. This was not wholly to my liking. I was no natural leader of men. I could not slap people on the back and make friends of strangers. I could not easily break down an inherited reserve; or at all times curb a biting, critical tongue. Nevertheless, having put my hand to the plow, I had to go on. The Niagara Movement with less momentum met in Boston in 1907 and in Oberlin in 1908. It began to suffer internal strain from the dynamic personality of Trotter and my inexperience with organizations. Finally it practically became merged with a new and enveloping organization.

This started with a lynching 100 years after the birth of Abraham Lincoln, in his birthplace. William English Walling dramatized the gruesome happening and a group of liberals formed a committee in New York, which I was invited to join. A conference was held in 1909. After the conference, a new organization, the National Association for the Advancement of Colored People, was formed, which without formal merger absorbed practically the whole membership of the Niagara Movement, save Trotter, who distrusted our white allies and their objects. With some hesitation I was asked to come as Director of Publications and Research, with the idea that my research work was to go on and with the further idea that my activities would be so held in check that the Association would not develop as an organ of attack upon Tuskegee— a difficult order; because how, in 1910, could one discuss the Negro problem and not touch upon Booker T. Washington and Tuskegee? But after all, as I interpreted the matter, it was a question of temperament and manner rather than of subject.

Here was an opportunity to enter the lists in a desperate fight aimed straight at the real difficulty: the question as to how far educated Negro opinion in the United States was going to have the right and opportunity to guide the Negro group. I did not hesitate because I could not. It was the voice without reply, and I went to New York.

One may consider these personal equations and this

clash of ideologies as biographical or sociological; as a matter of the actions and thoughts of certain men, or as a development of larger social forces beyond personal control. I suppose the latter aspect is the truer. My thoughts, the thoughts of Washington, Trotter and others, were the expression of social forces more than of our own minds. These forces or ideologies embraced more than our reasoned acts. They included physical, biological and psychological forces; habits, conventions and enactments. Opposed to these came natural reaction: the physical recoil of the victims, the unconscious and irrational urges, as well as reasoned complaints and acts. The total result was the history of our day. That history may be epitomized in one word—Empire; the domination of white Europe over black Africa and yellow Asia, through political power built on the economic control of labor, income and ideas. The echo of this industrial imperialism in America was the expulsion of black men from American democracy, their subjection to caste control and wage slavery. This ideology was triumphant in 1910.

CHAPTER 5. THE CONCEPT OF RACE

I WANT now to turn aside from the personal annals of this biography to consider the conception which is after all my main subject. The concept of race lacks something in personal interest, but personal interest in my case has always depended primarily upon this race concept and I wish to examine this now. The history of the development of the race concept in the world and particularly in America, was naturally reflected in the education offered me. In the elementary school it came only in the matter of geography when the races of the world were pictured: Indians, Negroes and Chinese, by their most uncivilized and bizarre representatives; the whites by some kindly and distinguished-looking philanthropist. In the elementary and high school, the matter was touched only incidentally, due I doubt not to the thoughtfulness of the teachers; and again my racial inferiority could not be dwelt upon because the single representative of the Negro race in the school did not happen to be in any way inferior to his fellows. In fact it was not difficult for me to excel them in many ways and to regard this as quite natural.

At Fisk, the problem of race was faced openly and essential racial equality asserted and natural inferiority strenuously denied. In some cases the teachers expressed this theory; in most cases the student opinion naturally forced it. At Harvard, on the other hand, I began to face scientific race dogma: first of all, evolution and the "Survival of the Fittest." It was continually stressed in the community and in classes that there was a vast difference in the development of the whites and the "lower" races; that this could be seen in the physical development of the Negro. I remember once in a museum, coming face to face with a demonstration: a series of skeletons arranged from a little monkey to a tall well-developed white man, with a Negro barely outranking a chimpanzee. Eventually in my classes stress was quietly transferred to brain weight and brain capacity, and at last to the "cephalic index."

In the graduate school at Harvard and again in Germany, the emphasis again was altered, and race became a matter of culture and cultural history. The history of the world was paraded before the observation of students. Which was the superior race? Manifestly that which had a history, the white race; there was some mention of Asiatic culture, but no course in Chinese or Indian history or culture was offered at Harvard, and quite unanimously in America and Germany, Africa was left without culture and without history. Even when the matter of mixed races was touched upon their evident and conscious inferiority was mentioned. I can never forget that morning in the class of the great Heinrich von Treitschke in Berlin. He was a big aggressive man, with an impediment in his speech which forced him to talk rapidly lest he stutter. His classes were the only ones always on time, and an angry scraping of feet greeted a late comer. Clothed in black, big, bushy-haired, peering sharply at the class, his words rushed out in a flood: "Mulattoes," he thundered, "are inferior." I almost felt his eyes boring into me, although probably he had not noticed me. "Sie fühlen sich niedriger!" "Their actions show it," he asserted. What contradiction could there be to that authoritative dictum?

The first thing which brought me to my senses in all this racial discussion was the continuous change in the proofs and arguments advanced. I could accept evolution and the survival of the fittest, provided the interval between advanced and backward races was not made too impossible. I balked at the usual "thousand years." But no sooner had I settled into scientific security here, than the basis of race distinction was changed without explanation, without apology. I was skeptical about brain weight; surely much depended upon what brains were weighed. I was not sure about physical measurements and social inquiries. For instance, an insurance actuary published in 1890 incontrovertible statistics showing how quickly and certainly the Negro race was dying out in the United States through sheer physical inferiority. I lived to see every assumption of Hoffman's "Race Traits and Tendencies" contradicted; but even before that, I doubted the statistical method which he had used. When the matter of race became a question of comparative culture, I was in revolt. I began to see that the cultural equipment attributed to any people depended largely on who estimated it; and conviction came later in a rush as I realized what in my education had been suppressed concerning Asiatic and African culture.

It was not until I was long out of school and indeed after the World War that there came the hurried use of the new technique of psychological tests, which were quickly adjusted so as to put black folk absolutely beyond the possibility of civilization. By this time I was unimpressed. I had too often seen science made the slave of caste and race hate. And it was interesting to see Odum, McDougall and Brigham eventually turn somersaults from absolute scientific proof of Negro inferiority to repudiation of the limited and questionable application of any test which pretended to measure innate human intelligence.

So far I have spoken of "race" and race problems quite as a matter of course without explanation or definition. That was our method in the nineteenth century. Just as I was born a member of a colored family, so too I was born a member of the colored race. That was obvious and no definition was needed. Later I adopted the designation "Negro" for the race to which I belong. It seemed more definite and logical. At the same time I was of course aware that all members of the Negro race were not black and that the pictures of my race which were current were not authentic nor fair portraits. But all that was incidental. The world was divided into great primary groups of folk who belonged naturally together through heredity of physical traits and cultural affinity.

I do not know how I came first to form my theories of race. The process was probably largely unconscious. The differences of personal appearance between me and my fellows, I must have been conscious of when quite young. Whatever distinctions came because of that did not irritate me; they rather exalted me because, on the whole, while I was still a youth, they gave me exceptional position and a chance to excel rather than handicapping me.

Then of course, when I went South to Fisk, I became a member of a closed racial group with rites and loyalties, with a history and a corporate future, with an art and philosophy. I received these eagerly and expanded them so that when I came to Harvard the theory of race separation was quite in my blood. I did not seek contact with my white fellow students. On the whole I rather avoided them. I took it for granted that we were training ourselves for different careers in worlds largely different. There was not the slightest idea of the permanent subordination and inequality of my world. Nor again was there any idea of racial amalgamation. I resented the assumption that we desired it. I frankly refused the possibility while in Germany and even in America gave up courtship with one "colored" girl because she looked quite white, and I should resent the inference on the street that I had married outside my race.

All this theory, however, was disturbed by certain facts in America, and by my European experience. Despite everything, race lines were not fixed and fast. Within the Negro group especially there were people of all colors. Then too, there were plenty of my colored friends who resented my ultra "race" loyalty and ridiculed it. They pointed out that I was not a "Negro," but a mulatto; that I was not a Southerner but a Northerner, and my object was to be an American and not a Negro; that race distinctions must go. I agreed with this in part and as an ideal, but I saw it leading to inner racial distinction in the colored group. I resented the defensive mechanism of avoiding too dark companions in order to escape notice and discrimination in public. As a sheer matter of taste I wanted the color of my group to be visible. I hotly championed the inclusion of two black school mates whose names were not usually on the invitation list to our social affairs. In Europe my friendships and close contact with white folk made my own ideas waver. The eternal walls between races did not seem so stern and exclusive. I began to emphasize the cultural aspects of race.

It is probably quite natural for persons of low degree, who have reached any status, to search feverishly for distinguished ancestry, as a sort of proof of their inherent desert. This is particularly true in America and has given rise to a number of organizations whose membership depends upon ancestors who have made their mark in the world. Of course, it is clear that there must be here much fable, invention and wishful thinking, facilitated by poor vital statistics and absence of written records. For the mass of Americans, and many Americans who have had the most distinguished careers, have been descended from people who were quite ordinary and even less; America indeed has meant the breaking down of class bars which imprisoned personalities and capabilities and allowing new men and new families to emerge. This is not, as some people assume, a denial of the importance of heredity and family. It is rather its confirmation. It shows us that the few in the past who have emerged are not necessarily the best; and quite certainly are not the only ones worthy of development and distinction; that, on the contrary, only a comparatively few have, under our present economic and social organization, had a chance to show their capabilities.

I early began to take a direct interest in my own family as a group and became curious as to that physical descent which so long I had taken for granted quite unquestioningly. But I did not at first think of any but my Negro ancestors. I knew little and cared less of the white forebears of my father. But this chauvinism gradually changed. There is, of course, nothing more fascinating than the question of the various types of mankind and their intermixture. The whole question of heredity and human gift depends upon such knowledge; but ever since the African slave trade and before the rise of modern biology and sociology, we have been afraid in America that scientific study in this direction might lead to conclusions with which we were loath to agree; and this fear was in reality because the economic foundation of the modern world was based on the recognition and preservation of so-called racial distinctions. In accordance with this, not only Negro slavery could be justified, but the Asiatic coolie profitably used and the labor classes in white countries kept in their places by low wage.

It is not singular then that here in America and in the West Indies, where we have had the most astonishing modern mixture of human types, scientific study of the results and circumstances of this mixture has not only lagged but been almost non-existent. We have not only not studied race and race mixture in America, but we have tried almost by legal process to stop such study. It is for this reason that it has occurred to me just here to illustrate the way in which Africa and Europe have been united in my family. There is nothing unusual about this interracial history. It has been duplicated thousands of times;

but on the one hand, the white folk have bitterly resented even a hint of the facts of this intermingling; while black folk have recoiled in natural hesitation and affected disdain in admitting what they know.

I am, therefore, relating the history of my family and centering it around my maternal great-great-grandfather, Tom Burghardt, and my paternal grandfather, Alexander Du Bois.

Absolute legal proof of facts like those here set down is naturally unobtainable. Records of birth are often nonexistent, proof of paternity is exceedingly difficult and actual written record rare. In the case of my family I have relied on oral tradition in my mother's family and direct word and written statement from my paternal grandfather; and upon certain general records which I have been able to obtain. I have no doubt of the substantial accuracy of the story that I am to tell.

Of my own immediate ancestors I knew personally only four: my mother and her parents and my paternal grandfather. One other I knew at second hand—my father. I had his picture. I knew what my mother told me about him and what others who had known him, said. So that in all, five of my immediate forebears were known to me. Three others, my paternal great-grandfather and my maternal great-grandfather and great-great-grandfather, I knew about through persons who knew them and through records; and also I knew many of my collateral relatives and numbers of their descendants. My known ancestral family, therefore, consisted of eight or more persons. None of these had reached any particular distinction or were known very far beyond their own families and localities.

They were divided into whites, blacks and mulattoes, most of them being mulattoes.

My paternal great-grandfather, Dr. James Du Bois, was white and descended from Chrétien Du Bois who was a French Huguenot farmer and perhaps artisan and resided at Wicres near Lille in French Flanders. It is doubtful if he had any ancestors among the nobility, although his white American descendants love to think so. He had two, possibly three, sons of whom Louis and Jacques came to America to escape religious persecution. Jacques went from France first to Leiden in the Netherlands, where he was married and had several children, including a second Jacques or James. In 1674 that family came to America and settled at Kingston, New York. James Du Bois appears in the Du Bois family genealogy as a descendant of Jacques in the fifth generation, although the exact line of descent is not clear; but my grandfather's written testimony establishes that James was a physician and a landholder along the Hudson and in the West Indies. He was born in 1750, or later. He may have been a loyalist refugee. One such refugee, Isaac Du Bois, was given a grant of five hundred acres in Eleuthera after the Revolutionary War.

The career of Dr. James Du Bois was chiefly as a plantation proprietor and slave owner in the Bahama Islands with his headquarters at Long Cay. Cousins of his named Gilbert also had plantations near. He never married, but had one of his slaves as his common-law wife, a small brown-skinned woman born on the island. Of this couple two sons were born, Alexander and John. Alexander, my grandfather, was born in 1803, and about 1810, possibly because of the death of the mother, the father brought both these boys to America and planned to give them the education of gentlemen. They were white enough in appearance to give no inkling of their African descent. They were entered in the private Episcopal school at Cheshire, Connecticut, which still exists there and has trained many famous men. Dr. James Du Bois used often to visit his sons there, but about 1812, on his return from a visit, he had a stroke of apoplexy and died. He left no will and his estate descended to a cousin.

The boys were removed from school and bound out as apprentices, my grandfather to a shoemaker. Their connection with the white Du Bois family ceased suddenly, and was never renewed. Alexander Du Bois thus started with a good common school and perhaps some high school training and with the instincts of a gentleman of his day. Naturally he passed through much inner turmoil. He became a rebel, bitter at his lot in life, resentful at being classed as a Negro and yet implacable in his attitude toward whites. Of his brother, John, I have only a picture. He may have been the John Du Bois who helped Bishop Payne to purchase Wilberforce University.

If Alexander Du Bois, following the footsteps of Alexander Hamilton, had come from the West Indies to the United States, stayed with the white group and married and begotten children among them, anyone in after years who had suggested his Negro descent would have been unable to prove it and quite possibly would have been laughed to scorn, or sued for libel. Indeed the legal advisers of the publishers of my last book could write: "We may assume as a general proposition that it is libelous to state erroneously that a white man or woman has colored blood." Lately in Congress the true story, in a WPA history, of miscegenation affecting a high historic personage raised a howl of protest.

Alexander Du Bois did differently from Hamilton. He married into the colored group and his oldest son allied himself with a Negro clan but four generations removed from Africa. He himself first married Sarah Marsh Lewis in 1823 and then apparently set out to make his way in Haiti. There my father was born in 1825, and his elder sister, Augusta, a year earlier, either there or just as the family was leaving the United States. Evidently the situation in Haiti did not please my grandfather or perhaps the death of his young wife when she was scarcely thirty turned him back to America. Within a year he married Emily Basset who seems to have been the widow of a man named Jacklyn and lived in New Milford. Leonard Bacon, a well-known Congregational clergyman, performed his second marriage.

The following year, Alexander began his career in the United States. He lived in New Haven, Springfield, Providence, and finally in New Bedford. For some time, he was steward on the New York-New Haven boat and insisted on better treatment for his colored help. Later about 1848 he ran a grocery store at 23 Washington Street, New Haven, and owned property at different times in the various cities where he lived. By his first wife, my grandmother, he had two children, and by his second wife, one daughter, Henrietta. Three or four children died in infancy. Alexander was a communicant of Trinity Parish, New Haven, and was enrolled there as late as 1845; then something happened, because in 1847 he was among that group of Negroes who formed the new colored Episcopal Parish of St. Luke, where he was for years their senior warden. Probably this indicates one of his bitter fights and rebellions, for nothing but intolerable insult would have led him into a segregated church movement. Alexander Crummell was his first rector here.

As I knew my grandfather, he was a short, stern, up-standing man, sparing but precise in his speech and stiff in manner, evidently long used to repressing his feelings. I remember as a boy of twelve, watching his ceremonious reception of a black visitor, John Freedom; his stately bow, the way in which the red wine was served and the careful almost stilted conversation. I had seen no such social cere-mony in my simple western Massachusetts home. The darkened parlor with its horsehair furniture became a very special and important place. I was deeply impressed. My grandfather evidently looked upon me with a certain misgiving if not actual distaste. I was brown, the son of his oldest son, Alfred, and Alfred and his father had never gotten on together.

The boy Alfred was a throwback to his white grand-father. He was small, olive-skinned and handsome and just visibly colored, with curly hair; and he was naturally a play-boy. My only picture of him shows him clothed in the uniform of the Union Army; but he never actually went to the front. In fact, Alfred never actually did much of anything. He was gay and carefree, refusing to settle long at any one place or job. He had a good elementary school training but nothing higher. I think that my father ran away from home several times. Whether he got into any very serious scrapes or not, I do not know, nor do I know whether he was married early in life; I imagine not. I think he was probably a free lance, gallant and lover, yielding only to marital bonds when he found himself in the rather strict clannishness of my mother's family. He was barber, merchant and preacher, but always irresponsible and charming. He had wandered out from eastern New England where his father lived and come to the Berkshire valley in 1867 where he met and married my brown mother.

The second wife of Alexander Du Bois died in 1865. His oldest daughter, Augusta, married a light mulatto and has descendants today who do not know of their Negro blood. Much later Alexander Du Bois married his third wife, Annie Green, who was the grandmother that I knew, and who knew and liked my father Alfred, and who brought me and my grandfather together. Alexander Du Bois died December 9, 1887, at the age of eighty-four, in New Bedford, and lies buried today in Oak Grove Cemetery near the Yale campus in New Haven, in a lot which he owned and which is next to that of Jehudi Ashmun of Liberian fame.

My father, by some queer chance, came into western Massachusetts and into the Housatonic Valley at the age of forty-two and there met and quickly married my brown mother who was then thirty-six and belonged to the Burghardt clan. This brings us to the history of the black Burghardts.

In 1694, Rev. Benjamin Wadsworth, afterwards president of Harvard College, made a journey through western Massachusetts, and says in regard to the present site of the town of Great Barrington, "Ye greatest part of our road this day was a hideous, howling wilderness." Here it was that a committee of the Massachusetts General Court confirmed a number of land titles in 1733-34, which had previously been in dispute between the English, Dutch, and Indians. In the "fifth division" of this land appears the name of a Dutchman, who signed himself as "Coenraet Borghghardt." This Borghghardt, Bogoert or Burghardt family has been prominent in Dutch colonial history and its descendants have been particularly identified with the annals of the little town of about five thousand inhabitants which today still lies among the hills of middle Berkshire.

Coenrod Burghardt seems to have been a shrewd pushing Dutchman and is early heard of in Kinderhook, together with his son John. This family came into possession of an African Negro named Tom, who had formerly belonged to the family of Etsons (Ettens?) and had come to the Burghardts by purchase or possibly by marriage. This African has had between one hundred and fifty and two hundred descendants, a number of whom are now living and reach to the eighth generation.

Tom was probably born about 1730. His granddaughter writes me that her father told her that Tom was born in Africa and was brought to this country when he was a boy. For many years my youthful imagination painted him as certainly the son of a tribal chief, but there is no warrant for this even in family tradition. Tom was probably just a stolen black boy from the West African Coast, nameless and lost, either a war captive or a tribal pawn. He was probably sent overseas on a Dutch ship at the time when their slave trade was beginning to decline and the vast English expansion to begin. He was in the service of the Burghardts and was a soldier in the Revolutionary War, going to the front probably several times; of only one of these is there official record when he appeared with the rank of private on the muster and payroll of Colonel John Ashley's Berkshire County regiment and Captain John Spoor's company in 1780. The company marched northward by order of Brigadier-General Fellows on an alarm when Fort Anne and Fort George were taken by the enemy. It is recorded that Tom was "reported a Negro." (Record Index of the Military Archives of Massachusetts, Vol. 23, p. 2.)

Tom appears to have been held as a servant and possibly a legal slave first by the family of Etsons or Ettens and then to have come into the possession of the Burghardts who settled at Great Barrington. Eventually, probably after the Revolutionary War, he was regarded as a freeman. There is record of only one son, Jacob Burghardt, who continued in the employ of the Burghardt family, and was born apparently about 1760. He is listed in the census of 1790 as "free" with two in his family. He married a wife named Violet who was apparently newly arrived from Africa and brought with her an African song which became traditional in the family. After her death, Jacob married Mom Bett, a rather celebrated figure in western Massachusetts history. She had been freed under the Bill of Rights of 1780 and the son of the judge who freed her wrote, "Even in her humble station, she had, when occasion required it, an air of command which conferred a degree of dignity and gave her an ascendancy over those of her rank, or color. Her determined and resolute character, which en-

abled her to limit the ravages of Shays's mob, was mani-
fested in her conduct and deportment during her whole
life. She claimed no distinction, but it was yielded to her
from her superior experience, energy, skill and sagacity.
Having known this woman as familiarly as I knew either
of my parents, I cannot believe in the moral or physical
inferiority of the race to which she belonged. The degradation of the African must have been otherwise caused
than by natural inferiority."

Family tradition has it that her husband, Jacob, took
part in suppressing this Shays's Rebellion. Jacob Burghardt
had nine children, five sons of whom one was my grandfather, and four daughters. My grandfather's brothers and
sisters had many children: Harlow had ten and Ira also
ten; Maria had two. Descendants of Harlow and Ira still
survive. Three of these sons, Othello, Ira, Harlow, and one
daughter Lucinda settled on South Egremont plain near
Great Barrington, where they owned small adjoining
farms. A small part of one of these farms I continue to
own.

Othello was my grandfather. He was born November
18, 1791, and married Sarah Lampman in 1811. Sarah was
born in Hillsdale, New York, in 1793, of a mother named
Lampman. There is no record of her father. She was probably the child of a Dutchman perhaps with Indian blood.
This couple had ten children, three sons and seven daughters. Othello died in 1872 at the age of eighty-one and
Sarah or Sally in 1877 at the age of eighty-six. Their sons
and daughters married and drifted to town as laborers and
servants. I thus had innumerable cousins up and down the
valley. I was brought up with the Burghardt clan and this

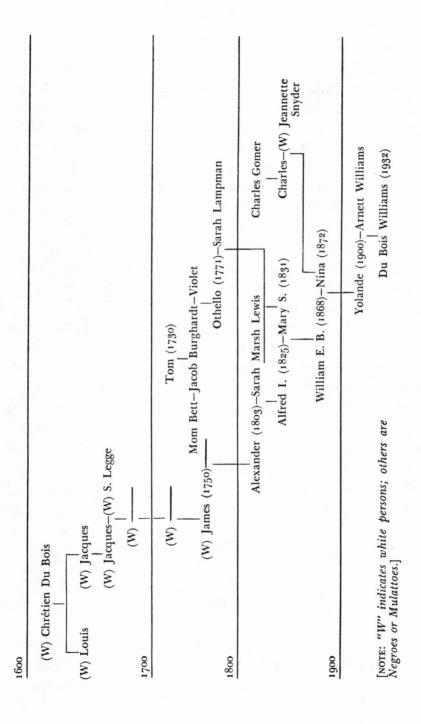

1600

(W) Chrétien Du Bois

(W) Louis   (W) Jacques

(W) Jacques—(W) S. Legge

(W)

(W)

1700

Tom (1730)

(W) James (1750)———

Mom Bett—Jacob Burghardt—Violet

Othello (1771)—Sarah Lampman

1800

Charles Gomer

Charles—(W) Jeannette Snyder

Alexander (1803)—Sarah Marsh Lewis

Alfred I. (1825)—Mary S. (1831)

William E. B. (1868)—Nina (1872)

Yolande (1900)—Arnett Williams

Du Bois Williams (1932)

1900

[NOTE: "W" indicates white persons; others are Negroes or Mulattoes.]

fact determined largely my life and "race." The white relationship and connections were quite lost and indeed unknown until long years after. The black Burghardts were ordinary farmers, laborers and servants. The children usually learned to read and write. I never heard or knew of any of them of my mother's generation or later who were illiterate. I was, however, the first one of the family who finished in the local high school. Afterward, one or two others did. Most of the members of the family left Great Barrington. Parts of the family are living and are fairly prosperous in the Middle West and on the Pacific Coast. I have heard of one or two high school graduates in the Middle West branch of the family.

This, then, was my racial history and as such it was curiously complicated. With Africa I had only one direct cultural connection and that was the African melody which my great-grandmother Violet used to sing. Where she learned it, I do not know. Perhaps she herself was born in Africa or had it of a mother or father stolen and transported. But at any rate, as I wrote years ago in the "Souls of Black Folk," "coming to the valleys of the Hudson and Housatonic, black, little, and lithe, she shivered and shrank in the harsh north winds, looked longingly at the hills, and often crooned a heathen melody to the child between her knees, thus:

> Do bana coba, gene me, gene me!
> Do bana coba, gene me, gene me!
> Ben d' nuli, nuli, nuli, nuli, ben d' le.

The child sang it to his children and they to their children's children, and so two hundred years it has traveled down to us and we sing it to our children, knowing as little as our fathers what its words may mean, but knowing well the meaning of its music."

Living with my mother's people I absorbed their culture patterns and these were not African so much as Dutch and New England. The speech was an idiomatic New England tongue with no African dialect; the family customs were New England, and the sex mores. My African racial feeling was then purely a matter of my own later learning and reaction; my recoil from the assumptions of the whites; my experience in the South at Fisk. But it was none the less real and a large determinant of my life and character. I felt myself African by "race" and by that token was African and an integral member of the group of dark Americans who were called Negroes.

At the same time I was firm in asserting that these Negroes were Americans. For that reason and on the basis of my great-great-grandfather's Revolutionary record I was accepted as a member of the Massachusetts Society of the Sons of the American Revolution, in 1908. When, however, the notice of this election reached the headquarters in Washington and was emphasized by my requesting a national certificate, the secretary, A. Howard Clark of the Smithsonian Institution, wrote to Massachusetts and demanded "proof of marriage of the ancestor of Tom Burghardt and record of birth of the son." He knew, of course, that the birth record of a stolen African slave could not possibly be produced. My membership was, therefore, suspended.

Countee Cullen sings:

> What is Africa to me:
> Copper sun or scarlet sea,

Jungle star or jungle track,
Strong bronzed men, or regal black
Women from whose loins I sprang
When the birds of Eden sang?
One three centuries removed
From the scenes his fathers loved,
Spicy grove, cinnamon tree,
What is Africa to me?

What is Africa to me? Once I should have answered the question simply: I should have said "fatherland" or perhaps better "motherland" because I was born in the century when the walls of race were clear and straight; when the world consisted of mutally exclusive races; and even though the edges might be blurred, there was no question of exact definition and understanding of the meaning of the word. One of the first pamphlets that I wrote in 1897 was on "The Conservation of Races" wherein I set down as the first article of a proposed racial creed: "We believe that the Negro people as a race have a contribution to make to civilization and humanity which no other race can make."

Since then the concept of race has so changed and presented so much of contradiction that as I face Africa I ask myself: what is it between us that constitutes a tie which I can feel better than I can explain? Africa is, of course, my fatherland. Yet neither my father nor my father's father ever saw Africa or knew its meaning or cared overmuch for it. My mother's folk were closer and yet their direct connection, in culture and race, became tenuous; still, my tie to Africa is strong. On this vast continent were born and lived a large portion of my direct ancestors going back a thousand years or more. The mark of their heritage is upon me in color and hair. These are obvious things, but of little meaning in themselves; only important as they stand for real and more subtle differences from other men. Whether they do or not, I do not know nor does science know today.

But one thing is sure and that is the fact that since the fifteenth century these ancestors of mine and their other descendants have had a common history; have suffered a common disaster and have one long memory. The actual ties of heritage between the individuals of this group, vary with the ancestors that they have in common and many others: Europeans and Semites, perhaps Mongolians, certainly American Indians. But the physical bond is least and the badge of color relatively unimportant save as a badge; the real essence of this kinship is its social heritage of slavery; the discrimination and insult; and this heritage binds together not simply the children of Africa, but extends through yellow Asia and into the South Seas. It is this unity that draws me to Africa.

When shall I forget the night I first set foot on African soil? I am the sixth generation in descent from forefathers who left this land. The moon was at the full and the waters of the Atlantic lay like a lake. All the long slow afternoon as the sun robed herself in her western scarlet with veils of misty cloud, I had seen Africa afar. Cape Mount—that mighty headland with its twin curves, northern sentinel of the realm of Liberia—gathered itself out of the cloud at half past three and then darkened and grew clear. On beyond flowed the dark low undulating land quaint with palm and breaking sea. The world grew black. Africa faded away, the stars stood forth curiously twisted—Orion in the zenith—the Little Bear asleep and the Southern Cross rising behind the horizon. Then afar, ahead, a lone light shone, straight at the ship's fore. Twinkling lights appeared below, around, and rising shadows. "Monrovia," said the Captain.

Suddenly we swerved to our left. The long arms of the bay enveloped us and then to the right rose the twinkling hill of Monrovia, with its crowning star. Lights flashed on the shore—here, there. Then we sensed a darker shading in the shadows; it lay very still. "It's a boat," one said. "It's two boats!" Then the shadow drifted in pieces and as the anchor roared into the deep, five boats outlined themselves on the waters—great ten-oared barges with men swung into line and glided toward us.

It was nine at night—above, the shadows, there the town, here the sweeping boats. One forged ahead with the flag—stripes and a lone star flaming behind, the ensign of the customs floating wide; and bending to the long oars, the white caps of ten black sailors. Up the stairway clambered a soldier in khaki, aide-de-camp of the President of the Republic, a customhouse official, the clerk of the American legation—and after them sixty-five lithe, lean black stevedores with whom the steamer would work down to Portuguese Angola and back. A few moments of formalities, greetings and good-bys and I was in the great long boat with the President's aide—a brown major in brown khaki. On the other side, the young clerk and at the back, the black barelegged pilot. Before us on the high thwarts were the rowers: men, boys, black, thin, trained in muscle and sinew, little larger than the oars in thickness, they bent their strength to them and swung upon them.

One in the center gave curious little cackling cries to keep up the rhythm, and for the spurts and the stroke, a call a bit thicker and sturdier; he gave a low guttural command now and then; the boat, alive, quivering, danced beneath the moon, swept a great curve to the bar to breast its narrow teeth of foam—"t'chick-a-tickity, t'chick-a-tickity," sang the boys, and we glided and raced, now between boats, now near the landing—now cast aloft at the dock. And lo! I was in Africa.

Christmas Eve, and Africa is singing in Monrovia. They are Krus and Fanti—men, women and children, and all the night they march and sing. The music was once the music of mission revival hymns. But it is that music now transformed and the silly words hidden in an unknown tongue—liquid and sonorous. It is tricked out and expounded with cadence and turn. And this is that same rhythm I heard first in Tennessee forty years ago: the air is raised and carried by men's strong voices, while floating above in obbligato, come the high mellow voices of women —it is the ancient African art of part singing, so curiously and insistently different.

So they come, gay appareled, lit by transparency. They enter the gate and flow over the high steps and sing and sing and sing. They saunter round the house, pick flowers, drink water and sing and sing and sing. The warm dark heat of the night steams up to meet the moon. And the night is song.

On Christmas Day, 1923, we walk down to the narrow, crooked wharves of Monrovia, by houses old and gray and step-like streets of stone. Before is the wide St. Paul River, double-mouthed, and beyond, the sea, white, curling on the sand. Before us is the isle—the tiny isle, hut-covered and guarded by a cotton tree, where the pioneers lived in 1821. We board the boat, then circle round—then up the river. Great bowing trees, festoons of flowers, golden blossoms, star-faced palms and thatched huts; tall spreading trees lifting themselves like vast umbrellas, low shrubbery with gray and laced and knotted roots—the broad, black, murmuring river. Here a tree holds wide fingers out and stretches them over the water in vast incantation; bananas throw their wide green fingers to the sun. Iron villages, scarred clearings with gray, sheet-iron homes staring, grim and bare, at the ancient tropical flood of green.

The river sweeps wide and the shrubs bow low. Behind, Monrovia rises in clear, calm beauty. Gone are the wharves, the low and clustered houses of the port, the tight-throated business village, and up sweep the villas and the low wall, brown and cream and white, with great mango and cotton trees, with lighthouse and spire, with porch and pillar and the color of shrubbery and blossom.

We climbed the upright shore to a senator's home and received his wide and kindly hospitality—curious blend of feudal lord and modern farmer—sandwiches, cake, and champagne. Again we glided up the drowsy river—five, ten, twenty miles and came to our hostess, a mansion of five generations with a compound of endless native servants and cows under the palm thatches. The daughters of the family wore, on the beautiful black skin of their necks, the exquisite pale gold chains of the Liberian artisan and the slim, black little granddaughter of the house had a wide pink ribbon on the thick curls of her dark hair, that lay like sudden sunlight on the shadows. Double porches, one above the other, welcomed us to ease. A native man, gay with Christmas and a dash of gin, sang and danced in the road. Children ran and played in the blazing sun. We sat at a long broad table and ate duck, chicken, beef, rice, plantain, collards, cake, tea, water and Madeira wine. Then we went and looked at the heavens, the uptwisted sky—Orion and Cassiopeia at zenith; the Little Bear beneath the horizon, now unfamiliar sights in the Milky Way—all awry, a-living—sun for snow at Christmas, and happiness and cheer.

The shores were lined with old sugar plantations, the buildings rotting and falling. I looked upon the desolation with a certain pain. What had happened, I asked? The owners and planters had deserted these homes and come down to Monrovia, but why? After all, Monrovia had not much to offer in the way of income and occupation. Was this African laziness and inefficiency? No, it was a specimen of the way in which the waves of modern industry broke over the shores of far-off Africa. Here during our Civil War, men hastened to raise sugar and supply New York. They built their own boats and filled the river and sailed the sea. But afterwards, Louisiana came back into the Union, colored Rillieux invented the vacuum pan; the sugar plantations began to spread in Cuba and the Sugar Trust monopoly of refining machinery, together with the new beet sugar industry, drove Liberia quickly from the market. What all this did not do, the freight rates finished. So sugar did not pay in Liberia and other crops rose and fell in the same way.

As I look back and recall the days, which I have called great—the occasions in which I have taken part and which have had for me and others the widest significance, I can remember none like the first of January, 1924. Once I took my bachelor's degree before a governor, a great college president, and a bishop of New England. But that was rather personal in its memory than in any way epochal. Once before the assembled races of the world I was called to speak in London in place of the suddenly sick Sir Harry Johnston. It was a great hour. But it was not greater than the day when I was presented to the President of the Negro Republic of Liberia.

Liberia had been resting under the shock of world war into which the Allies forced her. She had asked and been promised a loan by the United States to bolster and replace her stricken trade. She had conformed to every preliminary requirement and waited when waiting was almost fatal. It was not simply money, it was world prestige and protection at a time when the little republic was sorely beset by creditors and greedy imperial powers. At the last moment, an insurgent Senate peremptorily and finally refused the request and strong recommendation of President Wilson and his advisers, and the loan was refused. The Department of State made no statement to the world, and Liberia stood naked, not only well-nigh bankrupt, but peculiarly defenseless amid scowling and unbelieving powers.

It was then that the United States made a gesture of courtesy; a little thing, and merely a gesture, but one so unusual that it was epochal. President Coolidge, at the suggestion of William H. Lewis, a leading colored lawyer of Boston, named me, an American Negro traveler, Envoy Extraordinary and Minister Plenipotentiary to Liberia— the highest rank ever given by any country to a diplomatic agent in black Africa. And it named this Envoy the special representative of the President of the United States to the President of Liberia, on the occasion of his inauguration; charging the Envoy with a personal word of encouragement and moral support. It was a significant action. It had in it nothing personal. Another appointee would have been equally significant. But Liberia recognized the meaning. She showered upon the Envoy every mark of appreciation and thanks. The Commander of the Liberian Frontier Force was made his special aide, and a sergeant, his orderly. At ten a.m. New Year's morning, 1924, a company of the Frontier Force, in red fez and khaki, presented arms before the American Legation and escorted Solomon Porter Hood, the American Minister Resident, and myself as Envoy Extraordinary and my aide to the Presidential Mansion—a beautiful white, verandaed house, waving with palms and fronting a grassy street.

Ceremonials are old and to some antiquated and yet this was done with such simplicity, grace and seriousness that none could escape its spell. The Secretary of State met us at the door, as the band played the impressive Liberian National hymn, and soldiers saluted:

> All hail! Liberia, hail!
> In union strong, success is sure.
> We cannot fail.
> With God above,
> Our rights to prove,
> We will the world assail.

We mounted a broad stairway and into a great room that stretched across the house. Here in semi-circle were ranged the foreign consuls and the cabinet—the former in white, gilt with orders and swords; the latter in solemn black. Present were England, France, Germany, Spain, Belgium, Holland, and Panama, to be presented to me in order of seniority by the small brown Secretary of State with his perfect poise and ease. The President entered—frock-coated with the star and ribbon of a Spanish order on his breast. The American Minister introduced me, and I said:

"The President of the United States has done me the great honor of designating me as his personal representative on the occasion of your inauguration. In so doing, he has had, I am sure, two things in mind. First, he wished publicly and unmistakably to express before the world the interest and solicitude which the hundred million inhabitants of the United States of America have for Liberia. Liberia is a child of the United States, and a sister Republic. Its progress and success is the progress and success of democracy everywhere and for all men; and the United States would view with sorrow and alarm any misfortune which might happen to this Republic and any obstacle that was placed in her path.

"But special and peculiar bonds draw these two lands together. In America live eleven million persons of African descent; they are citizens, legally invested with every right that inheres in American citizenship. And I am sure that in this special mark of the President's favor, he has had in mind the wishes and hopes of Negro Americans. He knows how proud they are of the hundred years of independence which you have maintained by force of arms and by brawn and brain upon the edge of this mighty continent; he knows that in the great battle against color caste in America, the ability of Negroes to rule in Africa has been and ever will be a great and encouraging reenforcement. He knows that the unswerving loyalty of Negro Americans to their country is fitly accompanied by a pride in their race and lineage, a belief in the potency and promise of Negro blood which makes them eager listeners to every whisper of success from Liberia, and eager helpers in every movement for your aid and comfort. In a special sense, the moral burden of Liberia and the advancement and integrity of Liberia is the sincere prayer of America."

And now a word about the African himself—about this primitive black man: I began to notice a truth as I entered southern France. I formulated it in Portugal. I knew it as a great truth one Sunday in Liberia. And the Great Truth was this: efficiency and happiness do not go together in modern culture. Going south from London, as the world darkens it gets happier. Portugal is deliciously dark. Many leading citizens would have difficulty keeping off a Georgia "Jim Crow" car. But, oh, how lovely a land and how happy a people! And so leisurely. Little use of trying to shop seriously in Lisbon before eleven. It isn't done. Nor at noon; the world is lunching or lolling in the sun. Even after four p.m. one takes chances, for the world is in the Rocio. And the banks are so careless and the hotels so leisurely. How delightfully angry Englishmen get at the "damned, lazy" Portuguese!

But if this of Portugal, what of Africa? Here darkness descends and rests on lovely skins until brown seems luscious and natural. There is sunlight in great gold globules and soft, heavy-scented heat that wraps you like a garment. And laziness; divine, eternal, languor is right and good and true. I remember the morning; it was Sunday, and the night before we heard the leopards crying down there. Today beneath the streaming sun we went down into the gold-green forest. It was silence—silence the more mysterious because life abundant and palpitating pulsed all about us and held us drowsy captives to the day. Ahead the gaunt missionary strode, alert, afire, with his gun. He apologized for the gun, but he did not need to, for I saw the print of a leopard's hind foot. A monkey sentinel screamed, and I heard the whir of the horde as they ran.

Then we came to the village; how can I describe it? Neither London, nor Paris, nor New York has anything of its delicate, precious beauty. It was a town of the Veys and done in cream and pale purple—still, clean, restrained, tiny, complete. It was no selfish place, but the central abode of fire and hospitality, clean-swept for wayfarers, and best seats were bare. They quite expected visitors, morning, noon, and night; and they gave our hands a quick, soft grasp and talked easily. Their manners were better than those of Park Lane or Park Avenue. Oh, much better and more natural. They showed breeding. The chief's son—tall and slight and speaking good English—had served under the late Colonel Young. He made a little speech of welcome. Long is the history of the Veys and comes down from the Eastern Roman Empire, the great struggle of Islam and the black empires of the Sudan.

We went on to other villages—dun-colored, not so beautiful, but neat and hospitable. In one sat a visiting chief of perhaps fifty years in a derby hat and a robe, and beside him stood a shy young wife done in ebony and soft brown, whose liquid eyes would not meet ours. The chief was taciturn until we spoke of schools. Then he woke suddenly —he had children to "give" to a school. I see the last village fading away; they are plastering the wall of a home, leisurely and carefully. They smiled a good-by—not effusively, with no eagerness, with a simple friendship, as we glided under the cocoa trees and into the silent forest, the gold and silent forest.

And there and elsewhere in two long months I began to learn: primitive men are not following us afar, frantically waving and seeking our goals; primitive men are not behind us in some swift foot-race. Primitive men have already arrived. They are abreast, and in places ahead of us; in others behind. But all their curving advance line is contemporary, not prehistoric. They have used other paths and these paths have led them by scenes sometimes fairer, sometimes uglier than ours, but always toward the Pools of Happiness. Or, to put it otherwise, these folk have the leisure of true aristocracy—leisure for thought and courtesy, leisure for sleep and laughter. They have time for their children—such well-trained, beautiful children with perfect, unhidden bodies. Have you ever met a crowd of children in the east of London or New York, or even on the Avenue at Forty-second or One Hundred and Forty-second Street, and fled to avoid their impudence and utter ignorance of courtesy? Come to Africa, and see well-bred and courteous children, playing happily and never sniffling and whining.

I have read everywhere that Africa means sexual license. Perhaps it does. Most folk who talk sex frantically have all too seldom revealed their source material. I was in West Africa only two months, but with both eyes wide. I saw children quite naked and women usually naked to the waist—with bare bosom and limbs. And in those sixty days I saw less of sex dalliance and appeal than I see daily on Fifth Avenue. This does not mean much, but it is an interesting fact.

The primitive black man is courteous and dignified. If the platforms of Western cities had swarmed with humanity as I have seen the platforms swarm in Senegal, the police would have a busy time. I did not see one respectable quarrel. Wherefore shall we all take to the Big Bush? No. I prefer New York. But my point is that New York and London and Paris must learn of West Africa and may learn.

The one great lack in Africa is communication—communication as represented by human contact, movement of goods, dissemination of knowledge. All these things we have—we have in such crushing abundance that they have mastered us and defeated their real good. We meet human beings in such throngs that we cannot know or even understand them—they become to us inhuman, mechanical, hateful. We are choked and suffocated, tempted and killed by goods accumulated from the ends of the earth; our newspapers and magazines so overwhelm us with knowledge—knowledge of all sorts and kinds from particulars as to our neighbors' underwear to Einstein's mathematics—that one of the great and glorious joys of the African bush is to escape from "news."

On the other hand, African life with its isolation has deeper knowledge of human souls. The village life, the forest ways, the teeming markets, bring in intimate human knowledge that the West misses, sinking the individual in the social. Africans know fewer folk, but know them infinitely better. Their intertwined communal souls, therefore, brook no poverty nor prostitution—these things are to them un-understandable. On the other hand, they are vastly ignorant of what the world is doing and thinking, and of what is known of its physical forces. They suffer terribly from preventable disease, from unnecessary hunger, from the freaks of the weather.

Here, then, is something for Africa and Europe both to learn; and Africa is eager, breathless, to learn—while Europe? Europe laughs with loud guffaws. Learn of Africa? Nonsense. Poverty cannot be abolished. Democracy and firm government are incompatible. Prostitution is world old and inevitable. And Europe proceeds to use Africa as a means and not as an end; as a hired tool and welter of raw materials and not as a land of human beings.

I think it was in Africa that I came more clearly to see the close connection between race and wealth. The fact that even in the minds of the most dogmatic supporters of race theories and believers in the inferiority of colored folk to white, there was a conscious or unconscious determination to increase their incomes by taking full advantage of this belief. And then gradually this thought was metamorphosed into a realization that the income-bearing value of race prejudice was the cause and not the result of theories of race inferiority; that particularly in the United States the income of the Cotton Kingdom based on black slavery caused the passionate belief in

Negro inferiority and the determination to enforce it even by arms.

I have wandered afield from miscegenation in the West Indies to race blending and segregation in America and to a glimpse of present Africa. Now to return to the American concept of race. It was in my boyhood, as I have intimated, an adventure. In my youth, it became the vision of a glorious crusade where I and my fellows were to match our mettle against white folk and show them what black folk could do. But as I grew older the matter became more serious and less capable of jaunty settlement. I not only met plenty of persons equal in ability to myself but often with greater ability and nearly always with greater opportunity. Racial identity presented itself as a matter of trammels and impediments as "tightening bonds about my feet." As I looked out into my racial world the whole thing verged on tragedy. My "way was cloudy" and the approach to its high goals by no means straight and clear. I saw the race problem was not as I conceived, a matter of clear, fair competition, for which I was ready and eager. It was rather a matter of segregation, of hindrance and inhibitions, and my struggles against this and resentment at it began to have serious repercussions upon my inner life.

It is difficult to let others see the full psychological meaning of caste segregation. It is as though one, looking out from a dark cave in a side of an impending mountain, sees the world passing and speaks to it; speaks courteously and persuasively, showing them how these entombed souls are hindered in their natural movement, expression, and development; and how their loosening from prison would be a matter not simply of courtesy, sympathy, and help to them, but aid to all the world. One talks on evenly and logically in this way, but notices that the passing throng does not even turn its head, or if it does, glances curiously and walks on. It gradually penetrates the minds of the prisoners that the people passing do not hear; that some thick sheet of invisible but horribly tangible plate glass is between them and the world. They get excited; they talk louder; they gesticulate. Some of the passing world stop in curiosity; these gesticulations seem so pointless; they laugh and pass on. They still either do not hear at all, or hear but dimly, and even what they hear, they do not understand. Then the people within may become hysterical. They may scream and hurl themselves against the barriers, hardly realizing in their bewilderment that they are screaming in a vacuum unheard and that their antics may actually seem funny to those outside looking in. They may even, here and there, break through in blood and disfigurement, and find themselves faced by a horrified, implacable, and quite overwhelming mob of people frightened for their own very existence.

It is hard under such circumstances to be philosophical and calm, and to think through a method of approach and accommodation between castes. The entombed find themselves not simply trying to make the outer world understand their essential and common humanity but even more, as they become inured to their experience, they have to keep reminding themselves that the great and oppressing world outside is also real and human and in its essence honest. All my life I have had continually to haul my soul back and say, "All white folk are not scoundrels nor murderers. They are, even as I am, painfully human."

One development continually recurs: any person out-side of this wall of glass can speak to his own fellows, can assume a facile championship of the entombed, and gain the enthusiastic and even gushing thanks of the victims. But this method is subject to two difficulties: first of all, not being possibly among the entombed or capable of sharing their inner thought and experience, this outside leadership will continually misinterpret and compromise and complicate matters, even with the best of will. And secondly, of course, no matter how successful the outside advocacy is, it remains impotent and unsuccessful until it actually succeeds in freeing and making articulate the sub-merged caste.

Practically, this group imprisonment within a group has various effects upon the prisoner. He becomes provincial and centered upon the problems of his particular group. He tends to neglect the wider aspects of national life and human existence. On the one hand he is unselfish so far as his inner group is concerned. He thinks of himself not as an individual but as a group man, a "race" man. His loy-alty to this group idea tends to be almost unending and balks at almost no sacrifice. On the other hand, his atti-tude toward the environing race congeals into a matter of unreasoning resentment and even hatred, deep disbelief in them and refusal to conceive honesty and rational thought on their part. This attitude adds to the difficul-ties of conversation, intercourse, understanding between groups.

This was the race concept which has dominated my life, and the history of which I have attempted to make the leading theme of this book. It had as I have tried to show all sorts of illogical trends and irreconcilable tendencies. Perhaps it is wrong to speak of it at all as "a concept" rather than as a group of contradictory forces, facts and tendencies. At any rate I hope I have made its meaning to me clear. It was for me as I have written first a matter of dawning realization, then of study and science; then a matter of inquiry into the diverse strands of my own family; and finally consideration of my connection, physical and spiritual, with Africa and the Negro race in its homeland. All this led to an attempt to rationalize the racial concept and its place in the modern world.

CHAPTER 6. THE WHITE WORLD

THE majority of men resent and always have resented the idea of equality with most of their fellow men. This has had physical, economic, and cultural reasons: the physical fear of attack; the economic strife to avert starvation and secure protection and shelter; but more especially I presume the cultural and spiritual desire to be one's self without interference from others; to enjoy that anarchy of the spirit which is inevitably the goal of all consciousness. It is only in highly civilized times and places that the conception arises of an individual freedom and development, and even that was conceived of as the right of a privileged minority, and was based on the degradation, the exclusion, the slavery of most others. The history of tribes and clans, of social classes and all nations, and of race antipathies in our own world, is an exemplification of this fight against equality and inability even to picture its possibility.

The result is that men are conditioned and their actions forced not simply by their physical environment, powerful as mountains and rain, heat and cold, forest and desert always have been and will be. When we modify the effects of this environment by what we call the social environment, we have conceived a great and important truth. But even this needs further revision. A man lives today not

only in his physical environment and in the social environment of ideas and customs, laws and ideals; but that total
environment is subjected to a new socio-physical environment of other groups, whose social environment he shares
but in part.

A man in the European sixteenth century was born
not simply in the valley of the Thames or Seine, but in a
certain social class and the environment of that class made
and limited his world. He was then, consciously or not, not
fully a man; he was an artisan and until he complied with
the limitations of that class he was continually knocking
his hands, head and heart against an environment, composed of other classes, which limited what he could and
could not do and what he must do; and this greater group
environment was not a matter of mere ideas and thought;
it was embodied in muscles and armed men, in scowling
faces, in the majesty of judge and police and in human
law which became divine.

Much as I knew of this class structure of the world, I
should never have realized it vividly and fully if I had
not been born into its modern counterpart, racial segregation; first into a world composed of people with colored
skins who remembered slavery and endured discrimination; and who had to a degree their own habits, customs,
and ideals; but in addition to this I lived in an environment which I came to call the white world. I was not an
American; I was not a man; I was by long education and
continual compulsion and daily reminder, a colored man
in a white world; and that white world often existed
primarily, so far as I was concerned, to see with sleepless
vigilance that I was kept within bounds. All this made me

limited in physical movement and provincial in thought
and dream. I could not stir, I could not act, I could not
live, without taking into careful daily account the reaction
of my white environing world. How I traveled and where,
what work I did, what income I received, where I ate,
where I slept, with whom I talked, where I sought recreation, where I studied, what I wrote and what I could get
published—all this depended and depended primarily
upon an overwhelming mass of my fellow citizens in the
United States, from whose society I was largely excluded.

Of course, there was no real wall between us. I knew
from the days of my childhood and in the elementary
school, on through my walks in the Harvard yard and my
lectures in Germany, that in all things in general, white
people were just the same as I: their physical possibilities,
their mental processes were no different from mine; even
the difference in skin color was vastly overemphasized and
intrinsically trivial. And yet this fact of racial distinction
based on color was the greatest thing in my life and absolutely determined it, because this surrounding group, in
alliance and agreement with the white European world,
was settled and determined upon the fact that I was and
must be a thing apart.

It was impossible to gainsay this. It was impossible for
any time and to any distance to withdraw myself and look
down upon these absurd assumptions with philosophical
calm and humorous self-control. If, as happened to a friend
of mine, a lady in a Pullman car ordered me to bring her
a glass of water, mistaking me for a porter, the incident in
its essence was a joke to be chuckled over; but in its hard,

cruel significance and its unending inescapable sign of slavery, it was something to drive a man mad.

For long years it seemed to me that this imprisonment of a human group with chains in hands of an environing group, was a singularly unusual characteristic of the Negro in the United States in the nineteenth century. But since then it has been easy for me to realize that the majority of mankind has struggled through this inner spiritual slavery and that while a dream which we have easily and jauntily called democracy envisages a day when the environing group looses the chains and compulsion, and is willing and even eager to grant families, nations, subraces, and races equality of opportunity among larger groups, that even this grand equality has not come; and until it does, individual equality and the free soul is impossible. All our present frustration in trying to realize individual equality through communism, fascism, and democracy arises from our continual unwillingness to break the intellectual bonds of group and racial exclusiveness.

Thus it is easy to see that scientific definition of race is impossible; it is easy to prove that physical characteristics are not so inherited as to make it possible to divide the world into races; that ability is the monopoly of no known aristocracy; that the possibilities of human development cannot be circumscribed by color, nationality, or any conceivable definition of race; all this has nothing to do with the plain fact that throughout the world today organized groups of men by monopoly of economic and physical power, legal enactment and intellectual training are limiting with determination and unflagging zeal the development of other groups; and that the concentration particularly of economic power today puts the majority of mankind into a slavery to the rest.

There has been an understandable determination in the United States among both Negro and white thinkers to minimize and deny the realities of racial difference. The race problem has been rationalized in every way. It has been called the natural result of slavery; the effect of poverty and ignorance; the situation consequent upon lack of effort and thought on the part of Americans and of other races. But all this reasoning has its logical pitfalls: granted that poverty causes color prejudice, color prejudice certainly is a cause of poverty. Ignorance leads to exploitation and mistreatment, but the black child is more often forced into ignorance and kept there than the white child. Thus it is impossible for the clear-headed student of human action in the United States and in the world, to avoid facing the fact of a white world which is today dominating human culture and working for the continued subordination of the colored races.

It may be objected here that so general a statement is not fair; that there are many white folk who feel the unfairness and crime of color and race prejudice and have toiled and sacrificed to counteract it. This brings up the whole question of social guilt. When, for instance, one says that the action of England toward the darker races has been a course of hypocrisy, force and greed covering four hundred years it does not mean to include in that guilt many persons of the type of William Wilberforce and Granville Sharpe. On the other hand because British history has not involved the guilt of all Britons we cannot jump to the opposite and equally fallacious conclusion that there has been no guilt; that the development of the British Empire is a sort of cosmic process with no individual human being at fault. In the history of England, France, America, Germany and Italy, we have villains who have selfishly and criminally desired and accomplished what made for the suffering and degradation of mankind. We have had others who desired the uplift and worked for the uplift of all men. And we have had a middle class of people who sometimes ignorantly and sometimes consciously shifted the balance now here, and now there; and when, in the end, this balance of public opinion, this effective social action, has made for the degradation of mankind or in so far as it has done this, that part of England which has allowed this or made it possible is blood-guilty of the result. So in America, not the philosophy of Jefferson nor the crusade of Garrison nor the reason of Sumner was able to counterbalance the race superiority doctrines of Calhoun, the imperialism of Jefferson Davis, nor the race hate of Ben Tillman. As a result white America has crucified, enslaved, and oppressed the Negro group and holds them still, especially in the South, in a legalized position of inferior caste.

With the best will the factual outline of a life misses the essence of its spirit. Thus in my life the chief fact has been race—not so much scientific race, as that deep conviction of myriads of men that congenital differences among the main masses of human beings absolutely condition the individual destiny of every member of a group. Into the spiritual provincialism of this belief I have been born and this fact has guided, embittered, illuminated

and enshrouded my life. Yet, how shall I explain and
clarify its meaning for a soul? Description fails—I have
tried that. Yet, lest I omit the most important thing in
the life of an American Negro today and the only thing
that adequately explains his success, failures and foibles,
let me attempt its exposition by personifying my white
and colored environment.

✦

When, for example, the obsession of his race consciousness leaves him, my white friend, Roger Van Dieman
(who, I hasten to add, is an abstraction and integration
and never existed), is quite companionable; otherwise he is
impossible. He has a way of putting an excessive amount
of pity in his look and of stating as a general and incontrovertible fact that it is "horrible" to be an Exception.
By this he means me. He is more than certain that I prove
the rule. He is not a bright person, but of that famous
average, standardized and astonished at anything that even
seems original. His thesis is simple: the world is composed of Race superimposed on Race; classes superimposed on classes; beneath the whole thing is "Our Family"
in capitals, and under that is God. God seems to be a
cousin, or at least a blood relative, of the Van Diemans.

"Of course," he says, "you know Negroes are inferior."

I admit nothing of the sort, I maintain. In fact, having
known with some considerable intimacy both male and
female, the people of the British Isles, of Scandinavia, of
Russia, of Germany, north and south, of the three ends of
France and the two ends of Italy; specimens from the
Balkans and black and white Spain; the three great races

of Asia and the melange of Africa, without mentioning America, I sit here and maintain that black folk are much superior to white.

"You are either joking or mad," he says.

Both and neither. This race talk is, of course, a joke, and frequently it has driven me insane and probably will permanently in the future; and yet, seriously and soberly, we black folk are the salvation of mankind.

He regards me with puzzled astonishment and says confidentially:

"Do you know that sometimes I am half afraid that you really believe this? At other times I see clearly the inferiority complex."

The former after lunch, I reply, and the latter before.

"Very well," he says, "let's lunch."

Where? I ask quizzically, we being at the time in the Roaring Forties.

"Why—oh, well—their refusal to serve you lunch at least does not prove your superiority."

Nor yet theirs, I answer; but never mind, come with me to Second Avenue, where Labor lives and food is bad.

We start again with the salad.

"Now, superiority consists of what?" he argues.

Life is, I remark, (1) Beauty and health of body. (2) Mental clearness and creative genius. (3) Spiritual goodness and receptivity. (4) Social adaptability and constructiveness.

"Not bad," he answers. "Not bad at all. Now I contend that the white race conspicuously excels in beauty, genius, and construction, and is well abreast even in goodness."

And I maintain that the black race excels in beauty,

goodness, and adaptability, and is well abreast in genius.

"Sheer nonsense and pure balderdash. Compare the Venus of Milo and the Apollo Belvedere with a Harlem or Beale Street couple."

I retort: in short, compare humanity at its worst with the Ideal, and humanity suffers. But black folk in most attributes of physical beauty, in line and height and curve, have the same norms as whites and differ only in small details of color, hair and curve of countenance. Now can there be any question but that as colors, bronze, mahogany, coffee and gold are far lovelier than pink, gray, and marble? Hair is a matter of taste. Some will have it drab and stringy and others in a gray, woven, unmoving mass. Most of us like it somewhere between, in tiny tendrils, smoking curls and sweeping curves. I have loved all these varieties in my day. I prefer the crinkly kind, almost wavy, in black, brown, and glistening gold. In faces, I hate straight features; needles and razors may be sharp—but beautiful, never.

"All that is personal opinion. I prefer the colors of heaven and day: sunlight hair and sky-blue eyes; straight noses and thin lips, and that incomparable air of haughty aloofness and aristocracy."

And I, on the contrary, am the child of twilight and night, and choose intricately curly hair, black eyes, full and luscious features; and that air of humility and wonder which streams from moonlight. Add to this voices that caress instead of rasp, glances that appeal rather than repel, and a sinuous litheness of movement to replace Anglo-Saxon stalking—there you have my ideal. Of course, you can bury any human body in dirt and misery and make it horrible. I have seen the East End of London.

"Beauty seems to be simply opinion, if you put it that way."

To be sure. But whose opinion?

"Bother beauty. Here we shall never agree. But, after all, I doubt if it makes much difference. The real point is Brains: clear thinking, pure reason, mathematical precision and creative genius. Now, without blague, stand and acknowledge that here the white race is supreme."

Quite the contrary. I know no attribute in which the white race has more conspicuously failed. This is white and European civilization; and as a system of culture it is idiotic, addle-brained, unreasoning, topsy-turvy, without precision; and its genius chiefly runs to marvelous contrivances for enslaving the many, and enriching the few, and murdering both. I see absolutely no proof that the average ability of the white man's brain to think clearly is any greater than that of the yellow man or of the black man. If we take even that doubtful but widely heralded test, the frequency of individual creative genius (when a real racial test should be the frequency of ordinary common sense)—if we take the Genius as the savior of mankind, it is only possible for the white race to prove its own incontestable superiority by appointing both judge and jury and summoning its own witnesses.

I freely admit that, according to white writers, white teachers, white historians, and white molders of public opinion, nothing ever happened in the world of any importance that could not or should not be labeled "white." How silly. I place black iron-welding and village democracy, and yellow printing and state building, side by side with white representative government and the steam engine, and unhesitatingly give the palm to the first. I hand the first vast conception of the solar system to the Africanized Egyptians, the creation of Art to the Chinese, the highest conception of Religion to the Asiatic Semites, and then let Europe rave over the Factory system.

"But is not well-being more widely diffused among white folk than among yellow and black, and general intelligence more common?"

True, and why? Ask the geography of Europe, the African Slave Trade and the industrial technique of the nineteenth-century white man. Turn the thing around, and let a single tradition of culture suddenly have thrust into its hands the power to bleed the world of its brawn and wealth, and the willingness to do this, and you will have exactly what we have today, under another name and color.

"Precisely. Then, at least, the white race is more advanced and no more blameworthy than others because, as I insist, its native intelligence is greater. It is germ plasm, seed, that I am talking about. Do you believe in heredity?"

Not blindly; but I should be mildly surprised to see a dog born of a cat.

"Exactly; or a genius born of a fool."

No, no; on the contrary, I rather expect fools of geniuses and geniuses of fools. And while I stoutly maintain that cattiness and dogginess are as far apart as the East from the West, on the other hand, I just as strongly believe that the human ass and the superman have much in common and can often, if not always, spawn each other.

"Is it possible that you have never heard of the Jukes, or of the plain results of hereditary degeneration and the possibilities of careful breeding?"

It is not possible; they have been served up to me ad infinitum. But they are nothing. I know greater wonders: Lincoln from Nancy Hanks, Dumas from a black beast of burden, Kant from a saddler, and Jesus Christ from a manger.

"All of which, instead of disproving, is exact and definite proof of the persistence of good blood."

Precisely, and of the catholicity of its tastes; the method of proof is this: when anything good occurs, it is proof of good blood; when anything bad occurs, it is proof of bad blood. Very well. Now good and bad, native endowment and native deficiency, do not follow racial lines. There is good stock in all races and the outcropping of bad individuals, too; and there has been absolutely no proof that the white race has any larger share of the gifted strains of human heritage than the black race or the yellow race. To be sure, good seed proves itself in the flower and the fruit, but the failure of seed to sprout is no proof that it is not good. It may be proof simply of the absence of manure— or its excessive presence.

Granted, that when time began, there was hidden in a Seed that tiny speck that spelled the world's salvation, do you think today it would manifest itself crudely and baldly in a dash of skin color and a crinkle of hair? Is the subtle mystery of life and consciousness and of ability portrayed in any such slapdash and obvious marks of difference?

"Go out upon the street; choose ten white men and ten colored men. Which can carry on and preserve American civilization?"

The whites.

"Well, then."

You evidently consider that a compliment. Let it pass. Go out upon the street and choose ten men and ten women. Which could best run a Ford car? The men, of course; but hold. Fly out into the sky and look down upon ten children of Podunk and ten children of Chicago. Which would know most about elevated railroads, baseball, zoology, and movies?

"The point is visible, but beyond that, outside of mere experience and education, and harking back to native gift and intelligence, on your honor, which has most, white folk or black folk?"

There you have me deep in the shadows, beyond the benign guidance of words. Just what is gift and intelligence, especially of the native sort? And when we compare the gift of one human soul with that of another, are we not seeking to measure incommensurable things; trying to lump things like sunlight and music and love? And if a certain shadowy Over-soul can really compare the incomparable with some transcendental yardstick, may we not here emerge into a super-equality of man? At least this I can quite believe.

"But it is a pious belief, not more."

Not more; but a pious belief outweighs an impious unbelief.

Admitting that the problem of native human endowment is obscure, there is no corresponding obscurity in

spiritual values. Goodness and unselfishness; simplicity and
honor; tolerance, susceptibility to beauty in form, color,
and music; courage to look truth in the face; courage to
live and suffer in patience and humility, in forgiveness
and in hope; eagerness to turn, not simply the other cheek,
but the face and the bowed back; capacity to love. In all
these mighty things, the greatest things in the world,
where do black folk and white folk stand?

Why, man of mine, you would not have the courage to
live one hour as a black man in America, or as a Negro in
the whole wide world. Ah, yes, I know what you whisper
to such accusation. You say dryly that if we had good
sense, we would not live either; and that the fact that we
do submit to life as it is and yet laugh and dance and
dream, is but another proof that we are idiots.

This is the truly marvelous way in which you prove your
superiority by admitting that our love of life can only be
intelligently explained on the hypothesis of inferiority.
What finer tribute is possible to our courage?

What great works of Art have we made? Very few. The
Pyramids, Luxor, the Bronzes of Benin, the Spears of the
Bongo, "When Malinda Sings" and the Sorrow Song she
is always singing. Oh, yes, and the love of her dancing.

But art is not simply works of art; it is the spirit that
knows Beauty, that has music in its soul and the color
of sunsets in its headkerchiefs; that can dance on a flaming
world and make the world dance, too. Such is the soul of
the Negro.

Why, do you know the two finest things in the industry
of the West, finer than factory, shop or ship? One is the
black laborer's Saturday off. Neither the whip of the

driver, nor the starvation wage, nor the disgust of the Yankee, nor the call of the cotton crop, has yet convinced the common black variety of plantation laborer that one day in the week is enough for rest and play. He wants two days. And, from California to Texas, from Florida to Trinidad, he takes two days while the planter screams and curses. They have beaten the English slavey, the French and German peasants, and the North Italian contadini into twelve-hour, six-day slaves. They crushed the Chinese and Indian coolie into a twenty-four-hour beast of burden; they have even made the American, free, white and twenty-one, believe that daily toil is one of the Ten Commandments. But not the Negro. From Monday to Friday the field hand is a slave; then for forty-eight golden hours he is free, and through these same forty-eight hours he may yet free the dumb, driven cattle of the world.

Then the second thing, laughter. This race has the greatest of the gifts of God, laughter. It dances and sings; it is humble; it longs to learn; it loves men; it loves women. It is frankly, baldly, deliciously human in an artificial and hypocritical land. If you will hear men laugh, go to Guinea, "Black Bottom," "Niggertown," Harlem. If you want to feel humor too exquisite and subtle for translation, sit invisibly among a gang of Negro workers. The white world has its gibes and cruel caricatures; it has its loud guffaws; but to the black world alone belongs the delicious chuckle.

"But the State; the modern industrial State. Wealth of work, wealth of commerce, factory and mine, skyscrapers; New York, Chicago, Johannesburg, London and Buenos Aires!"

This is the best expression of the civilization in which the white race finds itself today. This is what the white world means by culture.

"Does it not excel the black and yellow race here?"

It does. But the excellence here raises no envy; only regrets. If this vast Frankenstein monster really served its makers; if it were their minister and not their master, god and king; if their machines gave us rest and leisure, instead of the drab uniformity of uninteresting drudgery; if their factories gave us gracious community of thought and feeling; beauty enshrined, free and joyous; if their work veiled them with tender sympathy at human distress and wide tolerance and understanding—then, all hail, White Imperial Industry! But it does not. It is a Beast! Its creators even do not understand it, cannot curb or guide it. They themselves are but hideous, groping higher Hands, doing their bit to oil the raging devastating machinery which kills men to make cloth, prostitutes women to rear buildings and eats little children.

Is this superiority? It is madness. We are the supermen who sit idly by and laugh and look at civilization. We, who frankly want the bodies of our mates and conjure no blush to our bronze cheeks when we own it. We, who exalt the Lynched above the Lyncher, and the Worker above the Owner, and the Crucified above Imperial Rome.

"But why have you black and yellow men done nothing better or even as good in the history of the world?"

We have, often.

"I never heard of it."

Lions have no historians.

"It is idiotic even to discuss it. Look around and see the

pageantry of the world. It belongs to white men; it is the expression of white power; it is the product of white brains. Who can have the effrontery to stand for a moment and compare with this white triumph, yellow and brown anarchy and black savagery?"

You are obsessed by the swiftness of the gliding of the sled at the bottom of the hill. You say: what tremendous power must have caused its speed, and how wonderful is Speed. You think of the rider as the originator and inventor of that vast power. You admire his poise and *sang-froid,* his utter self-absorption. You say: surely here is the son of God and he shall reign forever and forever.

You are wrong, quite wrong. Away back on the level stretches of the mountain tops in the forests, amid drifts and driftwood, this sled was slowly and painfully pushed on its little hesitating start. It took power, but the power of sweating, courageous men, not of demigods. As the sled slowly started and gained momentum, it was the Law of Being that gave it speed, and the grace of God that steered its lone, scared passengers. Those passengers, white, black, red and yellow, deserve credit for their balance and pluck. But many times it was sheer luck that made the road not land the white man in the gutter, as it had others so many times before, and as it may him yet. He has gone farther than others because of others whose very falling made hard ways iced and smooth for him to traverse. His triumph is a triumph not of himself alone, but of humankind, from the pusher in the primeval forests to the last flier through the winds of the twentieth century.

And so to leave our parable and come to reality. Great as has been the human advance in the last one thousand

years, it is, so far as native human ability, so far as intellectual gift and moral courage are concerned, nothing as
compared with any one of ten and more millenniums
before, far back in the forests of tropical Africa and in hot
India, where brown and black humanity first fought climate
and disease and bugs and beasts; where man dared simply
to live and propagate himself. There was the hardest and
greatest struggle in all the human world. If in sheer ex-
haustion or in desperate self-defense during this last moment of civilization he has rested, half inert and blinded
with the sweat of his efforts, it is only the silly onlooker
who sees but the passing moment of time, who can think
of him as subhuman and inferior.

All this is Truth, but unknown, unapprehended Truth.
Indeed, the greatest and most immediate danger of white
culture, perhaps least sensed, is its fear of the Truth, its
childish belief in the efficacy of lies as a method of human
uplift. The lie is defensible; it has been used widely
and often profitably among humankind. But it may be
doubted if ever before in the world so many intelligent
people believed in it so deeply. We deliberately and continuously deceive not simply others, but ourselves as to the
truth about them, us, and the world. We have raised
Propaganda to a capital "P" and elaborated an art, almost
a science, of how one may make the world believe what is
not true, provided the untruth is a widely wished-for thing
like the probable extermination of Negroes, the failure of
Japanese Imperialism, the incapacity of India for self-rule,
collapse of the Russian Revolution. When in other days
the world lied, it was a world that expected lies and con-

sciously defended them; when the world lies today it is to a world that pretends to love truth.

"In other words, according to you, white folk are about the meanest and lowest on earth."

They are human, even as you and I.

"Why don't you leave them, then? Get out, go to Africa or to the North Pole; shake the dust of their hospitality from off your feet?"

There are abundant reasons. First, they have annexed the earth and hold it by transient but real power. Thus, by running away, I shall not only not escape them, but succeed in hiding myself in out of the way places where they can work their deviltry on me without photograph, telegraph, or mail service. But even more important than this: I am as bad as they are. In fact, I am related to them and they have much that belongs to me—this land, for instance, for which my fathers starved and fought; I share their sins; in fine, I am related to them.

"By blood?"

By Blood.

"Then you are railing at yourself. You are not black; you are no Negro."

And you? Yellow blood and black has deluged Europe in days past even more than America yesterday. You are not white, as the measurements of your head will show.

"What then becomes of all your argument, if there are no races and we are all so horribly mixed as you maliciously charge?"

Oh, my friend, can you not see that I am laughing at you? Do you suppose this world of men is simply a great layer cake with superimposed slices of inferior and superior races, interlaid with mud?

No, no. Human beings are infinite in variety, and when they are agglutinated in groups, great and small, the groups differ as though they, too, had integrating souls. But they have not. The soul is still individual if it is free. Race is a cultural, sometimes an historical fact. And all that I really have been trying to say is that a certain group that I know and to which I belong, as contrasted with the group you know and to which you belong, and in which you fanatically and glorifyingly believe, bears in its bosom just now the spiritual hope of this land because of the persons who compose it and not by divine command.

"But what is this group; and how do you differentiate it; and how can you call it 'black' when you admit it is not black?"

I recognize it quite easily and with full legal sanction; the black man is a person who must ride "Jim Crow" in Georgia.

✦

My mythical friend Van Dieman is not my only white companion. I have others—many others; one and one especially I want to bring to your attention not because of his attitude toward me but rather because of his attitude toward himself. He represents the way in which my environing white group distorts and frustrates itself even as it strives toward Justice and all because of me. In other words, because of the Negro problem. The average reasonable, conscientious, and fairly intelligent white American faces continuing paradox.

This other friend of mine is free, white, and twenty-one. Which is to say—he is as free as the law and his income, his family and friends, and his formal and informal education allow. He is "white" so far as the records show and as tradition tells; he is not simply twenty-one—he is fifty-one. He is respectable, that is, he belongs to the Episcopal Church, the Union League and Harvard Clubs, and the Republican Party. He is educated, in the sense that he can read if he will, he can write in case his stenographer is absent and he has the privilege of listening to Metropolitan Opera on Tuesdays. He is a Son of the American Revolution, a reserve officer and a member of the American Legion. He reads the *Times* and the *Evening Post* (Saturday); he subscribes for the *Atlantic* and last year he read two books. He also began "Man the Unknown." He owns a home in Westchester assessed at fifty thousand; he drives a Buick. He associates quite often with a wife and a child of fifteen and more often with his fellow employees of the wholesale house which pays him ten thousand a year.

Frankly, my friend faces a dilemma. It is this: his pastor, the Reverend J. Simpson Stodges, D.D., preaches to him Sundays (except July, August and September) a doctrine that sounds like this (I say "sounds" because Dr. Stodges has explanations which mitigate the extremities of his ex cathedra statements): The Doctor asserts in sermons that Peace on Earth is the message of Christ, the Divine leader of men; that this means Good Will to all human beings; that it means Freedom, Toleration of the mistakes, sins and shortcomings of not only your friends but of your enemies. That the Golden Rule of Christianity is to treat others as you want to be treated and that finally you

should be willing to sacrifice your comfort, your convenience, your wealth and even your life for mankind; in
other words, that Poverty is better than riches and that the
meek shall inherit the earth.

Stated thus plainly, this is to my friend's mind pretty
stiff doctrine for an ordinary human being in A.D. 1940;
and while he believes it in a sense (having been reared in
a Godly and Presbyterian household and by a father who
spared no rods and spoiled no children), yet, as he puts it
to Dr. Stodges in his own parlor, Could a man live up to
all that today?

Now, Dr. Stodges out of the pulpit is a most companionable fellow; excellent family, good manners, Oxford accent
and Brooks Brothers to-order clothes. He plays keen golf,
smokes a rare weed and knows a Bronx cocktail from a
Manhattan. Well, the Doctor explained things rather satis-
factorily. This Christian business of Peace, Good Will, the
Golden Rule, Liberty and Poverty, was, of course, the
Ideal. But, bless your soul, man, we can't all always attain
the heights, much less live in their rarefied atmosphere.
Aim at 'em—that's the point, and in fact, at least live a
Gentleman with the "G" capitalized.

Now my friend is exceedingly anxious to be a gentleman. His father, to be sure, sneered at gentlemen and his
grandfather for certain obscure reasons both hated them
and denied their existence. His great-great-great-grand-
father, whose existence the Media Research Bureau had
discovered, was, however, high-bred enough to shoulder a
pitchfork against England. But at college, at his club, and
with his daily companions it appeared altogether desirable
to be genteel—to have manners, an "air," and a tailor. As

there was no one to preach gentility in plain words, my
friend has gathered this rather vague definition: a Gentleman relies on the Police and Law for protection and self-
assertion; he is sustained by a fine sense of Justice for himself and his Family, past and present; he is always courteous in public with "ladies first" and precedence to "gray
hairs"; and even in private, he minds his manners and dignity and resists his neighbor's wife; he is charitable, giving
to the needy and deserving, to the poor and proud, to in-
explicable artists and to the Church. He certainly does not
believe in the WPA or other alphabetical ways of encouraging laziness and waste and increasing his taxes. And
finally, without ostentation, he is exclusive; picking his
associates with care and fine discrimination and appearing
socially only where the Best People appear. All this calls
for money and a good deal of it. He does not want to be
vulgarly and ostentatiously rich. As millionaires go, he is
relatively poor, which is poverty as he understands it.

Now my friend knows that this conception lets one in
for a certain snobbishness and tendency toward "climb-
ing." And yet it does furnish atmosphere, comfort and a
reasonable rule of life for a modern man of position. It is
not, of course, the Christianity of the Gospels, nor the
career of the Knight Errant; but it is a good, honest,
middle path suited to good, honest, middle-aged men.

If the matter halted here, my friend might be vaguely
disappointed, but fairly well satisfied. After all, in the
workaday life we can't expect moral heroes in quantity.
But the trouble is, my friend saw the edges of the Great
War (from a swivel chair in America) and he belongs to
the American Legion. Also he reads the papers and con-

verses in club lobbies. From this he has assimilated a new and alarming code of action. As Americans we've got to be "prepared" for "defense." Well enough to think of a world of peace, but we haven't got it. Not only that, but the world is not preparing for peace. Everywhere and all over it is not only preparing for war—it is fighting. What is the sense of man, even though he be big, strong, well, sitting down empty-handed while around him are grouped a dozen men armed to the teeth with every device that brains and money can furnish? No, no, this will never do. We've got to have an army and a big army for a big country. We need a militia and a universal draft; we need several big seventy-five million dollar battle-ships with cruisers, airplane carriers and submersibles. We must play expensively at war with elaborate maneuvers. Defense, Preparedness—that's the word.

America must be prepared for all eventualities. England wants her trade, France wants her gold, Germany wants her markets, Russia wants her laborers remade into Bolsheviks. Italy wants her raw material; and above all— Japan! Japan is about to conquer the world for the yellow race and then she'll be ready to swallow America. We must, therefore, be prepared to defend ourselves.

In order to defend America and make an efficient, desirable country, we must have authority and discipline. This may not sound like the Good Will of the Christian but at bottom, it is. There is no use pretending any longer that all men are equal. We know perfectly well that Negroes, Chinamen, Mexicans and a lot of others who are presuming to exercise authority in this country are not our equals. Human beings should be considered as facts and not as possibilities and most of them have no possibilities. Unless, therefore, we have Efficiency—Ability at the top and submission and thrift at the bottom—we are going to come a cropper. Critics may sneer at this and call it caste or fascism, but a country and a world governed by gentlemen for gentlemen is after all the only one worth living in.

There may come some argument as to who should belong to this ruling caste of the Efficient. My friend does not want to be snobbish nor assume too much. Ability will rise. On the whole it would seem that well-bred persons of English descent and New England nurture are the kernel and hope of the land. There will, of course, be modifications in the membership of this group. Without doubt remnants of the Southern slave-holding aristocracy and some of the Mid-Western agrarian stock belong. But we have got to have the best at the top and we know pretty well who the best are.

This hierarchy we should defend vigorously. For this, deliberate propaganda is necessary and permissible; propaganda assists the truth and hurries it on; it may at times exaggerate and distort but all this is for a defensible end and newspapers, radio channels, and news distribution agencies should be owned and used for this end. Here comes the necessity of smoking out radicals. Radicals are insidious intellectuals, themselves usually unsuccessful misfits, envious of success and misled by cranks. They not only advocate impossible panaceas but they undermine the safety of the state. If honest and able, they are even more dangerous. They should be sternly dealt with.

Having thus established a country worth saving, patriotism comes next; and patriotism means standing by your country, thick and thin. It means not simply being an American but feeling proud of America and publicly asserting the fact from time to time. Also, it means seeing to it that other people are patriotic; looking about carefully when the "Star-Spangled Banner" is played to see who is sitting down and why; keeping a watchful eye on the flag. Americans traveling abroad, or at any rate white Americans, should, like the English, have such a panoply thrown about them that street urchins will be afraid to make faces and throw stones.

Finally, my friend learned that a nation must not only be powerful; that power must expand; more territory; more commerce; widened influence and that sort of thing. America must no longer be provincial. It must sit among the great powers of the earth, consulted for all world movements. In fact, it is not too much to think of this marvelous country as a sort of super-power, umpire of humanity, tremendous, irresistible.

Now all these things intrigue my friend. On his trip to Europe last summer he was made to feel more strongly his Americanism, partly in protest against the outrageous misunderstanding and apparent jealousy of America which he met, and partly from the complacency which swelled his breast when he noted what a great country America was in the eyes of Europe and how everybody was hanging on her lightest whisper. Would she please call a peace conference? Would she please restore the gold standard? Would she kindly sell her raw materials cheap? Would she please lend a helping hand in China and Africa? Would she forbear from completely swallowing South America? And so forth and so on.

But there was one difficulty about this code of Americanism which my friend learned; and that was that it led directly and inevitably to another code to which, theoretically, he was definitely opposed, but which, logically, he could not see his way to resist. It was not stated as clearly as any of the other codes; it certainly did not echo in Sunday sermons, although he sometimes suspected it lurked there. It did not enter into his definition of "gentleman" and seemed in fact opposed to it. And yet, somehow, all the gentlemen that he knew were strongly for it. It did seem bound up with his Americanism and yet there again, he resented the logical imputation.

The statement of this fourth code of action was found in unfinished assumption rather than plain words; in unfinished sentences, in novels, in editorials written for country papers by city scriveners; in organizations like the Ku Klux Klan which he thought was extremely silly; or the Security League, which was very respectable. This code rested upon the fact that he was a White Man. Now until my friend had reached the age of thirty he had not known that he was a white man, or at least he had not realized it. Certainly, so far as his skin was concerned, he knew that he was not black, brown, or very yellow. But it never occurred to him that there was any divine significance in that rather negative fact. But lately he had come to realize that his whiteness was fraught with tremendous responsibilities, age-old and infinite in future possibilities. It would seem that colored folks were a threat to the world. They were going to overthrow white folk by sheer weight of numbers, destroy their homes and marry their daughters.

It was this last point that particularly got upon his nerves. He had, as I've said, a girl of fifteen, rather pretty and fragile; and he and his wife were planning already certain advantageous family and economic alliances for the young miss. Much of their social life was already being guided to this end. Now, imagine a world where she would have to repel the advances of Japanese or Negroes!

He had noticed with some disturbed feeling that Negroes in particular were not nearly as agreeable and happy as they used to be. He had not for years been able to get a cheap, good colored cook and the last black yard man asked quite exorbitant wages. He now had white help. They were expensive but in fashion. He had had only last year to join in a neighborhood association to keep a Negro from buying a lot right in the next block!

Now all this led him to understand, if not to sympathize with, a code which began with War. Not only preparedness nor simply defense, but war against the darker races, carried out now and without too nice discrimination as to who were dark: war against the Riff, the Turk, Chinese, Japanese, Indians, Negroes, Mulattoes, Italians and South Americans. Recently this fact, which he knew perfectly well himself, has been confirmed by that great authority, Charles Lindbergh, who flew into wealth and omniscience through one trip to Paris. War and all that goes to implement war: We must hate our enemies. That sounds heathenish; but there can be no effective war, no determination to fight evil to the death, without full-bellied Hate! We need to lay emphasis upon "white": acting like a "White" man, doing things "white"; "white" angels, etc.; efforts to boost novels which paint white heroes, black devils and brown scoundrels with yellow souls; efforts to use the theater and the movies for the same reason; emphasis upon the race element in crime.

In this matter, too, there cannot unfortunately be too nice an honesty. Self-preservation is a First Law; the crimes and shortcomings of white people, while unfortunate, are incidental; news of them must be ignored or suppressed; crimes of colored people are characteristic and must be advertised as stern warnings. He had noted with surprise and satisfaction that the only place in the movies where Negroes were in special evidence was in jails. That was the only way to make that true which ought to be true and which was true but hidden. War, righteous Hate and then Suspicion. It was very easy to be deceived by other races; to think of the Negro as good-natured; of the Chinaman as simply "queer"; of the Japanese as "imitative." No. Look for low subtle methods and death-dealing ideals. Meet them by full-blooded contempt for other races. Teach this to children so that it will become instinctive. Then they won't get into trouble by playing artlessly with colored children or even with colored dolls unless, of course, they are attired as servants.

Next, Exploitation. No use wincing at the word. No sense in letting Roosevelt and the "New Deal" mislead you. The poor must be poor so that the Rich may be Rich. That's clear and true. It merely means using the world for the good of the world and those who own it; bringing out its wealth and abundance; making the lazy and shiftless and ignorant work for their soul's good and for the profit of their betters, who alone are capable of using Wealth to promote Culture.

And finally, Empire: the white race as ruler of all the world and the world working for it, and the world's wealth piled up for the white man's use. This may seem harsh and selfish and yet, of course, it was perfectly natural. Naturally white men would and must rule and any question of their ruling should be met and settled promptly. My friend had not thought that there was any question of this, and there was not before the first World War. There we made the wretched mistake of letting the colored folk dip in, and it turned their weak heads. They almost thought they won the war. He remembered his own disgust at seeing American Negroes actually tricked up as officers—shoulder-straps, Sam Browne belts, and all. He could not conceive of a world where white people did not rule colored people, and certainly if the matter actually came to a trial of force, would he not naturally have to stand for War, Hate, Suspicion and Exploitation in order to put over the Empire of the Whites?

The trouble was, however, that when my friend tabulated all of the codes which he at once and apparently simultaneously was to put in action, he found a most astonishing result, and here it is:

Christian	Gentleman	American	White Man
Peace	Justice	Defense	War
Good Will	Manners	Caste	Hate
Golden Rule	Exclusiveness	Propaganda	Suspicion
Liberty	Police	Patriotism	Exploitation
Poverty	Wealth	Power	Empire

Looking them over, he doesn't know what on earth to do. It is not only dilemma, it is almost quadri-lemma.

It is most astonishing!

Perhaps he might put a line between "Christian Gentle-man" on the one hand and the "American White Man" on the other, and so arrange a very tremendous and puzzling dilemma.

My friend comes and sits down with me and asks me frankly what to do about it. And I? Why, I appeal to you, Gentle Reader. What should he do about it?

My friend's fault is that he is logical. His reasoning is a clean, simple process like two plus two equal four. This is the cause of his present unrest. Other folk are deliciously impervious to reason. They are pacifists with the help of the police and backed by careful preparation for war. They are filled with Good Will for all men, provided these men are in their places and certain of them kept there by severe discountenance. In that case courtesy smooths human relations. They certainly aim to treat others as they want to be treated themselves, so far as this is consistent with their own necessarily exclusive position. This position must be maintained by propaganda inculcating a perfectly defensible contempt for inferiors and suspicion of strangers and radicals. They believe in liberty under a firm police system backed by patriotism and an organization of work which will yield profit to capital. And, of course, they believe in poverty so long as they have sufficient wealth. This they are certain is the way to make America the greatest country on earth for white supremacy.

This makes my friend tear his pale hair. "How can they do it?" he yells. "It ain't reasonable." I explained patiently: possibly they are playing acrostics. See how they might arrange their meanings?

Peace			
	Manners		
		Propaganda	
			Exploitation
Good Will			
	Exclusiveness		
		Patriotism	
			Empire

			Hate
		Propaganda	
	Police		
Poverty			
			War
		Caste	
	Exclusiveness		
Liberty			

"Fact is," I add, "I've heard them singing in St. Thomas's:

> The Prince of *Peace* goes forth to *War*
> A *Kingly Crown* to ga-a-ain!
> His *blood-red banner* floats afar.
> Who follows *in his Name!*"

"Your quotation is not exact," responds my literal friend.

"Perhaps not, but it comes to the same thing: they combine Peace, War, Empire, Bolshevism and Jesus Christ in one happy family."

My friend waves all this aside. "Outside of spoofing and horse-play," he insists, "it's all both reasonable and impossible. Take each column alone and it is to me absolutely convincing. I believe in it. Think of a world with

Peace, Good Will, Freedom, the Golden Rule and
Poverty! My God, what a Paradise, despite death and accident, cold and heat—what? That fellow Gandhi is the only
human leader today with the right idea. It's magnificent.
It's tremendous."

"Plain living and high thinking," I suggest.

"Of course," he responds, "only—well, one wants some
Beauty—travel, gowns, palaces, diamonds, and Grand
Opera—"

I intervene, "But don't forget the preceding lines:
'never to blend our pleasure or our pride, with sorrow of
the meanest thing that feels.' "

"But—well, that brings me down out of the clouds," he
complains. "This can't be a world of saints. We have got
to have wealth and servants. Servants must be cheap and
willing and the mean ought not to be so sensitive. Perhaps
they are not. But why not have a world of gentlemen—
well-policed, everybody in his place; all the rich, courteous
and generous and all the poor appreciative; propaganda
for the right, love of country and prosperous business;
White World leading the Colored as far as the darkies
can go. Certainly despite all your democracy, blood will
tell. Now that seems to be *practical*. They've got something like that in England. Or at least, they think they
have.

"But if I put this thing to the club, as man to man, no
sooner have I mentioned England than they're in arms.
England, dammit, has a bigger navy and merchant marine
than we, with which she monopolizes the world-carrying
trade; she patronizes and despises us, and then pats us on
the back when her chestnuts are red-hot; she rules a bigger

empire. And France won't pay us and has a big black army; and Russia is stirring up Revolution with a big Red army; and Germany! Good Lord! Hitler is anti-Christ. I tell you what, we got to watch out. America is the greatest nation on earth and the world is jealous of her. We got to be prepared if it takes a billion a year for powder and guns. We've got to be disciplined; a stern, severe code for the lazy and criminal; training for boy scouts and militia. We must put patriotism before everything—make 'em salute the flag, stop radical treason, keep out the dirty foreigners, disfranchise niggers and make America a Power!

"Well, I like America. Darn it! I *love* it. My father died for it, although not in war—and I am reasonably willing to. There's no doubt about it, lambs have got no business prowling about lions and—oh, Hell! Honest to God, what do you think Asia and Africa would do to us, if they got a chance?"

"Skin us alive," I answer cheerfully, loving the "us."

"Well, then! Skin them and skin 'em first and keep 'em skinned. I'm a He-White-Man, get me?

"Then, look at these other columns. Suppose they are not logical, correct, compelling. We cannot run this world without the police and courts of Justice. We must not be discourteous even to the pushing, careless, impudent American fellow-citizen, but something is due our own self-respect. Can we get on without being exclusive? I don't mean downright snobbishness, but be careful, nice, 'aristocratic' in the best meaning of the term. Finally, we of the upper class must have money. We must have it, no matter how we get it, or civilization is lost.

"Well, now, if we cannot do without these things, then, they must become our rule of life. But no sooner have you settled it this way than there comes that business of being an American. Can we give that up? Can we go in for Humanity and the International? Lord knows I'd like to but somehow, I can't see it. Suppose America disarmed like Denmark, gave up poison gas, big battleships and dinky little officers in khaki? Suppose we continue to neglect discipline for the mob and stop teaching thick and thin patriotism? I admit it isn't exactly honest business; America isn't so wonderful as nations go, but must we not make Americans believe it wonderful? Can we emphasize the fact that Lincoln told smutty stories and Washington held slaves and Jefferson begat bastards, and Webster drank more than was good for him? Suppose we did not become powerful as well as big? What is going to happen to us? Well, there you are. We've got to be Americans even if we give up being Christians and Gentlemen."

Or again, and here my friend gets a bit embarrassed and red in the face: "You see," he says to me confidentially, "I've got a little daughter, young yet, but a nice little thing. Probably she is going to be pretty, certainly is going to have some money from her aunt as well as a bit from me. She is being educated, and I may say rather expensively educated, in a private school. She may go in for art or some high class profession, or she may not; but certainly, I hope she will marry and marry well. There will be children and grandchildren and great-grandchildren and so on ad infinitum. Now, I tell you frankly, I want them all white. Even if she were a son, while the case wouldn't be so bad, still I don't want to think of colored folk sharing my blood. Can you for a moment conceive a world where brown men and dagoes were giving orders to white men and women? It would spell the end of civilization. Of course, there may be a few exceptions, but the mass of the colored world can't think, they can't rule, they can't direct, and we mustn't let them try. And to keep them from trying we've got to pound them back into their places every time they show their heads above the ramparts!"

Then my friend stopped. He turned red and grew apologetic. "Of course," he stammered, "I don't exactly mean you—you are an Exception, at least in some respects—"

"In some respects?" I rejoin helplessly. But my friend stiffened. Suddenly he ceased speaking and stared at the headlines in the evening paper. The world had gone to war again to defend Democracy!

✦

The democracy which the white world seeks to defend does not exist. It has been splendidly conceived and discussed, but not realized. If it ever is to grow strong enough for self-defense and for embracing the world and developing human culture to its highest, it must include not simply the lower classes among the whites now excluded from voice in the control of industry; but in addition to that it must include the colored peoples of Asia and Africa, now hopelessly imprisoned by poverty and ignorance. Unless these latter are included and in so far as they are not, democracy is a mockery and contains within itself the seeds of its own destruction.

Hitler is the late crude but logical exponent of white

world race philosophy since the Conference of Berlin in 1884. Europe had followed the high, ethical dream of a young Jew but twisted that ethic beyond recognition to any end that Europe wanted. If that end was murder, the "Son of God went forth to war!" If that end was slavery, God thundered, "Cursed be Canaan," and Paul echoed "Servants obey your masters!" If poverty was widespread and seemingly inevitable, Christ was poor and alms praiseworthy.

There persisted the mud-sill theory of society that civilization not only permitted but must have the poor, the diseased, the wretched, the criminal upon which to build its temples of light. Western Europe did not and does not want democracy, never believed in it, never practiced it and never without fundamental and basic revolution will accept it. Not the keen, the bold, the brave and the enlightened are the ones which modern individual struggle throws to the fore but rather the lucky and the strong.

How now, not so much in the judgment of the common man, but in the light of science, can the racial attitude of the white world be explained and rationalized and removed from the harsh judgment put upon it by the darker races today? Negroes in Africa, Indians in Asia, mulattoes and mestizoes in the West Indies, Central and South America, all explain the attitude of the white world as sheer malevolence; while the white people of the leading European countries honestly regard themselves as among the great benefactors of mankind and especially of colored mankind.

In this dilemma sociologists of earlier years took refuge in inventing a new entity, the group, which had action, guilt, praise and blame quite apart from the persons composing the group. It was of course a metaphysical hypothesis which had its uses in reasoning, but could not be regarded as corresponding to exact truth. No such group over-soul has been proven to exist.

The facts of the situation however as science today conceives it, are clear. The individual may act consciously and rationally and be responsible for what he does; but on the other hand many of his actions, and indeed, as we are coming to believe, most of his actions, are not rational and many of them arise from subconscious urges. It is our duty to assess praise and blame for the rational and conscious acts of men, but to regard the vast area of the subconscious and the irrational and especially of habit and convention which also produce significant action, as an area where we must apply other remedies and judgments if we would get justice and right to prevail in the world. Above all we must survey these vague and uncharted lands and measure their limits.

Looking at this whole matter of the white race as it confronts the world today, what can be done to make its attitudes rational and consistent and calculated to advance the best interests of the whole world of men? The first point of attack is undoubtedly the economic. The progress of the white world must cease to rest upon the poverty and the ignorance of its own proletariat and of the colored world. Thus industrial imperialism must lose its reason for being and in that way alone can the great racial groups of the world come into normal and helpful relation to each other. The present attitude and action of the white world is not based solely upon rational, deliberate intent. It is a matter of conditioned reflexes; of long followed habits, customs and folkways; of subconscious trains of reasoning and unconscious nervous reflexes. To attack and better all this calls for more than appeal and argument. It needs carefully planned and scientific propaganda; the vision of a world of intelligent men with sufficient income to live decently and with the will to build a beautiful world. It will not be easy to accomplish all this, but the quickest way to bring the reason of the world face to face with this major problem of human progress is to listen to the complaint of those human beings today who are suffering most from white attitudes, from white habits, from the conscious and unconscious wrongs which white folk are today inflicting on their victims. The colored world therefore must be seen as existing not simply for itself but as a group whose insistent cry may yet become the warning which awakens the world to its truer self and its wider destiny.

CHAPTER 7. THE COLORED WORLD WITHIN

NOT only do white men but also colored men forget the facts of the Negro's double environment. The Negro American has for his environment not only the white surrounding world, but also, and touching him usually much more nearly and compellingly, is the environment furnished by his own colored group. There are exceptions, of course, but this is the rule. The American Negro, therefore, is surrounded and conditioned by the concept which he has of white people and he is treated in accordance with the concept they have of him. On the other hand, so far as his own people are concerned, he is in direct contact with individuals and facts. He fits into this environment more or less willingly. It gives him a social world and mental peace. On the other hand and especially if in education and ambition and income he is above the average culture of his group, he is often resentful of its environing power; partly because he does not recognize its power and partly because he is determined to consider himself part of the white group from which, in fact, he is excluded. This weaving of words does not make the situation entirely clear and yet it does point toward its complications.

It is true, as I have argued, that Negroes are not in-

herently ugly nor congenitally stupid. They are not naturally criminal and their poverty and ignorance today have
clear and well-known and remediable causes. All this is
true; and yet what every colored man living today knows
is that by practical present measurement Negroes today
are inferior to whites. The white folk of the world are
richer and more intelligent; they live better; have better
government; have better legal systems; have built more
impressive cities, larger systems of communication and
they control a larger part of the earth than all the colored
peoples together.

Against this colored folk may certainly bring many
countervailing considerations. But putting these aside,
there remains the other fact that the mass of the colored
peoples in Asia and Africa, in North America and the
West Indies and in South America and in the South Sea
Islands are in the mass ignorant, diseased, and inefficient;
that the governments which they have evolved, even
allowing for the interested interference of the white
world, have seldom reached the degree of efficiency of
modern European governments; and that particularly in
the use, increase, and distribution of wealth, in the regulation of human services, they have at best fallen behind
the accomplishment of modern England, France and the
United States.

It may be said, and with very strong probability back
of such assertion, there is no reason to doubt, that whatever white folk have accomplished, black, brown and
yellow folk might have done possibly in differing ways
with different results. Certainly modern civilization is too
new and has steered too crooked a course and been too

much a matter of chance and fate to make any final judgment as to the abilities of humankind.

All this I strongly believe and yet today we are faced by these uncomforting facts: the ignorance, poverty and inefficiency of the darker peoples; the wealth, power and technical triumph of the whites. It is not enough when the colored people face this situation, that they decry resulting attitudes of the white world. There is a strong suspicion among themselves and a probability often asserted among whites, that were conditions reversed, blacks would have done everything to white people that white people have done to blacks; or going less far afield than this: if yellow folk in the future gain the domination of the world, their program might not be more philanthropic than that of the whites. But here again, this is not the question. Granting its possible truth, it is no answer to the present plight.

The present question is: What is the colored world going to do about the current situations? Present Negro attitudes can be illuminated by turning our attention for a space to colored America, to an average group of Negroes, say, in Harlem, not in their role of agitation and reform, but in their daily human intercourse and play. Imagine a conversation like this, of which I have heard dozens:

✦

"Just like niggers!"
"This is what colored people always do."
"What can you expect of the 'brother'?"
"I wish to God I had been born white!"

This interchange takes place at midnight. There are no white persons present. Four persons have spent an evening playing bridge, and now are waiting until a fifth, the hostess, brings in the supper. The apartment is small but comfortable; perhaps a little too full of conventional furniture, which does not altogether agree in pattern; but evidently the home of fairly well-to-do people who like each other and are enjoying themselves. But, of course, they have begun to discuss "the problem" which no group of American colored people can long keep from discussing. It is and must be the central interest of their lives.

There is a young colored teacher from the public schools of New York—well-paid and well-dressed, with a comely form and an arresting personality. She is from the South. Her mother had been servant and housekeeper in a wealthy Southern white family. Her grandmother had been a slave of their own grandfather. This teacher is complaining bitterly of her walk through Harlem that night; of the loud and vulgar talking; of the way in which the sidewalks were blocked; of the familiarity and even insults of dark loafers; of the insistent bad manners and resentful attitude of so many of these Harlem black folk.

The lawyer lights a cigar. "It certainly is a question where to live," he says. He had been educated at Fisk University and brought in contact for eight years with Northern white teachers. Then he had gone West and eventually studied law at the University of Michigan. He is big, dark, good-natured and well-dressed. He complains of the crowded conditions of living in Harlem; of the noise and dirt in any Negro community; of the fact that if you went out to a better class white neighborhood you could not rent, you had to buy; if you did buy, first you could place no mortgage; then the whites made your life a hell; if you survived this, the whites became panicky, sold to anyone for anything: pretty soon, in two, three, five years, people of all sorts and kinds came crowding in. Homes were transformed into lodging houses; undesirable elements became your neighbors. "I moved to a nice apartment on Sugar Hill last year. It had just been turned over to colored people. The landlord promised everything. I started out of the apartment last night; there was a pool of blood in front of my door, where there had been a drunken brawl and cutting the night before."

A young, slim, cream-colored physician, native of New York and a graduate of its schools, but compelled to go to Howard in order to finish the clinical work of his medical education, looked uncomfortable. "I don't mind going with colored people; I prefer it, if they are my kind; but if I go out to lunch here in Harlem, I get pork chops and yams which I do not like, served on a table cloth which is not clean, set down negligently by indifferent waiters. In the movies uptown here I find miscellaneous and often ill-smelling neighbors. On my vacation, where shall I— where can I go? The part of Atlantic City open to me, I continue to frequent, because I see so many charming friends of mine from all over the land; but always I get sick at heart not only at the discrimination on the board-walk, in the restaurants, on the beach, in the amusements —that is bad enough; but I gag at the kind of colored people always in evidence, against whom I want to dis-

criminate myself. We tried to support a colored section
of the beach; see who crowded in; we failed."

"Yes, but that is all pleasure or convenience," says the
fourth man. He was an insurance agent, playing a difficult
game of chance with people who made weekly payments
to him and then tried to beat him by malingering; or
with others who paid promptly and had their claims dis-
allowed by the higher-ups. "What I am bothered about,"
he says, "is this poverty, sickness and crime; the cheating
of Negroes not only by whites, but by Negroes themselves;
the hold-ups and murders of colored people by colored
people. I am afraid to go to some places to make my col-
lections. I don't know what is going to become of Negroes
at this rate."

Just then, the fifth member of the party, the wife of
the insurance agent, emerges from the kitchen where she
has been arranging the lunch. She is pretty and olive, a
little inclined to be fat. She was the daughter of dark
laborers who had gone to Boston after emancipation.
There she had been educated in the public schools and
was a social worker there before she married. She knew
how to cook and liked to, and is accompanied through the
swinging door by a delicious aroma of coffee, hot biscuits
and fried chicken. She has been listening to the conversation from outside and she came in saying, "What's got me
worried to death, is where I am going to send Junior to
school. Junior is bright and has got nice manners, if I do
say it; but I just can't send him to these Harlem schools.
I was visiting them yesterday; dirt, noise, bad manners,
filthy tales, no discipline, over-crowded. The teachers
aren't half trying. They purposely send green teachers

to Harlem for experience. I just can't send Junior there; but where can I send him?"

✦

This is a fairly characteristic colored group of the better class and they are voicing that bitter inner criticism of Negroes directed in upon themselves, which is widespread. It tends often to fierce, angry, contemptuous judgment of nearly all that Negroes do, say, and believe. Of course these words are seldom voiced in the presence of white folk. Every one of these persons, in the presence of whites, would eagerly and fiercely defend their "race."

Such complaints are the natural reaction of people toward the low average of culture among American Negroes. There is some exaggeration here, which the critics themselves, if challenged, would readily admit; and yet, there is sound basis for much of this criticism. Similar phenomena may be noticed always among undeveloped or suppressed peoples or groups undergoing extraordinary experience. None have more pitilessly castigated Jews than the Jewish prophets, ancient and modern. It is the Irish themselves who rail at "dirty Irish tricks." Nothing could exceed the self-abasement of the Germans during the *Sturm und Drang.*

Negro self-criticism recognizes a perfectly obvious fact and that fact is that most Negroes in the United States today occupy a low cultural status; both low in itself and low as compared with the national average in the land. There are cultured individuals and groups among them. All Negroes do not fall culturally below all whites. But if one selects any one of the obviously low culture groups

in the United States, the proportion of Negroes who belong to it will be larger than the Negro proportion in
the total population. Nor is there anything singular about
it; the real miracle would be if this were not so. Former
slavery, present poverty and ignorance, with the inevitable
resulting sickness and crime, are adequate social explanation.

This low social condition of the majority of Negroes is
not solely a problem of the whites; a question of historic
guilt in slavery and labor exploitation and of present discrimination; it is not merely a matter of the social uplift-
ing of an alien group within their midst; a problem of
social contact and political power. Howsoever it may be
thus rationalized and explained, it must be, at any current
moment, primarily an inner problem of the Negro group
itself, a condition from which they themselves are prime
sufferers, and a problem with which this group is forced
itself to grapple. No matter what the true reasons are, or
where the blame lies, the fact remains that among twelve
million American Negroes, there are today poverty, ignorance, bad manners, disease, and crime.

A determined fight has been made upon Negro ignorance, both within and without the group, and the results
have been notable. Nevertheless, this is still an ignorant
people. One in every six Negroes ten years of age and
over admitted in 1930 that he could not read and write.
It is probable that one in every three would have been
justified in confessing to practical illiteracy, to inexperience and lack of knowledge of the meaning of the modern
world. In the South not one-half the colored children
from five to sixteen are regularly in school and the ma-

jority of these schools are not good schools. Any poor, ignorant people herded by themselves, filled with more or less articulate resentment, are bound to be bad-mannered, for manners are a matter of social environment; and the mass of American Negroes have retrograded in this respect.

There has been striking improvement in the Negro death rate. It was better than that of most South American countries, of Italy, Japan and Spain even before the war. Nevertheless it is still bad and costly, and the toll in tuberculosis, pneumonia, heart disease, syphilis, and homicide is far too high. It is hard to know just what the criminal tendencies of the American Negroes are, for our crime statistics are woefully inadequate. We do know that in proportion to population three times as many Negroes are arrested as whites, but to what extent this measures prejudice and to what extent anti-social ills, who shall say? Many of these ought never to have been arrested; most of them are innocent of grave crimes; but the transgression of the poor and sick is always manifest among Negroes: disorder of all sorts, theft and burglary, fighting, breaking the gambling and liquor laws and especially fighting with and killing each other.

Above all the Negro is poor: poor by heritage from two hundred forty-four years of chattel slavery, by emancipation without land or capital and by seventy-five years of additional wage exploitation and crime peonage. Sudden industrial changes like the Civil War, the World War and the spree in speculation during the twenties have upset him. The Negro worker has been especially hard hit by the current depression. Of the nearly three million Negro families in the United States today, probably the bread-winners of a million are unemployed and another million on the lower margin of decent subsistence. Assuming a gradual restoration of fairly normal conditions it is probable that not more than two per cent of the Negro families in the United States would have an income of $2,500 a year and over; while fifty-eight per cent would have incomes between $500 and $2,500.

This social degradation is intensified and emphasized by discrimination; inability to get work, discrimination in pay, improbability of promotion, and more fundamentally, spiritual segregation from contact with manners, customs, incentives to effort despite handicaps. By outer pressure in most cases, Negroes must live among themselves; neighbors to their own people in segregated parts of the city, in segregated country districts. The segregation is not complete and most of it is customary rather than legal. Nevertheless, most Negroes live with Negroes, in what are on the whole the least pleasant dwelling places, although not necessarily always bad places in themselves.

This means that Negroes live in districts of low cultural level; that their contacts with their fellow men involve contacts with people largely untrained and ignorant, frequently diseased, dirty, and noisy, and sometimes antisocial. These districts are not usually protected by the police—rather victimized and tyrannized over by them. No one who does not know can realize what tyranny a low-grade white policeman can exercise in a colored neighborhood. In court his unsupported word cannot be disputed and the only defense against him is often mayhem and assassination by black criminals, with resultant hue and cry. City services of water, sewerage, garbage-removal, street-cleaning, lighting, noise and traffic regulation, schools and hospitalization are usually neglected or withheld. Saloons, brothels, and gambling seek these areas with open or tacit consent. No matter in what degree or in what way the action of the white population may increase or decrease these social problems, they remain the present problems which must be faced by colored people themselves and by colored people of widely different status.

It goes without saying that while Negroes are thus manifestly of low average culture, in no place nor at any time do they form a homogeneous group. Even in the country districts of the lower South, Allison Davis likens the group to a steeple with wide base tapering to a high pinnacle. This means that while the poor, ignorant, sick and anti-social form a vast foundation, that upward from that base stretch classes whose highest members, although few in number, reach above the average not only of the Negroes but of the whites, and may justly be compared to the better-class white culture. The class structure of the whites, on the other hand, resembles a tower bulging near the center with the lowest classes small in number as compared with the middle and lower middle classes; and the highest classes far more numerous in proportion than those among blacks. This, of course, is what one would naturally expect, but it is easily forgotten. The Negro group is spoken of continually as one undifferentiated low-class mass. The culture of the higher whites is often considered as typical of all the whites.

American Negroes again are of differing descent, from parents with varied education, born in many parts of the land and under all sorts of conditions. In differing degrees these folk have come through periods of great and vital social change; emancipation from slavery, migration from South to North, from country to city; changes in income and intelligence. Above this they have experienced widely different contacts with their own group and with the whites. For instance, during slavery the dark house servant came into close and intimate contact with the master class. This class itself differed in all degrees from cultured aristocrats to brutal tyrants. Many of the Negroes thus received ideals of gracious manners, of swaggering self-assertion, of conspicuous consumption. Later cultural contact came to the best of the Negroes through the mission schools in the South succeeding the war: the more simple and austere intellectual life of New England with its plain living and high thinking; its cleanliness and conscience; this was brought into direct contact with educated Negro life. Its influence is still felt among the descendants of those trained at Fisk and Atlanta, Hampton and Talladega and a score of other schools.

These contacts between the white and colored groups in the United States have gradually changed. On the whole the better cultural contacts have lessened in breadth and time, and greater cultural segregation by race has ensued. The old bonds between servants and masters in the South disappeared. The white New England teachers gradually withdrew from the Southern schools partly by white Southern caste pressure, partly to make place for Negroes whom the Northern teachers had trained. The bonds that replaced these older contacts were less direct, more temporary and casual; and yet, these still involve considerable numbers of persons. In Northern public schools and colleges, numbers of white and colored youth come into direct contact, knowledge and sympathy. Various organizations, movements, and meetings bring white and colored people together; in various occupations they work side by side and in large numbers of cases they meet as employers and employed. Deliberate interracial movements have brought some social contacts in the South.

Thus considerable intercourse between white and black folk in America is current today; and yet on the whole, the more or less clearly defined upper layers of educated and ambitious Negroes find themselves for the most part largely segregated and alone. They are unable, or at least unwilling on the terms offered, to share the social institutions of the cultured whites of the nation, and are faced with inner problems of contact with their own lower classes with which they have few or no social institutions capable of dealing.

The Negro of education and income is jammed beside the careless, ignorant and criminal. He recoils from appeal to the white city even for physical protection against his anti-social elements, for this, he feels, is a form of self-accusation, of attack on the Negro race. It invites the smug rejoinder: "Well, if you can't live with niggers, how do you expect us to?" For escape of the Negro cultured to areas of white culture, with the consequent acceleration of acculturation, there is small opportunity. There is little or no chance for a Negro family to remove to a quiet neighborhood, to a protected suburb or a college town. I tried once to buy a home in the Sage Foundation development at Forest Hills, Long Island. The project was designed for the class of white-collar workers to which I belonged. Robert De Forest and his directors hesitated, but finally and definitely refused, simply and solely because of my dark skin.

What now is the practical path for the solution of the problem? Usually it has been assumed in such cases that the culture recruits rising from a submerged group will be received more or less willingly by corresponding classes of neighboring or enveloping groups. Of course it is clear in the case of immigrant groups and other disadvantaged clusters of folk that this process is by no means easy or natural. Much bitter frustration and social upheaval continually arise from the refusal of the upper social layers to receive recruits from below. Nevertheless, in the United States it has been impossible long or entirely to exclude the better classes of the Irish, the Italians, the Southern poor whites. In the case of the Negro, the unwillingness is greater and public opinion supports it to such a degree, that admission of black folk to cultured circles is slow and difficult. It still remains possible in the United States for a white American to be a gentleman and a scholar, a Christian and a man of integrity, and yet flatly and openly refuse to treat as a fellow human being any person who has Negro ancestry.

The inner contradiction and frustration which this involves is curious. The younger educated Negroes show here vastly different interpretations. One avoids every appearance of segregation. He will not sit in a street car beside a Negro; he will not frequent a Negro church; he will join few, if any, Negro organizations. On the other hand, he will take every opportunity to join in the political and cultural life of the whites. But he pays for this and pays dearly. He so often meets actual insult or more or less veiled rebuffs from the whites that he becomes nervous and truculent through expectation of dislike, even when its manifestation does not always appear. And on the other hand, Negroes more or less withdraw from associating with him. They suspect that he is "ashamed of his race."

Another sort of young educated Negro forms and joins Negro organizations; prides himself on living with "his people"; withdraws from contact with whites, unless there is no obvious alternative. He too pays. His cultural contacts sink of necessity to a lower level. He becomes provincial in his outlook. He attributes to whites a dislike and hatred and racial prejudice of which many of them are quite unconscious and guiltless.

Between these two extremes range all sorts of interracial patterns, and all of them theoretically follow the idea that Negroes must only submit to segregation "when forced." In practically all cases the net result is a more or less clear and definite crystallization of the culture elements among colored people into their own groups for social and cultural contact.

The resultant path which commends itself to many whites is deliberate and planned cultural segregation of the upper classes of Negroes not only from the whites of all classes, but from their own masses. It has been said time and time again: if certain classes of Negroes do not like the squalor, filth and crime of Negro slums, instead of trying to escape to better class white neighborhoods, why do they not establish their own exclusive neighborhoods?

In other words, why does not the Negro race build up a class structure of its own, parallel to that of the whites, but separate; and including its own social, economic and religious institutions?

The arresting thing about this advice and program is that even when not planned, this is exactly what Negroes are doing and must do even in the case of those who theoretically resent it. The group with whose conversation this chapter started is a case in point. They form a self-segregated culture group. They have come to know each other partly by chance, partly by design, but form a small integrated clique because of similar likes and ideas, because of corresponding culture. This is happening all over the land among these twelve million Negroes. It is not a matter yet of a few broad super-imposed social classes, but rather of smaller cliques and groups gradually integrating and extending out of their neighborhoods into neighboring districts and cities. In this way a distinct social grouping has long been growing among American Negroes and recent studies have emphasized what we all knew, and that is that the education and acculturation of the Negro child is more largely the result of the training through contact with these cultural groups than it is of the caste-conditioned contacts with whites.

The question now comes as to how far this method of acculturation should and could go, and by what conscious planning the uplift of the Negro race can be accomplished through this means. Is cultural separation in the same territory feasible? To force a group of various levels of culture to segregate itself, will certainly retard its advance, since it must put energy not simply into social advance, but in the vast and intricate effort to duplicate, evolve, and contrive new social institutions to maintain their advance and guard against retrogression.

There can be two theories here: one that the rise of a talented tenth within the Negro race, whether or not it succeeds in escaping to the higher cultural classes of the white race, is a threat to the development of the whole Negro group and hurts their chances for salvation. Or it may be said that the rise of classes within the Negro group is precisely a method by which the level of culture in the whole group is going to be raised. But this depends upon the relations that develop between these masses and the cultural aims of the higher classes.

Many assume that an upper social class maintains its status mainly by reason of its superior culture. It may, however, maintain its status because of its wealth and political power and in that case its ranks can be successfully invaded only by the wealthy. In white America, it is in this direction that we have undoubtedly changed the older pattern of social hierarchy. Birth and culture still count, but the main avenue to social power and class domination is wealth: income and oligarchic economic power, the consequent political power and the prestige of those who own and control capital and distribute credit. This makes a less logical social hierarchy and one that can only be penetrated by the will and permission of the ruling oligarchy or the chances of gambling. Education, thrift, hard work and character undoubtedly are influential, but they are implemented with power only as they gain wealth; and as land, natural resources, credit and capital are increasingly monopolized, they gain wealth by permission of the dominating wealthy class.

If now American Negroes plan a vertical parallel of such a structure and such processes, they will find it practically impossible. First of all, they have not the wealth; secondly, they have not the political power which wealth manipulates, and in the realm of their democratic power they are not only already partly disfranchised by law and custom, but they suffer the same general limitation of democratic power in income and industry, in which the white masses are imprisoned.

There would be greater possibility of the Negro imitating the class structure of the white race if those whites who advise and encourage it were ready to help in its accomplishment, ready to furnish the Negro the broadest opportunity for cultural development and in addition to this to open the way for them to accumulate such wealth and receive such income as would make the corresponding structure secure. But, of course, those who most vehemently tell the Negro to develop his own classes and social institutions, have no plan or desire for such help. First of all, and often deliberately, they curtail the education and cultural advantage of black folk and they do this because they are not convinced of the cultural ability or gift of Negroes and have no hope nor wish that the mass of Negroes can be raised even as far as the mass of whites have been. It is this insincere attitude which especially arouses the ire and resentment of the culture groups among American Negroes.

When the Negro despairs of duplicating white development, his despair is not always because the paths to this development are shut in his face, but back of this lurks too often a lack of faith in essential Negro possibilities, parallel to similar attitudes on the part of the whites. Instead of this proving anything concerning the truth, it is simply a natural phenomenon. Negroes, particularly the better class Negroes, are brought up like other Americans despite the various separations and segregations. They share, therefore, average American culture and current American prejudices. It is almost impossible for a Negro boy trained in a white Northern high school and a white college to come out with any high idea of his own people or any abiding faith in what they can do; or for a Negro trained in the segregated schools of the South wholly to escape the deadening environment of insult and caste, even if he happens to have the good teachers and teaching facilities, which poverty almost invariably denies him. He may rationalize his own individual status as exceptional. He can well believe that there are many other exceptions, but he cannot ordinarily believe that the mass of Negro people have possibilities equal to the whites.

It is this sort of thing that leads to the sort of self-criticism that introduces this chapter. My grandfather, Alexander Du Bois, was pushed into the Negro group. He resented it. He wasn't a "Negro," he was a man. He would not attend Negro picnics or join a Negro church, and yet he had to. Now, his situation in 1810 was much different from mine in 1940, because the Negro group today is much more differentiated and has distinct cultural elements. He could go to a Negro picnic today and associate with interesting people of his own level. So much so, indeed, that some Negro thinkers are beginning to be afraid that we will become so enamored of our own internal social contacts, that we will cease to hammer at the doors of the larger group, with all the consequent loss of breadth through lack of the widest cultural contact; and all the danger of ultimate extinction through exacerbated racial repulsions and violence. For any building of a segregated Negro culture in America in those areas where it is by law or custom the rule and where neglect to take positive action would mean a slowing down or stoppage or even retrogression of Negro advance, unusual and difficult and to some extent unprecedented action is called for.

To recapitulate: we cannot follow the class structure of America; we do not have the economic or political power, the ownership of machines and materials, the power to direct the processes of industry, the monopoly of capital and credit. On the other hand, even if we cannot follow this method of structure, nevertheless we must do something. We cannot stand still; we cannot permit ourselves simply to be the victims of exploitation and social exclusion. It is from this paradox that arises the present frustration among American Negroes.

Historically, beginning with their thought in the eighteenth century and coming down to the twentieth, Negroes have tended to choose between these difficulties and emphasize two lines of action: the *first* is exemplified in Walker's Appeal, that tremendous indictment of slavery by a colored man published in 1829, and resulting very possibly in the murder of the author; and coming down through the work of the Niagara Movement and the National Association for the Advancement of Colored People in our day. This program of organized opposition to the action and attitude of the dominant white group, includes ceaseless agitation and insistent demand for equality: the equal right to work, civic and political equality, and social equality. It involves the use of force of every sort: moral suasion, propaganda and where possible even physical resistance.

There are, however, manifest difficulties about such a program. First of all it is not a program that envisages any direct action of Negroes themselves for the uplift of their socially depressed masses; in the very conception of the program, such work is to be attended to by the nation and Negroes are to be the subjects of uplift forces and agencies to the extent of their numbers and need. Another difficulty is that the effective organization of this plan of protest and agitation involves a large degree of inner union and agreement among Negroes. Now for obvious reasons of ignorance and poverty, and the natural envy and bickering of any disadvantaged group, this unity is difficult to achieve. In fact the efforts to achieve it through the Negro conventions of 1833 and thereafter during the fifties; during Reconstruction, and in the formation of the early Equal Rights League and Afro-American Council, were only partly successful.

The largest measure of united effort in the demand for Negro rights was attempted by the NAACP in the decade between 1914 and 1924. The difficulty even in that case was the matter of available funds. The colored people are not today able to furnish enough funds for the kind of campaign against Negro prejudice which is demanded; or at least the necessity of large enough contributions is not clear to a sufficient number of Negroes. Moreover, even if there were the necessary unity and resources available, there are two assumptions usually made in such a campaign, which are not quite true; and that is the assumption on one hand that most race prejudice is a matter of ignorance to be cured by information; and on the other hand that much discrimination is a matter of deliberate deviltry and unwillingness to be just. Admitting widespread ignorance concerning the guilt of American whites for the plight of the Negroes; and the undoubted existence of sheer malevolence, the present attitude of the whites is much more the result of inherited customs and of those irrational and partly subconscious actions of men which control so large a proportion of their deeds. Attitudes and habits thus built up cannot be changed by sudden assault. They call for a long, patient, well-planned and persistent campaign of propaganda.

Moreover, until such a campaign has had a chance to do its work, the minority which is seeking emancipation must remember that they are facing a powerful majority. There is no way in which the American Negro can force this nation to treat him as equal until the unconscious cerebration and folkways of the nation, as well as its rational deliberate thought among the majority of whites, are willing to grant equality.

In the meantime of course the agitating group may resort to a campaign of countermoves. They may organize and collect resources and by every available means teach the white majority and appeal to their sense of justice; but at the very best this means a campaign of waiting and the colored group must be financially able to afford to wait and patient to endure without spiritual retrogression while they wait.

The *second* group effort to which Negroes have turned is more extreme and decisive. One can see it late in the eighteenth century when the Negro union of Newport, Rhode Island, in 1788 proposed to the Free African Society of Philadelphia a general exodus to Africa on the part at least of free Negroes. This "back to Africa" movement has recurred time and time again in the philosophy of American Negroes and has commended itself not simply to the inexperienced and to demagogues, but to the prouder and more independent type of Negro; to the black man who is tired of begging for justice and recognition from folk who seem to him to have no intention of being just and do not propose to recognize Negroes as men. This thought was strong during the active existence of the Colonization Society and succeeded in convincing leading Negroes like John Russworm, the first Negro college graduate, and Lott Carey, the powerful Virginia preacher. Then it fell into severe disrepute when the objects of the Colonization Society were shown by the Abolitionists to be the perpetuation rather than the amelioration of American slavery.

Later, just before the Civil War, the scheme of migration to Africa or elsewhere was revived and agents sent out to South America, Haiti and Africa. After the Civil War and the disappointments of Reconstruction came Bishop Turner's proposal and recently the crazy scheme of Marcus Garvey. The hard facts which killed all these proposals were first lack of training, education and habits on the part of ex-slaves which unfitted them to be pioneers; and mainly that tremendous industrial expansion of Europe which made colonies in Africa or elsewhere about the last place where colored folk could successfully seek freedom and equality.

These extreme plans tended always to fade to more moderate counsel. First came the planned inner migration of the Negro group: to Canada, to the North, to the West, to cities everywhere. This has been a vast and continuing movement, affecting millions and changing and modifying the Negro problems. One result has been a new system of racial integrations. Groups of Negroes in their own clubs and organizations, in their own neighborhoods and schools, were formed, and were not so much the result of deliberate planning as the rationalization of the segregation into which they were forced by racial prejudice. These groups became physical and spiritual cities of refuge, where sometimes the participants were inspired to efforts for social uplift, learning and ambition; and sometimes reduced to sullen wordless resentment. It is toward this sort of group effort that the thoughts and plans of Booker T. Washington led. He did not advocate a deliberate and planned segregation, but advised submission to segregation in settlement and in work, in order that this bending to the will of a powerful majority might bring from that majority gradually such sympathy and sense of justice that in the long run the best interests of the Negro group would be served; particularly as those interests were, he thought, inseparable from the best interests of the dominant group. The difficulty here was that unless the dominant group saw its best interests bound up with those of the black minority, the situation was hopeless; and in any case the

danger was that if the minority ceased to agitate and resist oppression it would grow to accept it as normal and
inevitable.

A *third* path of the advance which lately I have been
formulating and advocating can easily be mistaken for a
program of complete racial segregation and even nation-
alism among Negroes. Indeed it has been criticized as
such. This is a misapprehension. First, ignoring other
racial separations, I have stressed the economic discrimination as fundamental and advised concentration of planning
here. We need sufficient income for health and home; to
supplement our education and recreation; to fight our
own crime problem; and above all to finance a continued,
planned and intelligent agitation for political, civil and
social equality. How can we Negroes in the United States
gain such average income as to be able to attend to these
pressing matters? The cost of this program must fall first
and primarily on us, ourselves. It is silly to expect any
large number of whites to finance a program which the
overwhelming majority of whites today fear and reject.
Setting up as a bogey-man an assumed proposal for an
absolute separate Negro economy in America, it has been
easy for colored philosophers and white experts to dismiss
the matter with a shrug and a laugh. But this is not so
easily dismissed. In the first place we have already got a
partially segregated Negro economy in the United States.
There can be no question about this. We not only build
and finance Negro churches, but we furnish a considerable
part of the funds for our segregated schools. We furnish
most of our own professional services in medicine, phar-
macy, dentistry and law. We furnish some part of our food

and clothes, our home building and repairing and many retail services. We furnish books and newspapers; we furnish endless personal services like those of barbers, beauty shop keepers, hotels, restaurants. It may be said that this inner economy of the Negro serves but a small proportion of its total needs; but it is growing and expanding in various ways; and what I propose is to so plan and guide it as to take advantage of certain obvious facts.

It is of course impossible that a segregated economy for Negroes in the United States should be complete. It is quite possible that it could never cover more than the smaller part of the economic activities of Negroes. Nevertheless, it is also possible that this smaller part could be so important and wield so much power that its influence upon the total economy of Negroes and the total industrial organization of the United States would be decisive for the great ends toward which the Negro moves.

We are of course obsessed with the vastness of the industrial machine in America, and with the way in which organized wealth dominates our whole government, our education, our intellectual life and our art. But despite this, the American economic class structure—that system of domination of industry and the state through income and monopoly—is breaking down; not simply in America but in the world. We have reached the end of an economic era, which seemed but a few years ago omnipotent and eternal. We have lived to see the collapse of capitalism. It makes no difference what we may say, and how we may boast in the United States of the failures and changed objectives of the New Deal, and the prospective rehabilitation of the rule of finance capital; that is but wishful

t fond hope?

thinking. In Europe and in the United States as well as in Russia the whole organization and direction of industry is changing. We are not called upon to be dogmatic as to just what the end of this change will be and what form the new organization will take. What we are sure of is the present fundamental change.

There faces the American Negro therefore an intricate and subtle problem of combining into one object two difficult sets of facts: his present racial segregation which despite anything he can do will persist for many decades; and his attempt by carefully planned and intelligent action to fit himself into the new economic organization which the world faces.

This plan of action would have for its ultimate object, full Negro rights and Negro equality in America; and it would most certainly approve, as one method of attaining this, continued agitation, protest and propaganda to that end. On the other hand my plan would not decline frankly to face the possibility of eventual emigration from America of some considerable part of the Negro population, in case they could find a chance for free and favorable development unmolested and unthreatened, and in case the race prejudice in America persisted to such an extent that it would not permit the full development of the capacities and aspirations of the Negro race. With its eyes open to the necessity of agitation and to possible migration, this plan would start with the racial grouping that today is inevitable and proceed to use it as a method of progress along which we have worked and are now working. Instead of letting this segregation remain largely a matter of chance and unplanned development, and allowing its objects and results to rest in the hands of the white majority or in the accidents of the situation, it would make the segregation a matter of careful thought and intelligent planning on the part of Negroes.

The object of that plan would be two-fold: first to make it possible for the Negro group to await its ultimate emancipation with reasoned patience, with equitable temper and with every possible effort to raise the social status and increase the efficiency of the group. And secondly and just as important, the ultimate object of the plan is to obtain admission of the colored group to co-operation and incorporation into the white group on the best possible terms.

This planned and deliberate recognition of self-segregation on the part of colored people involves many difficulties which have got to be faced. First of all, in what lines and objects of effort should segregation come? This choice is not wide, because so much segregation is compulsory: most colored children, most colored youth, are educated in Negro schools and by Negro teachers. There is more education by race today than there was in the latter part of the nineteenth century; partly because of increased racial consciousness, and partly because more Negroes are applying for education and this would call for larger social contact than ever before, if whites and Negroes went to the same schools.

On the other hand this educational segregation involves, as Negroes know all too well, poorer equipment in the schools and poorer teaching than colored children would have if they were admitted to white schools and treated with absolute fairness. It means that their contact with the better-trained part of the nation, a contact which spells quicker acculturation, is lessened and shortened; and that above all, less money is spent upon their schools. They must submit to double taxation in order to have a minimum of decent equipment. The Rosenwald school houses involved such double taxation on the Negro. The Booker T. Washington High School in Atlanta raises thousands of dollars each year by taxation upon colored students and parents, while city funds furnish only salaries, buildings, books and a minimum of equipment. This is the pattern throughout the South. On the other hand with the present attitude of teachers and the public, even if colored students were admitted to white schools, they would not in most cases receive decent treatment nor real education.

It is not then the theory but a fact that faces the Negro in education. He has group education in large proportion and he must organize and plan these segregated schools so that they become efficient, well-housed, well-equipped, with the best of teachers and with the best results on the children; so that the illiteracy and bad manners and criminal tendencies of young Negroes can be quickly and effectively reduced. Most Negroes would prefer a good school with properly paid colored teachers for educating their children, to forcing their children into white schools which met them with injustice and humiliation and discouraged their efforts to progress.

So too in the church, the activities for ethical teaching, character-building, and organized charity and neighborliness, which are largely concentrated in religious organizations, are segregated racially more completely than any other human activity; a curious and eloquent commentary upon modern Christianity. These are the facts and the colored church must face them. It is facing them only in part today because a large proportion of the intelligent colored folk do not co-operate with the church and leave the ignorant to make the church a seat of senseless dogma and meaningless ceremonies together with a multitude of activities which have no social significance and lead to no social betterment. On the other hand the Negro church does do immense amounts of needed works of charity and mercy among the poor; but here again it lacks funds.

There has been a larger movement on the part of the Negro intelligentsia toward racial grouping for the advancement of art and literature. There has been a distinct plan for reviving ancient African art through an American Negro art movement; and more especially a thought to use the extremely rich and colorful life of the Negro in America and elsewhere as a basis for painting, sculpture and literature. This has been partly nullified by the fact that if these new artists expect support for their art from the Negro group itself, that group must be deliberately trained and schooled in art appreciation and in willingness to accept new canons of art and in refusal to follow the herd instinct of the nation. Instead of this artistic group following such lines, it has largely tried to get support for the Negro art movement from the white public often with disastrous results. Most whites want Negroes to amuse them; they demand caricature; they demand jazz; and torn between these allegiances: between the extraordinary reward for entertainers of the white world, and meager encouragement to honest self-expression, the artistic movement among American Negroes has accomplished something, but it has never flourished and never will until it is deliberately planned. Perhaps its greatest single accomplishment is Carter Woodson's "Negro History Week."

In the same way there is a demand for a distinct Negro health movement. We have few Negro doctors in proportion to our population and the best training of Negro doctors has become increasingly difficult because of their exclusion from the best medical schools of America. Hospitalization among Negroes is far below their reasonable health needs and the individual medical practitioner depending upon fees is the almost universal pattern in this group. What is needed is a carefully planned and widely distributed system of Negro hospitals and socialized medicine with an adequate number of doctors on salary, with the object of social health and not individual income. "Negro Health Week," originating in Tuskegee, is a step in this direction. The whole planned political program of intelligent Negroes is deliberate segregation of their vote for Negro welfare. William L. Dawson, former alderman of Chicago, recently said, "I am not playing Party politics but race politics"; he urged, irrespective of party, adherence to political groups interested in advancing the political and economic rights of the Negro.

The same need is evident in the attitude of Negroes toward Negro crime; obsessed by the undoubted fact that crime is increased and magnified by race prejudice, we ignore the other fact that we have crime and a great deal of it and that we ourselves have got to do something about it; what we ought to do is to cover the Negro group with the services of legal defense organizations in order to counteract the injustice of the police and of the magistrate courts; and then we need positive organized effort to reclaim young and incipient malefactors. There is little organized effort of that sort among Negroes today, save a few Negro reformatories with meager voluntary support and grudging state aid.

From all the foregoing, it is evident that economic planning to insure adequate income is the crying need of Negroes today. This does not involve plans that envisage a return to the old patterns of economic organization in America and the world. This is the American Negro's present danger. Most of the well-to-do with fair education do not realize the imminence of profound economic change in the modern world. They are thinking in terms of work, thrift, investment and profit. They hope with the late Booker T. Washington to secure better economic conditions for Negroes by wider chances of employment and higher wages. They believe in savings and investment in Negro and in general business, and in the gradual evolution of a Negro capitalist class which will exploit both Negro and white labor.

The younger and more intelligent Negroes, realizing in different degrees and according to their training and acquaintance with the modern world the profound economic change through which the world is passing and is destined to pass, have taken three different attitudes: first, they have been confronted with the Communist solution of present social difficulties. The Communist philosophy was a program for a majority, not for a relatively small minority; it presupposed a class structure based on exploitation of the overwhelming majority by an exploiting minority; it advised the seizure of power by this majority and the future domination of the state by and for this majority through the dictation of a trusted group, who would hold power until the people were intelligent and experienced enough to rule themselves by democratic methods.

This philosophy did not envisage a situation where instead of a horizontal division of classes, there was a vertical fissure, a complete separation of classes by race, cutting square across the economic layers. Even if on one side this color line, the dark masses were overwhelmingly workers, with but an embryonic capitalist class, nevertheless the split between white and black workers was greater than that between white workers and capitalists; and this split depended not simply on economic exploitation but on a racial folk-lore grounded on centuries of instinct, habit and thought and implemented by the conditioned reflex of visible color. This flat and incontrovertible fact, imported Russian Communism ignored, would not discuss. American Negroes were asked to accept a complete dogma without question or alteration. It was first of all emphasized that all racial thought and racial segregation must go and that Negroes must put themselves blindly under the dictatorship of the Communist Party.

American Communists did thoroughly and completely obliterate the color bar within their own party ranks, but by so doing, absolutely blocked any chance they might have had to attract any considerable number of white workers to their ranks. The movement consequently did not get far. First, because of the natural fear of radical action in a group made timid through the heredity of slavery; but also and mainly because the attempt to abolish American race prejudice by a phrase was impossible even for the Communist Party. One result of Communistic agitation among Negroes was, however, far-reaching; and that was to impress the younger intellectuals with the fact that American Negroes were overwhelmingly workers, and that their first duty was to associate themselves with the white labor movement, and thus seek to bridge the gap of color, and eradicate the deep-seated racial instincts.

This formed a second line of action, more in consonance with conservative Negro thought. In accordance with this thought and advice and the pressure of other economic motives, Negro membership in labor unions has increased and is still increasing. This is an excellent development, but it has difficulties and pitfalls. The American labor movement varies from closed skilled labor groups, who are either nascent capitalists or stooges, to masses of beaten, ignorant labor outcasts, quite as helpless as the Negroes. Moreover among the working white masses the same racial repulsion persists as in the case of other cultural contacts. This is only natural. The white laborer has been trained to dislike and fear black labor; to regard the Negro as an unfair competitor, able and willing to degrade the price of labor; and even if the Negro prove a good union man, his treatment as an equal would involve equal status, which the white laborer through his long cultural training bitterly resents as a degradation of his own status. Under these circumstances the American Negro faces in the current labor movement, especially in the A F of L and also even in the CIO, the current racial patterns of America.

To counteract this, a recent study of Negro unionism suggests that like the Jews with their United Hebrew Trades, so the Negroes with a United Negro Trades should fight for equality and opportunity within the labor ranks. This illustrates exactly my plan to use the segregation technique for industrial emancipation. The Negro has but one clear path: to enter the white labor movement wherever and whenever he can; but to enter fighting still within labor ranks for recognition and equal treatment. Certainly unless the Negro by his organization and discipline is in position to bring to the movement something beside ignorance, poverty and ill-health, unionization in itself is no panacea.

There has come a third solution which is really a sophisticated attempt to dodge the whole problem of color in economic change; this proposal says that Negroes should join the labor movement, and also so far as possible should join themselves to capital and become capitalists and employers; and in this way, gradually the color line will dissolve into a class line between employers and employees.

Of course this solution ignores the impending change in capitalist society and hopes whatever that change may be, Negroes will benefit along with their economic class. The difficulty here is threefold: not only would there be the same difficulties of the color line in unions, but additional difficulties and exclusion when Negroes as small capitalists seek larger power through the use of capital and credit. The color bar there is beyond present hope of scaling.

But in addition to that, this plan will have inserted into the ranks of the Negro race a new cause of division, a new attempt to subject the masses of the race to an exploiting capitalist class of their own people. Negro labor will be estranged from its own intelligentsia, which represents black labor's own best blood; upper class Negroes and Negro labor will find themselves cutting each other's throats on opposite sides of a desperate economic battle, which will be but replica of the old battle which the white world is seeking to outgrow. Instead of forging ahead to a new relation of capital and labor, we would relapse into the old discredited pattern.

It seems to me that all three of these solutions are less hopeful than a fourth solution and that is a racial attempt to use the power of the Negro as a consumer not only for his economic uplift but in addition to that, for his economic education. What I propose is that into the interstices of this collapse of the industrial machine, the Negro shall search intelligently and carefully and farsightedly plan for his entrance into the new economic world, not as a continuing slave but as an intelligent free man with power in his hands.

I see this chance for planning in the role which the Negro plays as a consumer. In the future reorganization of industry the consumer as against the producer is going to become the key man. Industry is going to be guided according to his wants and needs and not exclusively with regard to the profit of the producers and transporters. Now as a consumer the Negro approaches economic equality much more nearly than he ever has as producer. Organizing then and conserving and using intelligently the power which twelve million people have through what they buy, it is possible for the American Negro to help in the rebuilding of the economic state.

The American Negro is primarily a consumer in the sense that his place and power in the industrial process is low and small. Nevertheless, he still has a remnant of his political power and that is growing not only in the North but even in the South. He has in addition to that his economic power as a consumer, as one who can buy goods with some discretion as to what goods he buys. It may truly be said that his discretion is not large but it does exist and it may be made the basis of a new instrument of democratic control over industry.

The cultural differentiation among American Negroes has considerably outstripped the economic differences, which sets this group aside as unusual and at the same time opens possibilities for institutional development and changes of great importance. Fundamental in such change would be the building up of new economic institutions suited to minority groups without wide economic differences, and with distinct cultural possibilities.

The fact that the number of Negro college graduates has increased from 215 between 1876 and 1880 to 10,000 between 1931 and 1935 shows that the ability is there if it can act. In addition to mental ability there is demanded an extraordinary moral strength, the strength to endure discrimination and not become discouraged; to face almost universal disparagement and keep one's soul; and to sacrifice for an ideal which the present generation will hardly see fulfilled. This is an unusual demand and no one can say off-hand whether or not the present generation of

American Negroes is equal to it. But there is reason to believe that if the high emotional content of the Negro soul could once be guided into channels that promise success, the end might be accomplished.

Despite a low general level of income, Negroes probably spend at least one hundred and fifty million a month under ordinary circumstances, and they live in an era when gradually economic revolution is substituting the consumer as the decisive voice in industry rather than the all-powerful producer of the past. Already in the Negro group the consumer interest is dominant. Outside of agriculture the Negro is a producer only so far as he is an employee and usually a subordinate employee of large interests dominated almost entirely by whites. His social institutions, therefore, are almost entirely the institutions of consumers and it is precisely along the development of these institutions that he can move in general accordance with the economic development of his time and of the larger white group, and also in this way evolve unified organization for his own economic salvation.

The fact is, as the Census of 1930 shows, there is almost no need that a modern group has which Negro workers already trained and at work are not able to satisfy. Already Negroes can raise their own food, build their own homes, fashion their own clothes, mend their own shoes, do much of their repair work, and raise some raw materials like tobacco and cotton. A simple transfer of Negro workers, with only such additional skills as can easily be learned in a few months, would enable them to weave their own cloth, make their own shoes, slaughter their own meat, prepare furniture for their homes, install electrical appliances, make their own cigars and cigarettes.

Appropriate direction and easily obtainable technique and capital would enable Negroes further to take over the whole of their retail distribution, to raise, cut, mine and manufacture a considerable proportion of the basic raw material, to man their own manufacturing plants, to process foods, to import necessary raw materials, to invent and build machines. Processes and monopolized natural resources they must continue to buy, but they could buy them on just as advantageous terms as their competitors if they bought in large quantities and paid cash, instead of enslaving themselves with white usury.

Large numbers of other Negroes working as miners, laborers in industry and transportation, could without difficulty be transferred to productive industries designed to cater to Negro consumers. The matter of skill in such industries is not as important as in the past, with industrial operations massed and standardized.

Without doubt, there are difficulties in the way of this program. The Negro population is scattered. The mouths which the Negro farmers might feed might be hundreds or thousands of miles away, and carpenters and mechanics would have to be concentrated and guaranteed a sufficiency of steady employment. All this would call for careful planning and particularly for such an organization of consumers as would eliminate unemployment, risk and profit. Demand organized and certain must precede the production and transportation of goods. The waste of advertising must be eliminated. The difference between actual cost and selling price must disappear, doing away with exploitation of labor which is the source of profit.

All this would be a realization of democracy in industry led by consumers' organizations and extending to planned production. Is there any reason to believe that such democracy among American Negroes could evolve the necessary leadership in technique and the necessary social institutions which would so guide and organize the masses that a new economic foundation could be laid for a group which is today threatened with poverty and social subordination?

In this process it will be possible to use consumers' organizations already established among the whites. There are such wholesale and manufacturing plants and they welcome patronage; but the Negro co-operative movement cannot rest here. If it does, it will find that quite unconsciously and without planning, Negroes will not be given places of authority or perhaps even of ordinary co-operation in these wider institutions; and the reason will be that white co-operators will not conceive it probable that Negroes could share and guide this work. This the Negro must prove in his own wholesale and manufacturing establishments. Once he has done this and done it thoroughly, there will gradually disappear much of the discrimination in the wider co-operative movement. But that will take a long time.

Meantime, this integration of the single consumers' co-operative into wholesales and factories will intensify the demand for selected leaders and intelligent democratic control over them—for the discovery of ability to manage, of character, of absolute honesty, of inspirational push not toward power but toward efficiency, of expert knowledge in the technique of production and distribution and of scholarship in the past and present of economic development. Nor is this enough. The eternal tendency of such leadership is, once it is established, to assume its own technocratic right to rule, to begin to despise the mass of people who do not know, who have no idea of difficulties of machinery and processes, who succumb to the blandishments of the glib talker, and are willing to select people not because they are honest and sincere but because they wield the glad hand.

Now these people must not be despised, they must be taught. They must be taught in long and lingering conference, in careful marshaling of facts, in the willingness to come to decision slowly and the determination not to tyrannize over minorities. There will be minorities that do not understand. They must patiently be taught to understand. There will be minorities who are stubborn, selfish, self-opinionated. Their real character must be so brought out and exhibited until the overwhelming mass of people who own the co-operative movement and whose votes guide and control it will be able to see just exactly the principles and persons for which they are voting.

The group can socialize most of its professional activities. Certain general and professional services they could change from a private profit to a mutual basis. They could mutualize in reality and not in name, banking and insurance, law and medicine. Health can be put upon the same compulsory basis that we have tried in the case of education, with universal service under physicians paid if possible by the state, or helped by the state, or paid entirely by the group. Hospitals can be as common as churches and used to far better advantage. The legal profession can be socialized and instead of being, as it is now, a defense of property and of the anti-social aggressions of wealth, it can become as it should be, the defense of the young, poor, ignorant and careless.

Banking should be so arranged as to furnish credit to the honest in emergencies or to put unneeded savings to useful and socially necessary work. Banking should not be simply and mainly a method of gambling, theft, tyranny, exploitation and profit-making. Our insurance business should cease to be, as it so largely is, a matter of deliberate gambling and become a co-operative service to equalize the incidence of misfortune equitably among members of the whole group without profit to anybody.

Negroes could not only furnish pupils for their own schools and colleges, but could control their teaching force and policies, their textbooks and ideals. By concentrating their demand, by group buying and by their own plants they could get Negro literature issued by the best publishers without censorship upon expression and they could evolve Negro art for its own sake and for its own beauty and not simply for the entertainment of white folk.

The American Negro must remember that he is primarily a consumer; that as he becomes a producer, it must be at the demand and under the control of organized consumers and according to their wants; that in this way he can gradually build up the absolutely needed co-operation in occupations. Today we work for others at wages pressed down to the limit of subsistence. Tomorrow we may work for ourselves, exchanging services, producing an increasing proportion of the goods which we consume and being re-

warded by a living wage and by work under civilized conditions. This will call for self-control. It will eliminate
the millionaire and even the rich Negro; it will put the
Negro leader upon a salary which will be modest as American salaries go and yet sufficient for a life under modern
standards of decency and enjoyment. It will eliminate
also the pauper and the industrial derelict.

To a degree, but not completely, this is a program of
segregation. The consumer group is in important aspects
a self-segregated group. We are now segregated largely
without reason. Let us put reason and power beneath this
segregation. Here comes tremendous opportunity in the
Negro housing projects of New York, Chicago, Atlanta
and a dozen other centers; in re-settlement projects like
the eight all-Negro farmers' colonies in six Southern states
and twenty-three rural projects in twelve states. Rail if
you will against the race segregation here involved and
condoned, but take advantage of it by planting secure
centers of Negro co-operative effort and particularly of
economic power to make us spiritually free for initiative
and creation in other and wider fields, and for eventually
breaking down all segregation based on color or curl of
hair.

There are unpleasant eventualities which we must face
even if we succeed. For instance, if the Negro in America
is successful in welding a mass or large proportion of his
people into groups working for their own betterment and
uplift, they will certainly, like the Jews, be suspected of
sinister designs and inner plotting; and their very success
in cultural advance be held against them and used for further and perhaps fatal segregation. There is, of course,

always the possibility that the plan of a minority group may be opposed to the best interests of a neighboring or enveloping or larger group; or even if it is not, the larger and more powerful group may think certain policies of a minority are inimical to the national interests. The possibility of this happening must be taken into account.

The Negro group in the United States can establish, for a large proportion of its members, a co-operative commonwealth, finding its authority in the consensus of the group and its intelligent choice of inner leadership. It can see to it that not only no action of this inner group is opposed to the real interests of the nation, but that it works for and in conjunction with the best interests of the nation. It need draw no line of exclusion so long as the outsiders join in the consensus. Within its own group it can, in the last analysis, expel the anti-social and hand him over to the police force of the nation. On the other hand it can avoid all appearance of conspiracy, of seeking goals incompatible with the general welfare of the nation, it can court publicity, it can exhibit results, it can plead for co-operation. Its great advantage will be that it is no longer as now attempting to march face forward into walls of prejudice. If the wall moves, we can move with it; and if it does not move it cannot, save in extreme cases, hinder us.

Have we the brains to do this?

Here in the past we have easily landed into a morass of criticism, without faith in the ability of American Negroes to extricate themselves from their present plight. Our former panacea emphasized by Booker T. Washington was flight of class from mass in wealth with the idea of escaping the masses or ruling the masses through power placed by white capitalists into the hands of those with larger income. My own panacea of earlier days was flight of class from mass through the development of a Talented Tenth; but the power of this aristocracy of talent was to lie in its knowledge and character and not in its wealth. The problem which I did not then attack was that of leadership and authority within the group, which by implication left controls to wealth—a contingency of which I never dreamed. But now the whole economic trend of the world has changed. That mass and class must unite for the world's salvation is clear. We who have had least class differentiation in wealth, can follow in the new trend and indeed lead it.

Most Negroes do not believe that this can be done. They not only share American public opinion in distrusting the inherent ability of the Negro group, but they see no way in which the present classes who have proven their intelligence and efficiency can gain leadership over their own people. On the contrary, they fear desperately a vulgarization of emerging culture among them, by contact with the ignorant and anti-social mass. This fear has been accentuated by recent radical agitation; unwashed and unshaven black demagogues have scared and brow-beaten cultured Negroes; have convinced them that their leadership can only be secured through demagoguery. It is for this reason that we see in large Northern centers like Chicago and New York, intelligent, efficient Negroes conniving with crime, gambling and prostitution, in order to secure control of the Negro vote and gain place and income for black folk. Their procedure is not justified by

the fact that often excellent and well-trained Negro officials are thus often raised to power. The price paid is deliberate surrender of any attempt at acculturation of the
mass in exchange for increased income among the few.

Yet American Negroes must know that the advance of
the Negro people since emancipation has been the extraordinary success in education, technique and character
among a small number of Negroes and that the emergence
of these exceptional men has been largely a matter of
chance; that their triumph proves that down among the
mass, ten times their number with equal ability could be
discovered and developed, if sustained effort and sacrifice
and intelligence were put to this task. That, on the contrary, today poverty, sickness and crime are choking the
paths to Negro uplift, and that salvation of the Negro race
is to come by planned and sustained efforts to open ways
of development to those who now form the unrisen mass
of the Negro group.

That this can be done by force, by the power of wealth
and of the police is true. Along that path of progress most
of the nineteenth century acculturation of the masses of
men has come; but it has been an unsatisfactory, unsteady
method. It has not developed the majority of men to anywhere near the top of their possibilities, and it has piti-
fully submerged certain groups among whites, and colored
groups, like Negroes in America, the West Indies and
Africa. Here comes then a special chance for a new trial
of democratic development without force among some of
the worst victims of force. How can it be done? It can be
done through consumers' groups and the mutual interests
that these members have in the success of the groups. It

can bring the cultured face to face with the untrained and it can accomplish by determined effort and planned foresight the acculturation of the many through the few, rather than the opposite possibility of pulling the better classes down through ignorance, carelessness, and crime.

It is to be admitted this will be a real battle. There are chances of failure, but there are also splendid chances of success. In the African communal group, ties of family and blood, of mother and child, of group relationship, made the group leadership strong, even if not always toward the highest culture. In the case of the more artificial group among American Negroes, there are sources of strength in common memories of suffering in the past; in present threats of degradation and extinction; in common ambitions and ideals; in emulation and the determination to prove ability and desert. Here in subtle but real ways the communalism of the African clan can be transferred to the Negro American group, implemented by higher ideals of human accomplishment through the education and culture which have arisen and may further arise through contact of black folk with the modern world. The emotional wealth of the American Negro, the nascent art in song, dance, and drama can all be applied, not to amuse the white audience, but to inspire and direct the acting Negro group itself. I can conceive no more magnificent nor promising crusade in modern times. We have a chance here to teach industrial and cultural democracy to a world that bitterly needs it.

A nation can depend on force and therefore carry through plans of capitalistic industry, or state socialism, or co-operative commonwealth, despite the opposition of large and powerful minorities. They can use police and the militia to enforce their will, but this is dangerous. In the long run force defeats itself. It is only the consensus of the intelligent men of good will in a community or in a state that really can carry out a great program with absolute and ultimate authority. And by that same token, without the authority of the state, without force of police and army, a group of people who can attain such consensus is able to do anything to which the group agrees.

It is too much to expect that any such guiding consensus will entirely eliminate dissent, but it will make agreement so overwhelming that eventual clear irrational dissent can safely be ignored. When real and open democratic control is intelligent enough to select of its own accord on the whole the best, most courageous, most expert and scholarly leadership, then the problem of democracy within the Negro group is solved and by that same token the possibility of American Negroes entering into world democracy and taking their rightful place according to their knowledge and power is also sure. Here then is the economic ladder by which the American Negro, achieving new social institutions, can move pari passu with the modern world into a new heaven and a new earth.

CHAPTER 8. PROPAGANDA
AND WORLD WAR

MY discussions of the concept of race, and of the white and colored worlds, are not to be regarded as digressions from the history of my life; rather my autobiography is a digressive illustration and exemplification of what race has meant in the world in the nineteenth and twentieth centuries. It is for this reason that I have named and tried to make this book an autobiography of race rather than merely a personal reminiscence, with the idea that peculiar racial situation and problems could best be explained in the life history of one who has lived them. My living gains its importance from the problems and not the problems from me.

Nothing illustrates this more than my experiences from the time I left Atlanta until the period of reconstruction after the first World War. These days were the climacteric of my pilgrimage. I had come to the place where I was convinced that science, the careful social study of the Negro problems, was not sufficient to settle them; that they were not basically, as I had assumed, difficulties due to ignorance but rather difficulties due to the determination of certain people to suppress and mistreat the darker races. I believed that this evil group formed a minority and a small minority of the nation and of all civilized peoples, and that once the majority of well-meaning folk realized their evil machinations, we would be able to secure justice.

A still further step I was not yet prepared to realize must be taken: not simply knowledge, not simply direct repression of evil, will reform the world. In long, indirect pressure and action of various and intricate sorts, the actions of men which are not due to lack of knowledge nor to evil intent, must be changed by influencing folkways, habits, customs and subconscious deeds. Here perhaps is a realm of physical and cosmic law which science does not yet control. But of all this in 1910 I had no clear concept. It took twenty more years of living and striving to bring this revolution to my thought. Stepping, therefore, in 1910, out of my ivory tower of statistics and investigation, I sought with bare hands to lift the earth and put it in the path in which I conceived it ought to go. Little did I realize in August, 1910, that the earth was about to be shaken with earthquake, deluged with blood, whipped and starved into disaster, and that race hate and wholesale color and group subordination, not only was a prime cause of this disaster, but emphasized and sharpened its course and hindered consequent recovery.

These were the years between the Roosevelts, including the administration of Taft, the two reigns of Wilson, the interlude of Harding and Coolidge and the disaster of Hoover. The United States was living not to itself, but as part of the strain and stress of the world. I knew something of Europe in these days. I went to the Paris Exposition in 1900 with the stipend that I had received for an exhibit on Negro development prepared in my office. By grace of an English friend, Frances Hoggan, I roamed through England, Scotland and a bit of France in 1906 on a bicycle and saw the Island of Skye and Edinburgh, the Lake and Shakespeare countries and London. I saw a Europe of past beauty and present culture, fit as I fondly dreamed to realize a democracy in which I and my people could find a welcome place.

I came home rested and ready to follow the steps that led from the Niagara Movement meeting of 1906 to the Negro conference of 1909. These steps were not only the indirect ones illustrated by the difficulty of raising money for the Atlanta work, but also the series of events which led to the New York conference. Lynching continued in the United States but raised curiously enough little protest. Three hundred twenty-seven victims were publicly murdered by the mob during the years 1910 to 1914, and in 1915 the number leaped incredibly to one hundred in one year. The pulpit, the social reformers, the statesmen continued in silence before the greatest affront to civilization which the modern world has known. In 1909 William English Walling and his wife Anna Strunsky went out to investigate a lynching and anti-Negro riot in Springfield, Illinois, the birthplace of Abraham Lincoln. The upheaval took place on the one hundredth anniversary of his birth. Eventually one hundred seventeen indictments were brought in against the rioters but there was almost no actual punishment.

Walling protested in the press. He asked America if the time had not come when the work of the Great Emancipator must be finished and the Negro race not simply in law and theory, but in fact, set free. Working with Mary White Ovington, Charles Edward Russell and Oswald Garrison Villard, after meetings and correspondence, he and others called a conference in New York City. The timeliness of such a conference and such action was manifest by the formation of the Niagara Movement in 1905 and its great meeting at Harper's Ferry in 1906. Heartened and at the same time warned by the Niagara Movement, the conference of 1909 invited the members of that body to participate. They were heartened by the fact that young radical opinion among Negroes saw the necessity of immediate organized intelligent effort to complete the emancipation of the Negro; but they were also warned that this radical movement had been initiated in direct opposition to the policy and action of the greatest Negro leader since the Civil War. To a degree never before accomplished, this Negro had united liberal opinion North and South in friendliness for the Negro and it was doubtful if any organization could make headway on an anti-Washington platform. The Niagara Movement itself had made little progress, beyond its inspirational fervor, toward a united and constructive program of work.

It was therefore not without misgiving that the members of the Niagara Movement were invited into the new conference, but all save Trotter and Ida Wells Barnett came to form the backbone of the new organization. In 1910 this was incorporated as the National Association for the Advancement of Colored People. It was inevitable that I should be offered an executive position in this organization; but there again many felt that I must not be allowed to direct its policy too openly against Mr. Washington and that the work which I did should as far as possible be a continuation of what I had done in studying the American Negro and making his accomplishment known.

This was in direct accord with my own desires and plans. I did not wish to attack Booker Washington; I wished to give him credit for much good, but to oppose certain of his words and policies which could be interpreted against our best interests; I wanted to do this through propaganda of the truth and for this reason I wished to continue in New York so far as possible my studies in Atlanta, and to add to this a periodical of fact and agitation which I should edit.

I tried to accomplish this with help of the Slater Fund and actually edited the four last studies of the Atlanta series from New York with the collaboration of Augustus Dill who succeeded me in Atlanta. But President Ware was strongly advised to cut the University off from the National Association for the Advancement of Colored People entirely, and did so in 1915. The studies ceased in 1917.

I arrived in New York to find a bare office; the treasurer, Mr. Villard, said frankly: "I don't know who is going to pay your salary; I have no money." The secretary then in charge was alarmed about her own job and suspicious of my designs; and a generally critical, if not hostile, public expected the National Association to launch a bitter attack upon Booker T. Washington and Tuskegee. I placated the secretary by disclaiming any design or desire for executive work; and I heartened the treasurer, a newspaper man, by my plan to publish a periodical which should be the organ of the Association. There was, however, opposition to this. First of all, magazines of this sort were costly and the organization had no money. Secondly, organs are usually of doubtful efficiency. My good friend, Albert E. Pillsbury, then Attorney-General of Massachusetts, wrote feelingly: "If you have not decided upon a periodical, for heaven's sake don't. They are as numerous as flies." And he meant, to conclude, about as useful.

My first job was to get the *Crisis* going; and arriving on August 1, 1910, I finally got the first copy off the press in November. Later I had the collaboration and advice of a young English woman, Mary McLean, then staff writer for the Sunday edition of the New York *Times*. I owe her more than I can say. The *Crisis* came at the psychological moment and its success was phenomenal. From the one thousand which I ventured to publish first, it went up a thousand a month until by 1918 (due, of course, to special circumstances) we published and sold over a hundred thousand.

In November, 1913, and at my earnest solicitation, Augustus G. Dill, who had succeeded me at Atlanta University, left his academic work and came to be business manager of the *Crisis* magazine. From then until early in 1928 he gave to the work his utmost devotion and to him was due much of its phenomenal business success. In five years the *Crisis* became self-supporting, January 1, 1916, with an annual income increasing from $6,500 in 1911 to $24,000 in 1915. Its total income during these years was over $84,000, and it circulated nearly a million and a half copies, net paid circulation. It reached every state in the Union, beside Europe, Africa, and the South Seas.

With this organ of propaganda and defense and with its legal bureau, lecturers and writers, the National Association for the Advancement of Colored People was able to organize one of the most effective assaults of liberalism upon prejudice and reaction that the modern world has seen. We secured extraordinary helpers: great lawyers like Moorfield Storey and Louis Marshall; earnest liberals like Milholland, John Haynes Holmes, and Jane Addams; sympathetic friends from the whole land.

Naturally the real and effective work of the organization was done by the group which centered in the office first at 20 Vesey Street, and then at 70 Fifth Avenue, where we stayed until Ginn and Company's Southern patrons forced us to move to 69. These persons were assiduous in their attendance, unfailing in their interest, and gave a large amount of their time to the work. As a result the organization was not a secretary-dominated center, with the power in the hands of one man. It was an intelligent group of considerable size which was willing and eager to learn and help.

There was one initial difficulty common to all interracial effort in the United States. Ordinarily the white members of a committee formed of Negroes and whites become dominant. Either by superior training or their influence or their wealth they take charge of the committee, guide it and use the colored membership as their helpers and executive workers in certain directions. Usually if the opposite policy is attempted, if the Negroes attempt to dominate and conduct the committee, the whites become dissatisfied and gradually withdraw. In the NAACP it was our primary effort to achieve an equality of racial influence without stressing race and without allowing undue predominance to either group. I think we accomplished this for a time to an unusual degree.

The members studied the situations. They were expert in various lines of inquiry and effort, once we had settled down to effective work. The outstanding members of this inner group were Oswald Garrison Villard, Mary Ovington, William English Walling, Paul Kennaday, Joel Spingarn, and Charles Edward Russell. Villard became chairman of the board but in 1913 was not wholly in agreement with me and was replaced by a young man to whom I have dedicated this book and who stands out vividly in my mind as a scholar and a knight.

With the combined aid of these workers and many others, we could, through the *Crisis* and our officers, our secretaries and friends, place consistently and continuously before the country a clear-cut statement of the legitimate aims of the American Negro and the facts concerning his condition. We began to organize his political power and make it influential and we started a campaign against lynching and mob law which was the most effective ever organized and eventually brought the end of the evil in sight. Especially we gained a series of court victories before the highest courts of the land which perhaps never have been equaled; beginning with the overthrow of the vicious "Grandfather Clauses" in 1916 and the breaking of the backbone of residential segregation in 1917.

One of the first difficulties that the National Association met was bound to be the matter of its attitude toward Mr. Washington. I carefully tried to avoid any exaggeration of differences of thought; but to discuss the Negro question in 1910 was to discuss Booker T. Washington and almost before we were conscious of the inevitable trends, we were challenged from Europe. Mr. Washington was in

Europe in 1910 and made some speeches in England on his usual conciliatory lines. John Milholland, who had been so dominant in the organization of the National Association, immediately wrote me and said that American Negroes must combat the idea that they were satisfied with conditions. I, therefore, wrote an appeal to England and Europe, under the signature of a group of colored friends so as not to involve the NAACP officially:

"If Mr. Booker T. Washington, or any other person, is giving the impression abroad that the Negro problem in America is in process of satisfactory solution, he is giving an impression which is not true. We say this without personal bitterness toward Mr. Washington. He is a distinguished American and has a perfect right to his opinion. But we are compelled to point out that Mr. Washington's large financial responsibilities have made him dependent on the rich charitable public and that, for this reason, he has for years been compelled to tell, not the whole truth, but that part of it which certain powerful interests in America wish to appear as the truth. In flat contradiction, however, to the pleasant pictures thus pointed out, let us not forget that the consensus of opinion among eminent European scholars who know the race problem in America, from De Tocqueville to Von Halle, De Laveleys, Archer and Johnston, is that it forms the gravest of American problems. We black men who live and suffer under present conditions, and who have no reason, and refuse to accept reasons for silence, can substantiate this nearly unanimous testimony."

In further emphasis of this statement and in anticipation of the meeting of the proposed Races Congress, Mr.

Milholland arranged that I should go early to London and make some addresses. The plan simmered down to an address before the Lyceum Club, the leading woman's club of London. There it encountered opposition. An American woman member wrote: "I think there is serious objection to entertaining Dr. Du Bois at the Lyceum." The result was an acrimonious controversy from which I tried to withdraw gently but was unable. Finally led by Her Highness, the then Ranee of Sarawak and Dr. Etta Sayre, a luncheon was held at the Lyceum Club with a bishop and two countesses; several knights and ladies, and men like Maurice Hewlett and Sir Harry Johnston; I was the chief speaker.

The Races Congress, held in July, 1911, in London, would have marked an epoch in the cultural history of the world, if it had not been followed so quickly by the World War. As it was, it turned out to be a great and inspiring occasion, bringing together representatives of numerous ethnic and cultural groups, and new and frank conceptions of the scientific bases of racial and social relations of people.

The Congress was planned with meticulous care and thoroughness by the clear-sighted Gustav Spiller, the organizer, working under the auspices of the English Ethical Culture movement. The papers of the Congress were printed and put into the hands of the delegates before the meeting and yet kept from general publication. An extraordinary number of distinguished persons took part and, together with Felix Adler, I was named as co-secretary to represent the United States. To be sure the Congress encountered a certain air of questioning and lack of high official sanction. There were even those in England who professed to think that it had something to do with horse-racing; but even papers like the *Times* had to notice its impressive meetings and the caliber of the participants. There were dramatic incidents like the arraignment of Christianity by the delegate from Ceylon, "where every prospect pleases and only man is vile."

I had not only my regular assigned part, but due to the sudden illness of Sir Harry Johnston from his chronic tropical fever, represented him at one of the chief sessions and made a speech which gained wide reading. Thus I had a chance twice to address the Congress and I wrote one of the two poems which greeted the assembly:

> Save us, World-Spirit, from our lesser selves,
> Grant us that war and hatred cease,
> Reveal our souls in every race and hue;
> Help us, O Human God, in this Thy Truce,
> To make Humanity divine.

Even while the Races Congress was meeting came the forewarning of coming doom: in a characteristic way a German war vessel sailed into an African port, notifying the world that Germany was determined to have larger ownership and control of cheap black labor; a demand camouflaged as the need of "a place in the sun." I fancied at the time that I knew my Europe pretty well, but familiarity with the dangers of the European scene had bred contempt of disaster. I thought with other philosophers that a general European war was impossible. The economic and cultural strands among the nations had grown too strong to be snapped by war. World peace, world organization, conference and conciliation, the gradual breaking down of trade barriers, the spread of civilization to backward peoples, the emancipation of suppressed groups like the American Negro—seem to me the natural, the inevitable path of world progress. I did not assess at the right value the envy and jealousy of those imperial powers which did not share profit in colored labor, nor did I realize that the intertwining threads of culture bound colored folk in slavery to, and not in mutual co-operation with, the whites.

Indeed it was not easily possible for the student of international affairs trained in white institutions and by European ideology to follow the partially concealed and hidden action of international intrigue, which was turning colonial empire into the threat of armed competition for markets, cheap materials and cheap labor. Colonies still meant religious and social uplift in current propaganda. There were indications of strain in the determination of Germany to increase her sea power and to rival England in the technique of her manufactures. It was evident that the understanding between England and France both in Africa and in Asia was relegating Germany to a second place in colonial imperialism. It was evident too that the defeat of Russia by Japan had given rise to a fear of colored revolt against white exploitation.

The general outlines of this I had followed, but like most of the world I was thrown into consternation when later with sudden and unawaited violence, world war burst in 1914. I had come to New York and the editorship of the *Crisis* during the administration of Taft. William Taft, fat, genial and mediocre, had no grasp of world affairs nor international trends. Despite his Philippine experience, he began his reactionary administration by promising the South that he would appoint no Federal official to whom the Southern people were opposed; and thus blandly announced that eight million black Southerners were not people. Not only this but his handling of the revolt of irritated and goaded black soldiers at Brownsville, Texas, and his general cynical attitude toward the race problem led me to one of my first efforts to make political solution of the race problem.

Returning to New York after the Races Congress, I was faced by the political campaign of 1912. Disappointed at the attitude of Taft, I turned eagerly toward Roosevelt and the "Bull Moose" movement, thinking that I saw there a splendid chance for a third party movement, on a broad platform of votes for Negroes and the democratization of industry. Sitting in the office of the *Crisis,* I wrote out a proposed plank for the Progressives to adopt at their Chicago meeting in 1912: "The Progressive Party recognizes that distinctions of race or class in political life have no place in a democracy. Especially does the party realize that a group of 10,000,000 people who have in a generation changed from a slave to a free labor system, re-established family life, accumulated $1,000,000,000 of real property, including 20,000,000 acres of land, and reduced their illiteracy from 80 to 30 per cent, deserves and must have justice, opportunity and a voice in their own government. The party, therefore, demands for the Americans of Negro descent the repeal of unfair discriminatory laws and the right to vote on the same terms on which other citizens vote."

This was taken to Chicago by my friend and fellow official of the NAACP, Joel Spingarn, and supported by two other directors of the Association, Dr. Henry Moskowitz and Jane Addams. They worked in vain for its adoption. Theodore Roosevelt would have none of it. He told Mr. Spingarn frankly that he should be careful of "that man Du Bois," who was in his opinion a "dangerous" person. The "Bull Moose" convention not only refused to adopt a plank anything like this, but refused to seat most of the colored delegates. They elected a Southern "lily-white" to run on the ticket with Mr. Roosevelt, and finally succeeded in splitting the Republican Party and giving Woodrow Wilson an opportunity of becoming President of the United States.

Immediately Bishop Walters of the African Zion Church, who had joined the Democratic Party in 1909, approached me with the idea that Mr. Wilson might be influenced in the Negro's behalf. I proposed, if he could, to throw the weight of the *Crisis* against Roosevelt and Taft, and for Wilson. Bishop Walters went to see Wilson. He secured from him in October, 1912, a categorical expression over his signature "of his earnest wish to see justice done the colored people in every matter; and not mere grudging justice, but justice executed with liberality and cordial good feeling. . . . I want to assure them that should I become President of the United States they may count upon me for absolute fair dealing, for everything by which I could assist in advancing the interests of their race in the United States."

I espoused the cause of Woodrow Wilson, fully aware of the political risk involved and yet impelled to this path by the reaction of Taft and disappointment at Roosevelt.

I resigned from New York Local No. 1 of the Socialist Party which I had joined, to escape discipline for not voting the Socialist ticket. I could not let Negroes throw away votes. I wrote in the *Crisis* just before the election: "We sincerely believe that even in the face of promises disconcertingly vague, and in the face of the solid caste-ridden South, it is better to elect Woodrow Wilson President of the United States and prove once for all if the Democratic Party dares to be democratic when it comes to black men. It has proven that it can be in many Northern states and cities. Can it be in the nation? We hope so, and we are willing to risk a trial."

We estimated that in the North a hundred thousand black voters had supported Woodrow Wilson in 1912, and had been so distributed in strategic places as to do much to help his election. This was an unusually successful effort to divide the Negro vote; but as many Negroes had feared it brought disappointment and encouraged unexpected reaction. Among minor indications of this reaction was Wilson's odd demand of Bishop Walters. The Bishop had been called to the White House for consultation concerning the colored people in 1915. "By the way," said the President, "what about that letter that I wrote you during the campaign. I do not seem to remember it." "I have it right here," said the Bishop eagerly, and handed it to him. The President forgot to return it.

With the accession of Woodrow Wilson to the presidency in 1913 there opened for the American Negro a period, lasting through and long after the World War and culminating in 1919, which was an extraordinary test for their courage and a time of cruelty, discrimination and wholesale murder. For this there were several causes: the return to power for the first time since the Civil War of the Southern Democracy; secondly, the apprehension and resentment aroused in the South by the campaign of the NAACP; but above and beyond that, the rising economic rivalry between colored and white workers in the United States and back of this the whole economic stress of the modern world with its industrial imperialism.

The Southern white workers had for years been lashed into enmity against the Negro by Tillman, Vardaman, Blease, and Jeff Davis of Arkansas. Representatives of these Southern workers, now seated in Congress, proceeded to demand stricter legal and economic caste; and at the meeting of Wilson's first Congress there came the greatest flood of bills proposing discriminatory legislation against Negroes that has ever been introduced into an American Congress. There were no less than twenty bills advocating "Jim Crow" cars in the District of Columbia, race segregation of Federal employees, excluding Negroes from commissions in the army and navy, forbidding the intermarriage of Negroes and whites, and excluding all immigrants of Negro descent.

Quite suddenly the program for the NAACP, which up to this time had been more or less indefinite, was made clear and intensive. Every ounce of effort was made not only against lynching and segregation, but against this new proposed discriminatory legislation in Congress and in a dozen different states, where with evident collusion similar legislation had been proposed. Most of this legislation was eventually killed; in only one state was such a measure—an anti-intermarriage bill—passed; but in Washington one proposal was put through by executive order: Wilson proceeded to segregate nearly all of the colored Federal employees, of whom there were a considerable number, herding them so far as possible in separate rooms with separate eating and toilet facilities. This was a serious reversal of Federal usage and despite repeated assaults, much of this segregation still remains in the departments of the national capital. When the militant Monroe Trotter headed a delegation to protest to the President this segregation of colored officeholders, Wilson angrily dismissed him, declaring his language "insulting."

We found that our political efforts were abortive for a reason which, while possible, did not seem to us probable. We had calculated that increased independence in the Negro vote would bring a bid for the Negro vote from opposing parties; but it did not until many years later. Indeed, it was not until the re-election of the second Roosevelt in 1936 that the Negro vote in the North came to be eagerly contended for by the two major parties. In 1914 we tried to make congressional candidates declare themselves as to our demands, but were only partially successful. The Sixty-fourth Congress saw eleven bills introduced advocating color caste and the state legislatures continued to be bombarded by similar legislation. Thus, in 1916, we found ourselves politically helpless. We had no choice. We could vote for Wilson who had segregated us or for Hughes who, despite all our requests, remained doggedly dumb on our problems.

The spread of disaster throughout the world shown by the Chinese Revolution of 1912 and the Balkan War of 1913, and the World War of 1914, was illustrated in the

United States by the meeting of the National Conference of Charities and Correction in Memphis in May, 1914. Not only were there no accommodations for colored delegates, but the conference refused even to put in the agenda anything touching the race problem. As a result, Joel Spingarn, William Pickens and myself went down to Memphis and advertised during the conference a public meeting "for all persons who love the truth and dare to hear it." A large crowd of persons black and white, including many delegates to the conference, were present.

For some time after the opening of the World War, its possible influence upon the Negro race in America was not clear. However, this world convulsion found America spiritually ill-prepared to cope with it, so far as race difficulties were concerned. In 1912 there arose the agitation for residential race segregation. It grew out of the fact that Negroes, as they increased in intelligence and property holding, were dissatisfied with the living quarters, where by long custom they had been confined in the chief cities of the land. In Baltimore came one of their first efforts to buy their way out of the back alleys and the slums into the better-paved, better-lighted main streets. This movement was encouraged by the wish of many of the owners of this property to move to newly developed suburban districts. A fierce conflict developed and Baltimore, by city ordinance, proceeded to segregate Negroes by law. This agitation throughout the North was increased by the emigration of Southern Negroes. Cheap foreign labor had been cut off by the war and Northern manufacturers began to encourage migration from the South. The stream began as soon as the European war opened. It caused not only increasing congestion in the colored districts of the North; it also began to deplete the supply of agricultural labor and common city labor in the South, and to encourage racial friction according to current social patterns.

Beginning in Baltimore this agitation with a series of ordinances and laws spread West, North and South. For a period of ten years it called for every resource and ingenuity on the part of the National Association for the Advancement of Colored People to fight the legislation in courts, to repel mob violence on home-buyers, and to seek a supporting white public opinion.

But all this was but a prelude to deeper and more serious race oppression. The United States seized Haiti in 1915. It was not alone the intrinsic importance of the country, but Haiti stood with Liberia as a continuing symbol of Negro revolt against slavery and oppression, and capacity for self-rule; and the sudden extinction of its independence by a President whom we had helped to elect, followed by exploitation at the hands of New York City banks and plundering speculators, and the killing of at least three thousand Haitians by American soldiers, was a bitter pre-war pill.

That same year occurred another, and in the end, much more insidious and hurtful attack: the new technique of the moving picture had come to America and the world. But this method of popular entertainment suddenly became great when David Griffith made the film "The Birth of a Nation." He set the pace for a new art and method: the thundering horses, the masked riders, the suspense of plot and the defense of innocent womanhood; all this was thrilling even if melodramatic and overdrawn. This would have been a great step in the development of a motion-picture art, if it had not happened that the director deliberately used as the vehicle of his picture one of the least defensible attacks upon the Negro race, made by Thomas Dixon in his books beginning with the "Leopard's Spots," and in his play "The Clansman." There was fed to the youth of the nation and to the unthinking masses as well as to the world a story which twisted the emancipation and enfranchisement of the slave in a great effort toward universal democracy, into an orgy of theft and degradation and wide rape of white women.

In combating this film, our Association was placed in a miserable dilemma. We had to ask liberals to oppose freedom of art and expression, and it was senseless for them to reply: "Use this art in your own defense." The cost of picture making and the scarcity of appropriate artistic talent made any such immediate answer beyond question. Without doubt the increase of lynching in 1915 and later was directly encouraged by this film. We did what we could to stop its showing and thereby probably succeeded in advertising it even beyond its admittedly notable merits. The combined result of these various events caused a sudden increase of lynching. The number of mob murders so increased that nearly one hundred Negroes were lynched during 1915 and a score of whites, a larger number than had occurred for more than a decade.

The year 1916 brought one decided note of hope. The Supreme Court of the United States, after having dodged the plain issue for a decade, finally at our insistence and with the help of our corps of lawyers headed by Moorfield Storey, handed down a decision which outlawed the infamous "Grandfather Clauses" of the disfranchising constitutions of the South. These clauses had given an hereditary right to vote to white illiterates while excluding colored illiterates. To overbalance this sign of hope there came, however, continued prevalence of lynching in unusually serious form. Five Negroes in Lee County, Georgia, were lynched en masse and there came the horrible public burning of Jesse Washington in Waco, Texas, before a mob of thousands of men, women and children. "While a fire was being prepared of boxes, the naked boy was stabbed and the chain put over the tree. He tried to get away, but could not. He reached up to grab the chain and they cut off his fingers. The big man struck the boy on the back of the neck with a knife just as they were pulling him up on the tree. Mr. —— thought that was practically the death blow. He was lowered into the fire several times by means of the chain around his neck. Someone said they would estimate the boy had about twenty-five stab wounds, each one of them death-dealing."

In October, Anthony Crawford, well-to-do colored farmer of South Carolina, worth $20,000, and the owner of four hundred acres of land, was set upon and whipped for "impudence" in refusing to agree to a price for his cotton seed; he was then jailed, mobbed, mutilated and killed, and his family driven out of the county.

The death of Booker Washington in 1915 coincided with a change in Negro attitudes. The political defeat of Roosevelt and Taft had deprived Mr. Washington of his political influence. The Tuskegee Machine gradually ceased to function, and Tuskegee came to realize its natural place as a center of education rather than of propaganda. For some time Mr. Washington's general influence among American Negroes, especially in the face of the rising importance of the NAACP and the *Crisis,* had waned. Once he had said a word seeming to condone residential segregation which raised a storm; but on the whole the Washington controversy began to subside. The morning that I heard of Mr. Washington's death I knew that an era in the history of the American Negro had ended, and I wrote:

"The death of Mr. Washington marks an epoch in the history of America. He was the greatest Negro leader since Frederick Douglass, and the most distinguished man, white or black, who has come out of the South since the Civil War. His fame was international and his influence far-reaching. Of the good that he accomplished there can be no doubt: he directed the attention of the Negro race in America to the pressing necessity of economic development; he emphasized technical education, and he did much to pave the way for an understanding between the white and the darker races.

"On the other hand, there can be no doubt of Mr. Washington's mistakes and shortcomings: he never adequately grasped the growing bond of politics and industry; he did not understand the deeper foundations of human training, and his basis of better understanding between white and black was founded on caste.

"We may generously and with deep earnestness lay on the grave of Booker T. Washington, testimony of our thankfulness for his undoubted help in the accumulation of Negro land and property, his establishment of Tuskegee and spreading of industrial education, and his compelling of the white South to think at least of the Negro as a possible man. On the other hand, in stern justice, we must lay on the soul of this man a heavy responsibility for the consummation of Negro disfranchisement, the decline of the Negro college and public school, and the firmer establishment of color caste in this land."

By the middle of the year 1916, it was evident to thinking people that the American Negroes were achieving a unity in thought and action, partly caused by the removal of Mr. Washington's powerful personality and partly because of pressure of outward circumstances. This realization was not entirely voluntary on our part; it was forced upon us by the concentration of effort and unity of thought which rising race segregation, discrimination and mob murder were compelling us to follow. We had to stand together; we were already in 1916 standing together to an extent unparalleled since Reconstruction. Joel Spingarn was among the first to realize this and he proposed to call in August a conference of persons interested in the race problem at his beautiful home Troutbeck, in the peace and quiet of Amenia, where once John Burroughs dreamed and wrote. Here colored and white men of all shades of opinion might sit down, and rest and talk, and find agreement so far as possible with regard to the Negro problems.

The Amenia Conference, as Spingarn conceived it, was to be "under the auspices of the NAACP," but wholly independent of it, and the invitations definitely said this. They were issued by Mr. Spingarn personally, and the guests were assured that they would not be bound by any program of the NAACP. Thus the Conference was intended primarily to bring about as large a degree as possible of unity of purpose among Negro leaders and to do this regardless of its effect upon any organization, although, of course, most of us hoped that some central organization and preferably the NAACP would eventually represent this new united purpose.

One can hardly realize today how difficult and intricate a matter it was to arrange such a conference, to say who should come and who should not, to gloss over old hurts and enmities. About two hundred invitations to white and colored people were actually issued, and sixty or more persons expressed their willingness to attend, including not only many founders of the Niagara Movement, but close personal friends of Booker Washington. There were messages of good will from many who could not attend: from Taft, Roosevelt, Hughes, Woodrow Wilson, and others.

I doubt if ever before so small a conference of American Negroes had so many colored men of distinction who represented at the same time so complete a picture of all phases of Negro thought. Its very completeness in this respect was its salvation. If it had represented one party or clique it would have been less harmonious. As it was, we all learned what the majority of us knew. None of us in the present pressure of race hate could afford to hold uncompromising and unchangeable views. It was, after all, a matter of emphasis. We all believed in thrift, we all wanted the Negro to vote, we all wanted the laws enforced, we all wanted to abolish lynching, we all wanted assertion of our essential manhood; but how to get these things—there, of course, must be wide divergence of opinion.

The Conference marked the beginning of the new era. As we said in our resolutions: "The Amenia Conference believes that its members have arrived at a virtual unanimity of opinion in regard to certain principles and that a more or less definite result may be expected from its deliberations."

Probably on account of our meeting the Negro race was more united and more ready to meet the problems of the world than it could possibly have been without these beautiful days of understanding. How appropriate that so fateful a thing should have taken place in the midst of so much quiet and beauty, in a place of poets and fishermen, of dreamers and farmers, a place far apart and away from the bustle of the world and the centers of activity.

As if in anticipation of the whirl of circumstances and stress of soul through which the next few years were to thrust me, at the very beginning of the year 1917, I went down into the valley of the shadow of death. Save for typhoid fever at the age of seventeen, I had never been sick, but now a serious operation was indicated and a second one seemed advisable following fast upon the first. I came to know what hospitals and the magic of modern surgery were. I lay for two or three weeks shrouded by the curtains of pain and then arose apparently as strong as ever, if not stronger, for the fight ahead. I needed my strength for the fight came with a surge.

Finally and in a sense inevitably, the World War actually touched America. With our participation and in anticipation of it came an extraordinary exacerbation of race hate and turmoil. Beginning with increased lynchings in 1915, there came in 1916 lynching, burning and murder.

In 1917 came the draft with its discrimination and mob rule; in 1918, the turmoil and discrimination of actual war; and finally in 1919 the worst experience of mob law and race hate that the United States had seen since Reconstruction.

The war was preceded by a spy scare—a national psychosis of fear that German intrigue would accomplish among Negroes that disloyalty and urge toward sabotage and revenge which their situation and treatment would certainly justify. It was not so much that this fear had any real support in fact; it was rather that it had every justification in reason. It was succeeded by witch-hunting—feverish endeavor to find out who dared to think differently from the increasingly major thought of the nation. Not only did Germans suffer and other foreigners, but Negroes were especially suspected. Suspicious state and Federal agents invaded even the offices of the *Crisis* and the National Association for the Advancement of Colored People and asked searching questions: "Just what, after all, were our objects and activities?" I took great satisfaction in being able to sit back in my chair and answer blandly, "We are seeking to have the Constitution of the United States thoroughly and completely enforced." It took some ingenuity, even for Southerners, to make treason out of that.

Then came the refusal to allow colored soldiers to volunteer into the army; but we consoled ourselves there by saying, "Why should we want to fight for America or America's friends; and how sure could we be that America's enemies were our enemies too?" With the actual declaration of war in April, 1917, and the forced draft May

18, the pattern of racial segregation which our organization had been fighting from the beginning was written into law and custom. The races by law must be mustered and trained separately. Eighty-three thousand Negro draftees, raised at the first call, had to go into separate units, and so far as possible, separate encampments. Hundreds of colored unfortunates found themselves called with no place prepared where they could be legally received. Colored militia units already enrolled in the North were sent South to be insulted and kicked in Southern cantonments, while thousands of draftees were engulfed in a hell of prejudice and discrimination. Not only that, but hundreds of Negroes were drafted regardless of their home duties and physical health. The government had to dismiss the Draft Board of Atlanta in a body for flagrant and open race discrimination. When sent to camp, a concerted effort was made to train Negro draftees as laborers and not as soldiers. There have been few periods in the history of the American Negro when he has been more discouraged and exasperated.

The National Association fought with its back to the wall and with all its energies, failing in some cases, and in some cases having conspicuous and unexpected success. From the beginning of the war, however, the efforts of the Association involved, in a sense, a retreat from the high ideal toward which it aimed and yet a retreat absolutely necessary and pointing the way to future deployment of its forces in the offensive against race hate. The situation arose in our attempt to secure decent treatment in encampments for colored draftees; to see that a reasonable proportion of them went to the front as soldiers bearing arms, and not merely as laborers; and to assure, above all, that some Negroes should act as commissioned officers in the army.

The opposition to Negro officers was intense and bitter; but on the other hand, the administration was alarmed. After all, this nation, with its diverse ethnic elements, with a large number of Germans and Slavs who at best could not be enthusiastic supporters of the Allies, did not dare further to complicate the situation by driving ten million Negroes into justifiable protest and opposition.

In May a conference of Negro organizations called in Washington adopted resolutions which I wrote: "We trace the real cause of this World War to the despising of the darker races by the dominant groups of men, and the consequent fierce rivalry among European nations in their effort to use darker and backward people for purposes of selfish gain regardless of the ultimate good of the oppressed. We see permanent peace only in the extension of the principle of government by the consent of the governed, not simply among the smaller nations of Europe, but among the natives of Asia and Africa, the Western Indies and the Negroes of the United States."

Efforts at last were made to placate the Negroes. First they were given a representative in Washington in the person of Emmett Scott, formerly private secretary to Booker T. Washington; Mr. Scott was without actual power, but he had access to the Secretary of War so as to be able to lay before him directly complaints voiced by the Negroes. Negroes were promised enrollment not merely as stevedores, but as actual soldiers, and also two full divisions of Negro soldiers, the Ninety-second and

Ninety-third, were planned. Immediately this brought up the question of Negro officers.

In the so-called Ninety-third Division, a number of Negro units from the organized state militia who had been drafted into the war, already had Negro officers. Two regiments of draftees with white officers were added, and these units were early hurried to France and incorporated with French troops. The complete organization of this Ninety-third Division was never actually accomplished and most of the higher Negro officers were gradually dismissed on various excuses.

On the other hand, the Ninety-second Division of Negro draftees was actually organized and immediately a demand arose for Negro officers over these troops. The official answer was a decided negative: there were no trained Negro officers—or at most, only two or three; there were no camps where new Negro officers could be trained and it was illegal under the draft law to train them in camps with white officers.

Our Association itself here hesitated. It had fought segregation and discrimination in the army valiantly, but lost. Then when, as the only alternative, we must accept a separate officers' training camp or no Negro officers, many members demurred at openly advocating segregation. Had it not been for Joel Spingarn, chairman of our Board, no Negro officers would have been trained or appointed. But Spingarn started a country-wide crusade, aided wholeheartedly by the *Crisis*. First of all, he got the Negro students interested. He spoke at Howard and corresponded with students at Fisk, Atlanta, and elsewhere. They arose en masse to demand a Negro officers' camp and the campus of Howard was even offered as a place for it.

The War Department squirmed. We had to fight even to be segregated. We fell out among ourselves. A large and important section of the Negro press led by the *Afro-American* and the *Chicago Defender* firmly opposed a Negro officers' camp on any terms. We struggled from March until May, and then suddenly a camp was opened for the training of Negro officers at Des Moines, Iowa.

The man eminently fitted and almost selected by fate for the heading of this camp was a black man, Charles Young, then lieutenant-colonel in the regular United States Army. He had an unblemished army record and a splendid character. He had recently accompanied Pershing in the Mexican foray and received distinguished commendation from the future commander-in-chief of the American Expeditionary Force. He was strong, fit, and only 49 years of age, and in the accelerated promotion of war-time would have been a general in the army by 1918. This, of course, the army did not propose to have, and although the Des Moines camp was established in May, the medical board of the army in June, when Young came up for examination for his colonelcy, hastened to retire him for "high blood pressure." It was a miserable ruse. An entire corps of white officers was appointed to train the colored cadets. Only colored captains and lieutenants were to be trained; the high officers were to be white.

Even then our difficulties were not finished; there was segregation against the cadets within and without their camp. General Ballou tried to lay down certain general rules as to what Negroes should strive for. A three-month period of training ensued. At the end of that time, after hesitation, it was decided to add another month. There was widespread suspicion that the War Department did not intend actually to commission these officers. I went down to Washington and talked with the Secretary of War, Newton Baker. He said coldly, "We are not trying by this war to settle the Negro problem." "True," I retorted, "but you are trying to settle as much of it as interferes with winning the war."

Finally, October 14, 1917, six hundred thirty-nine Negro officers were commissioned: 106 captains, 329 first lieutenants and 204 second lieutenants. It was as Champ Clark, Speaker of the House, said, a "new day" for the Negro and despite all we had been through, we felt tremendously uplifted.

In the very hour of our exaltation, the whirlwind struck us again; or perhaps I might better say, throughout this period the succession of uplift and downfall was continuous and bewildering. The very month that the Des Moines camp was authorized, a Negro was publicly burned alive in Tennessee under circumstances unusually atrocious. The mobbing and burning were publicly advertised in the press beforehand. Three thousand automobiles brought the audience, including mothers carrying children. Ten gallons of gasoline were poured over the wretch and he was burned alive, while hundreds fought for bits of his body, clothing, and the rope.

The migration of Negro workers out of the South had increased steadily. It was opposed by illegal and legal methods throughout the South, but by 1917 it had expanded to a stream and from my own travel and observation, I calculated that during the year at least a quarter of a million workers had migrated from South to North. In July came the first Northern repercussion in the East St. Louis riot, when one hundred twenty-five Negroes were killed by their white fellow laborers; their homes looted and destroyed; and hundreds of others maimed. It was a riot notable for its passion, cruelty and obvious economic motive.

In helpless exasperation we turned to symbolism and staged in New York City, and on Fifth Avenue, a silent parade to protest against mobs and lynching. Many hesitated to join us, but thousands fell in line, men, women, and children, headed by the officials of the National Association and other prominent Negroes.

In September of 1917 came another terrible occurrence arising out of the war. The Twenty-fourth colored Infantry of the regular army had been quartered at Houston, Texas. It was treated by the white population with discrimination and insult, and then kept from retaliating by being disarmed. Contrary to all army regulations, a soldier in Federal uniform could be insulted with impunity. At last some of these soldiers, goaded into desperation, broke into rioting, seized arms, and killed seventeen whites. As a result thirteen Negro soldiers were hanged, forty-one imprisoned for life, and forty others held for trial.

In my effort to reconstruct in memory my thought and the fight of the National Association for the Advancement of Colored People during the World War, I have difficulty in thinking clearly. In the midst of arms, not only laws but ideas are silent. I was, in principle, opposed to war. Everyone is. I pointed out in the *Atlantic Monthly* in 1915 how the partition of Africa was a cause of the conflict. Through my knowledge of Germany, I wished to see her militarism defeated and for that reason when America entered the war I believed we would in reality fight for democracy including colored folk and not merely for war investments.

But my main attention and interest was distracted from the facts of the war in Europe to the struggle of Color Caste in America and its repercussions on the conflict. Our partial triumph in this conflict often heartened me. I felt for a moment during the war that I could be without reservation a patriotic American. The government was making sincere efforts to meet our demands. They had commissioned over seven hundred Negro officers; we had been given representation in the Departments of War and Labor; the segregation ordinances had been mostly suppressed and even the Red Cross had reluctantly promised to use Negro nurses, although it later broke its word; Newton Baker, Secretary of War, tried to be fair and just; Wilson, overcoming long reluctance at last, spoke out against lynching. At other times I was bowed down and sickened by the public burnings, the treatment of colored troops and the widespread mob law.

At one of my periods of exaltation in July, 1918, after Negro officers had been commissioned, after news of achievement by our soldiers already in France began to come over the cables, and just as President Wilson was breaking his long silence on lynching, I wrote the editorial "Close Ranks."—"That which the German power represents today spells death to the aspirations of Negroes and all darker races for equality, freedom and democracy. Let us not hesitate. Let us, while this war lasts, forget our special grievances and close our ranks shoulder to shoulder with our own white fellow citizens and the allied nations that are fighting for democracy. We make no ordinary sacrifice, but we make it gladly and willingly with our eyes lifted to the hills."

The words were hardly out of my mouth when strong criticism was rained upon it. Who was I to talk of forgetting grievances, when my life had been given to protest against them? I replied in August, "First, This is Our Country: we have worked for it, we have suffered for it, we have fought for it; we have made its music, we have tinged its ideals, its poetry, its religion, its dreams; we have reached in this land our highest modern development and nothing, humanly speaking, can prevent us from eventually reaching here the full stature of our manhood. Our country is at war. The war is critical, dangerous and world-wide. If this is OUR country, then this is OUR war. We must fight it with every ounce of blood and treasure. . . . But what of our wrongs, cry a million voices with strained faces and bitter eyes. Our wrongs are still wrong. War does not excuse disfranchisement, 'Jim Crow' cars and social injustices, but it does make our first duty clear. It does say deep to the heart of every Negro American:— We will not bargain with our loyalty. We will not profiteer with our country's blood. We will not hesitate the fraction of a second when the God of Battles summons his dusky warriors to stand before the armposts of His Throne. Let them who call for sacrifice in this awful hour of Pain fight for the rights that should be ours; let them who make the laws writhe beneath each enactment that oppresses us,—but we? Our duty lies inexorable and splendid before us, and we shall not shirk."

I am less sure now than then of the soundness of this war attitude. I did not realize the full horror of war and its wide impotence as a method of social reform. Perhaps, despite words, I was thinking narrowly of the interest of my group and was willing to let the world go to hell, if the black man went free. Today I do not know; and I doubt if the triumph of Germany in 1918 could have had worse results than the triumph of the Allies. Possibly passive resistance of my twelve millions to any war activity might have saved the world for black and white. Almost certainly such a proposal on my part would have fallen flat and perhaps slaughtered the American Negro body and soul. I do not know. I am puzzled.

The recent death of Joel Spingarn brings vividly to my mind the influence which he had at that time upon my thought and action. I do not think that any other white man ever touched me emotionally so closely as Joel Spingarn. He was one of those vivid, enthusiastic but clear-thinking idealists which from age to age the Jewish race has given the world. He had learned of the National Association for the Advancement of Colored People just after a crisis in his life and he joined us eagerly, ready for a new fight, a new thrill and new allegiances. I was both fascinated by his character and antagonized by some of his quick and positive judgments.

We fought each other continually in the councils of the Association, but always our admiration and basic faith in each other kept us going hand in hand. We disagreed over the editorial power which I should have in the conduct of the *Crisis* and yet the *Crisis* had no firmer friend than Spingarn. Of greatest influence on me undoubtedly was Spingarn's attitude toward the war. He was fired with consuming patriotism, he believed in America and feared Germany. He wanted me and my people not merely as a matter of policy, but in recognition of a fact, to join wholeheartedly in the war. It was due to his advice and influence that I became during the World War nearer to feeling myself a real and full American than ever before or since. Not only did Spingarn work for the better treatment of Negro soldiers, for the commissioning of Negro officers, but he himself took training at Plattsburg and entered the army as a major. He was assigned to the Intelligence Department in Washington and worked out a bold and farsighted plan.

His basic idea was that his department would be a center for guiding the government into such an attitude and such action toward the Negroes that their loyalty, co-operation and sense of unity with the country would be assured. He urged on Secretary Baker not only the commissioning of Negro officers, but the placating of the Negro press and the appointment of Negroes to positions of authority in the government. He urged that President Wilson break his long silence and say a clear sharp word against lynching. Especially did he want me associated with him in his unit of the Intelligence Department, to be used for my firsthand knowledge of the American Negro and my ability to express their needs and plan a consistent program.

I was more than astonished when, June first, I was called to the War Department and asked if I would accept a captaincy in a bureau of the General Staff for the purpose "of far-reaching constructive effort to satisfy the pressing grievances of colored Americans." Urged by Spingarn, I replied that I would accept, provided that I could retain general oversight of the *Crisis* magazine. The military authorities saw no objection to this. But the board of directors of the NAACP, while recognizing that I ought and indeed must accept this offer, were not all of them convinced that I should retain control of the *Crisis*.

Fortunately the matter never came to an issue. Reaction and suspicion against Spingarn arose in the War Department. Late in 1917, his persistent energy and overwork had put him in the hospital and subjected him to a dangerous operation. On his recovery he had gone back to his project. Now, however, reluctance arose in Washington so far as I was concerned: many Negroes feared that once in the clutches of the war machine, my freedom of utterance would be curbed and instead of being able to influence the government toward a recognition of Negro rights, I would be reduced to the role of a cog in their organization of war spies. White Southern influence, on the other hand, was aghast when it learned from Negro sources just who it was that the War Department was about to add to its staff, and what my activities and words in the past had been. Spingarn was even urging that instead of being merely a captain I should be given from the first a commission as major, so as to be of equal rank with most of the fellow officers in his division. The final result was that the establishment of the new bureau was postponed since its broad scope might "lead beyond the proper limits of military activities." I was left to my work in the

Crisis which was probably by far the best result; while Spingarn went to the front as major in the AEF.

In the midst of this phantasmagoria of war, race hate and mob-law, I finished fifty years of living. Life, with all its difficulties and disappointments, was still good. With all its bitter fruit I enjoyed it. Above all, my soul-child, the *Crisis,* prospered. In the years from 1916 to 1919, the *Crisis* expanded enormously, reaching one year a net paid circulation of over 100,000 copies. Its income in 1920 was over $77,000 and it had sold since 1910 four and a half million copies. This was the peak of its material prosperity.

During the year I had one of my curiously seldom intimate contacts with fellow human beings across the color line. In all this chronicle of the events of my life I have said little of interracial contact, because it was limited. At Atlanta University there were white teachers and we mingled freely and nearly forgot color differences. When I came to New York my acquaintance with white people was not large, and outside the pleasant and close contacts with co-workers in the office, I met white people chiefly as I lectured and attended conferences and committees, and at radical and Socialist dinners. Once in a while, I had tea in Miss Ovington's studio; more often Mary McLean and I sat in my office or in her rooms and planned the *Crisis.* It was only now and then that outside of the work of the Association, I was invited to or sought the company of white folk.

During the Races Congress in London, 1911, I had my broadest contact with white folk of position in the modern world. I met the kindly but rather ineffective Lord Weardale and was entertained at dinner by the Buxtons where I met Sir Roger Casement, afterward hanged. I came to know Fisher Unwin who married Cobden's daughter, and later I met H. G. Wells, whose friendship has lasted over many years. Mrs. Havelock Ellis became one of my acquaintances. I visited her cottage in the country and afterward she came to see me and dined with me in New York. I deeply enjoyed this social contact; but in America, I met little that was analogous. In part this was my own fault. I early assumed that most Americans did not wish my personal acquaintance or contact with me except in purely business relations, and that many of them would repay any approach on my part with deliberate insult, while most of them would be at least embarrassed. Probably I was often wrong in this assumption, but I was right often enough to prove to myself that my rule was wise and a great help to my own peace and quiet. Consequently on the street, in travel, in public assembly and the like, where I came in contact with white people, I spoke to them only when it was necessary, and then briefly. For the most part I did not speak at all, unless they addressed me. This whole assumption and attitude may be explained as arising from an inferiority complex; but it seems to me that in my case it was born mainly of humiliating experience, and involved on my part no attempt to conceal an inferiority of which I certainly was never consciously aware.

In 1918 I had a dinner in Boston with Glendower Evans, Margaret Deland and William James. It was small and intimate and thoroughly enjoyable. I would like to have known other and wider circles of Americans in this manner, but it was not easily possible. Only by something like accident and at long intervals did I emerge from my colored world. On my fiftieth birthday I was given a dinner which brought me in pleasant contact not only with many colored friends but with white folk, many of whom I did not think knew or appreciated my work. Up to this time I had never seen Theodore Roosevelt; but in November, 1918, I presided at a meeting in Carnegie Hall where he spoke together with Irvin Cobb and Knecht of the French High Commission. I remember my words of introduction. "I have the honor to present—Theodore Roosevelt." This was his last public speech.

Immediately after the Armistice came an unexpected change in my life program. Out of a clear sky the board of directors of the NAACP asked me to go to France for the purpose of investigating the treatment of Negro soldiers and for collecting and perfecting the historic record of their participation in the war. Already I and a number of Negroes in the United States had been talking of the advisability and necessity of having the American Negro and the Negroes of the world represented in some way before the Peace Congress. The problems of Africa were going to be discussed; the question of the color bar was coming up; but there was no provision, so far as we could see, to allow the Negro to speak for himself. We proposed sending delegates in some capacity, but at the time war restrictions made this impossible. When it was learned that I was to go, I was delegated to be their representative and I determined to call in Paris a Pan-African Congress.

Only quick and adroit work on the part of myself and friends got me the chance of joining the newspaper men on George Creel's press boat "Orizaba." There was every disposition to refuse me, even as a representative of the *Crisis* magazine. But it happened that President Wilson was sending on that same boat Robert R. Moton, principal of Tuskegee and successor to Booker T. Washington. His duty was to speak to the returning Negro soldiers, pacify them and forestall any attempt at agitation or open expression of resentment on their return to the United States. Under these circumstances my request also to go could hardly be denied.

Thus without premeditation I was thrown into direct touch with what I came later to know was the real crux of the problems of my time; and that is the widespread effort of white Europe to use the labor and material of the colored world for its own wealth and power. My plan to have Africa in some way voice its complaints to the world during the Peace Congress at Versailles, was an ambitious project conceived in time of war, without political backing and indeed without widespread backing of any kind. Had it not been for one circumstance, it would have utterly failed; and that circumstance was that black Africa had the right to send from Senegal a member to the French Parliament.

This member, Blaise Diagne, as high commissioner during the World War had caused a hundred eighty thousand black soldiers to come from Africa to Europe to stand the shock of the German onslaught in Flanders Field. He stood high in French public esteem. With infinite difficulty and with the studied opposition of America, I succeeded in getting through him the consent of Clemenceau to hold in February, 1919, at the Grand Hotel in Paris, a

Pan-African Congress of fifty-seven delegates, including sixteen American Negroes, twenty West Indians, and twelve Africans. France, Belgium, and Portugal were represented by officials. The English government refused passports to English delegates, and the American Secretary of State assured Negro delegates that no congress would be held. My greatest helper in this Congress was Madame Calman-Levy, widow of the Paris publisher. This quiet, charming woman became enthusiastic over the idea of my Congress and brought together in her salon groups of interested persons including Otlet and Fontaine of Belgium and several French officials.

The results of this meeting were small. But it had some influence. I talked with Colonel House and a number of lower officials among the French, English and Portuguese. On the other hand, there came increasing disillusion. I saw the mud and dirt of the trenches; I heard from the mouths of soldiers the kind of treatment that black men got in the American army; I was convinced and said that American white officers fought more valiantly against Negroes than they did against the Germans. I still believe this was largely true. I collected some astonishing documents of systematic slander and attack upon Negroes and demands upon the French for insulting attitudes toward them. Not daring to transport these myself, I sent them to America in the hands of my friend, Frederic Howe. Later when I published these documents in America, the government started to interfere by refusing the *Crisis* mailing facilities. Then realizing that this was a partial confession of guilt, the Post Office withdrew its prohibition. We sold 100,000 copies that month.

The whole history of the American Negro and other black folk in the World War, has never been written. I collected while I was in France and since a mass of documents covering this episode in our history. They deserve publication, not simply as a part of the Negro's history, but as an unforgettable lesson in the spiritual lesions of race conflict during a critical period of American history. I hope sometime that a careful history based on these documents may see the light.

John Rolfe wrote that the last of August, 1619, there came to Virginia "a dutch man of warre that sold us twenty Negars." These Negroes were not slaves and they were not the first Negroes who saw America; but their descendants became slaves and they formed the first permanent black settlers in the United States. As early as October, 1918, I planned a national Negro celebration of the Tercentenary of the landing of these Negroes; but alas, almost exactly three hundred years later there occurred race riots in Chicago and Washington which were among the worst in their significance that the Negro had encountered during his three hundred years of slavery and emancipation.

The year 1919 was for the American Negro one of extraordinary and unexpected reaction. This reaction had two main causes: first, the competition of emigrating Negro workers, pouring into Northern industry out of the South and leaving the Southern plantations with a shortage of their customary cheap labor. The other cause was the resentment of American soldiers, especially those from the South, at the recognition and kudos which Negroes received in the World War; and particularly their treatment in France. In the last case, the sex motive, the brutal sadism into which race hate always falls, was all too evident. The facts concerning the year 1919 are almost unbelievable as one looks back upon them today. During that year seventy-seven Negroes were lynched, of whom one was a woman and eleven were soldiers; of these, fourteen were publicly burned, eleven of them being burned alive.

That year there were race riots large and small in twenty-six American cities including thirty-eight killed in a Chicago riot of August; from twenty-five to fifty in Phillips County, Arkansas; and six killed in Washington. For a day, the city of Washington in July, 1919, was actually in the hands of a black mob fighting against the aggression of the whites with hand grenades.

The white secretary of the NAACP was mobbed in Texas in 1919, where he had gone for investigation and eventually resigned his position, because of the hopelessness of the race situation as he had viewed it. James Weldon Johnson, who had been our Field Secretary, was selected to succeed him. I hated to see the fine soul of a poet and litterateur thus dulled and frayed in the rough work of actual propaganda and agitation. Johnson made an excellent secretary, but at fatal cost to his health and strength. In Arkansas, despite the slaughter of Negroes, ninety-four other victims were arrested; twelve were condemned to death, and eighty sentenced to imprisonment. On top of that, not only did the agitation for residential segregation increase, but there was an open and wide revival of the Ku Klux Klan.

In north Georgia a reign of terror began. Governor Dorsey in April, 1921, called a conference of citizens in

Atlanta and placed before them one hundred thirty-five examples of mistreatment of Negroes in Georgia within two years. He made no effort to collect all cases and said that if he had, the number could be multiplied. "In some counties the Negro is being driven out as though he were a wild animal; in others he is being held as a slave; in others no Negroes remain. In only two of the one hundred and thirty-five cases cited is the 'usual crime' against white women involved."

In 1919 the National Association staged a determined fight on lynching and concentrated all its energy in this direction. A national Conference on lynching was called in May, 1919, in New York City. The address to the nation was signed by one hundred fifty citizens including an ex-President of the United States, the attorney-general, governors of seven states, and heads of leading universities. The chief speaker at the Carnegie Hall meeting was the present Chief Justice of the United States. Mary Talbert started the anti-lynching crusade, raising a defense fund of $12,000; and James Weldon Johnson, secretary of the National Association for the Advancement of Colored People, succeeded in 1921 in forcing the Dyer Anti-lynching Bill on the attention of the Sixty-seventh Congress. Two thousand public meetings were held against lynching during that year and a thorough investigation of the causes of the Chicago riot was instigated and an investigation also headed by Mr. Johnson was made in Haiti where he charged that three thousand Haitians had been killed during the American occupation.

Meantime in the United States the battle of liberalism against race prejudice went on. I found myself trying to adjust war and post-war problems to the questions of racial justice; trying to show from the injustices of war time what the new vision must encompass; fighting mobs and lynching; encouraging Negro migration; helping woman suffrage; encouraging the new rush of young blacks to college; watching and explaining the political situation and traveling thousands of miles and lecturing in hundreds of centers.

The Dyer Anti-lynching Bill went through the House of Representatives and on to the floor of the Senate. There in 1924 it died with a filibuster and the abject surrender of its friends. It was not until years after that I knew what killed that anti-lynching bill. It was a bargain between the South and the West. By this bargain, lynching was let to go on uncurbed by Federal law, on condition that the Japanese be excluded from the United States.

Court cases kept pressing upon us: there were the Elaine riots and the Arkansas cases; there was the Sweet case in Detroit and, equally significant to my mind, although not to all my colleagues, the Sacco-Vanzetti case in Massachusetts. James Weldon Johnson, our secretary, raised from the public and the Garland Fund nearly $80,000 for a civil rights defense fund. We continued winning court victories, but somehow despite them, we did not seem to be getting far. We added to the "Grandfather" Case of 1916 and the Segregation Case of 1917 the victories in the Arkansas case, the white primary case and another segregation case in the high courts, in addition to the eventful freeing of Dr. Sweet and his family, who had been sentenced to death in Detroit for defending their home against a mob.

The most important work of the decade, as I now look back upon it, was my travel. Before 1918, I had made three trips to Europe; but now between 1918 and 1928 I made four more trips of extraordinary meaning: to France directly after the close of the war and during the Congress of Versailles; to England, Belgium, France and Geneva in the earliest days of the League of Nations; to Spain, Portugal and Africa in 1923 and 1924; and to Germany, Russia, and Constantinople in 1927. I could scarcely have encompassed a more vital part of the modern world picture than in those stirring journeys. They gave me a depth of knowledge and a breadth of view which was of incalculable value for realizing and judging modern conditions and, above all, the problem of race in America and in the world.

CHAPTER 9. REVOLUTION

AFTER the war, with most Americans, I was seeking to return to normalcy. I tried three paths, one of which represented an old ideal and ambition, the development of literature and art among Negroes through my own writing and the encouragement of others. The second path was new and had arisen out of war; and that was the development of the idea back of the Pan-African Congress. The third idea was quite new, and proved in a way of greater importance in my thinking than even the other two; and that was the economic rehabilitation and defense of the American Negro after the change and dislocation of war. Of course, it would have been impossible for me successfully to follow more than one of these paths and indeed with my work on the *Crisis* and for the National Association, perhaps I could do nothing but experiment in all three; but I did think that I might point ways for others to follow.

It had always been my ambition to write; to seek through the written word the expression of my relation to the world and of the world to me. I had begun that writing early; while at Fisk I had an article tentatively accepted by the *Century*, although it was never actually printed. Later while in college I wrote for various colored periodicals. Then after my graduation from Harvard came my first book. This work had been my doctor's thesis which I had succeeded in some degree in transforming from a dry historical treatise into readable literature. That was published in 1896 and to my gratification was the first volume in the Harvard Historical Studies. It was followed in 1899 by the "Philadelphia Negro," a huge volume of five hundred pages but not unreadable. And from 1897 to 1914, the sixteen Atlanta University Studies which I edited and largely wrote appeared, each varying in size from pamphlet to volume. They covered more than two thousand pages. Then came, in 1903, my collection of essays called "The Souls of Black Folk," of which I have spoken.

In 1909, I published my biography of John Brown which I regarded as one of the best things that I had done; but it met a curious fate. Unconsciously I had entrenched on the chosen field of a writer who controlled two powerful literary vehicles. He severely criticized the work, most unfairly as it seemed to me, and would give me no chance for rejoinder. In 1911, I tried my hand at fiction and published "The Quest of the Silver Fleece" which was really an economic study of some merit. Beginning in 1910, besides editing the *Crisis* continuously for twenty-three years, I published "The Negro," a sketch of racial history, in 1915; and a series of essays called "Darkwater" in 1920. In 1924, with the subvention of the publishing fund of the Knights of Columbus, I brought out "The Gift of Black Folk," basically sound as I believe, but too hurriedly done, with several unpardonable errors. The article on Georgia in "These United States" came the same year and a chapter in "The New Negro" in 1925. In 1928 came another novel, "Dark Princess," my favorite book. In addition to this I published a considerable number of magazine articles in many of the leading periodicals.

My writing up to this time and since has brought me but scant financial returns. From my twelve and more volumes I have not averaged altogether in forty years as much as five hundred dollars a year; but I have written what I wanted to say and not what men would rather hear. I have loved the writing and the chance to do it has fully repaid me and more.

More especially I tried to encourage other Negro writers through the columns of the *Crisis*. By 1920, we could point out that most of the young writers among American Negroes had made first publication in the columns of the *Crisis*. In the next few years we published work from Claude McKay, Langston Hughes, Jean Toomer, Countee Cullen, Anne Spencer, Abram Harris and Jessie Fauset. In 1924, through the generosity of Amy Spingarn, wife of Joel, we were enabled to offer a series of prizes for young Negro writers, and our contemporary, *Opportunity,* organ of the Urban League, offered similar prizes. For several years this competition went on until it grew into what has been called the renaissance of Negro literature, late in the twenties. Here again the World War and its aftermath balked us. No authentic group literature can rise save at the demand and with the support of the group which is calling for self-expression. The depression of industry, which came with a crash in 1929, was foreshadowed in the Negro group several years before, despite the apparent industrial boom. The circulation of the *Crisis* went down, the contributions to the National Association were curtailed and the New Negro literature was forced to place its dependence almost entirely upon a white audience and that audience had its own distinct patterns and preferences for Negro writing.

We were particularly proud to have had the chance to publish some bits of real literature; like that great poem of the black man's part in the war by Roscoe Jamison:

> These truly are the Brave,
> These men who cast aside
> Old memories, to walk the blood-stained pave
> Of Sacrifice, joining the solemn tide
> That moves away, to suffer and to die
> For Freedom—when their own is yet denied!
> O Pride! O Prejudice! When they pass you by,
> Hail them, the Brave, for you now crucified!

I sought to encourage the graphic arts not only by magazine covers with Negro themes and faces, but as often as I could afford, I portrayed the faces and features of colored folk. One cannot realize today how rare that was in 1910. The colored papers carried few or no illustrations; the white papers none. In many great periodicals, it was the standing rule that no Negro portrait was to appear and that rule still holds in some American periodicals. Through our "Men of the Month," our children's edition and our education edition, we published large numbers of most interesting and intriguing portraits.

In these days, 1920 and 1921, I made one effort toward which I look back with infinite satisfaction: an attempt in the *Brownie's Book* to furnish a little magazine for Negro children, in which my efforts were ably seconded by

Augustus Dill and Jessie Fauset; it was really a beautiful publication, but it did not pay its way.

In another realm of art I made essay. From my childhood I have been impressed with the beauty of Negro skin-color and astonished at the blindness of whites who cannot see it. In addition I recognized, not perhaps so much a native Negro dramatic ability, as lack of those inhibitions which keep most folk from natural self-expression. Combining these two things, I believed that the pageant, with masses of costumed colored folk and a dramatic theme carried out chiefly by movement, dancing and music, could be made effective. I even hoped that such a movement might be placed on a paying basis. I tried first in 1913, when New York made an appropriation to celebrate the fiftieth anniversary of emancipation. The colored contractor who handled my printing was head of the new colored Tammany organization in Harlem. He put me on the celebration committee and through all kinds of difficulties, I wrote and staged an historic pageant of the history of the Negro race, calling it "The Star of Ethiopia." Before a total attendance of thirty thousand persons, we played it on the floor of an armory with three hundred fifty actors. Led by Charles Burroughs, they did scenes whose imagery and beauty have not often been surpassed.

Encouraged by this response I undertook in 1915 to reproduce this in Washington. We used the great ball field of the American League, a massive background of an Egyptian temple painted by young Richard Brown, and a thousand actors. A committee of the most distinguished colored citizens of Washington co-operated with me. Audiences aggregating fourteen thousand saw the pageant. We faced every discouragement from rain to lack of funds. "Then," as I wrote, "it was, as it always is in things of this sort. Suddenly a great new spirit seemed born. The thing that you have exorcised becomes a living, mighty, moving spirit. It sweeps on and you hang trembling to its skirts. Nothing can stop it. It is. It will. Wonderfully, irresistibly the dream comes true. You feel no exaltation, you feel no personal merit. It is not yours. It is its own. You have simply called it, and it comes. I shall never forget that last night. Six thousand human faces looked down from the shifting blaze of lights and on the field the shimmering streams of colors came and went, silently, miraculously save for the great cloud of music that hovered over them and enveloped them. It was no mere picture: it was reality."

A difficulty, of course, with dramatic effort of this sort, was that it could not be made to pay unless organized with considerable capital. That I did not have and could not command. Nevertheless, once more I made the experiment in Philadelphia in 1916, to celebrate the one hundredth general conference of the African M. E. Church. "It was," says the *Friend's Intelligencer,* "a signal contribution to the fine art of pageantry." A settlement worker added: "I wish I could find the words I need to thank you for the beautiful thing you have given us in the pageant; but perhaps my best tribute is the very wordlessness, the tear-salted eyes with which I watched it, and shall always remember it. It was not only the pathos and the tragedy of the story that made the tears, but something deeper than that. In spite of the hurt, you'll keep right on being a poet, won't you, please?"

But alas, neither poetry nor pageants pay dividends, and in my case they scarcely paid expenses. My pageant died with an expiring gasp in Los Angeles in 1925. But it died not solely for lack of support; rather from the tremendous and expanding vogue of the motion picture and the power of the radio and loud speaker. We had no capital for entering into this field and indeed in face of monopoly, who has? Yet, my final pageant took place significantly in Hollywood Bowl, and was still a beautiful thing: "Hard and loving, costly and adventurous has been the effort that brought the 'Star of Ethiopia' to Los Angeles. It cost five thousand dollars and weeks of work; and doubt and travail, harsh words and with it, all curiously inwrought, a love and wonder, a working hand in hand and heart in heart, which paid. And sitting again tonight I see the trees darkly, solemnly uplifted to God; I hear the wild, sad music; and then comes thrilling the light—the light of dancing feet and soft, brown skins and beautiful, beautiful eyes: the eyes of Ethiopia on the Black Rock, beneath the gleaming of her sword."

Of the Pan-African Congresses, I have explained their rather hurriedly conceived beginning. I was convinced, however, by my experience in Paris in 1919 that here was a real vision and an actual need. Contacts of Negroes of different origins and nationality, which I had then and before at other congresses and the Races Congress were most inspiring. My plans as they developed had in them nothing spectacular nor revolutionary. If in decades or a century they resulted in such world organization of black men as would oppose a united front to European aggression, that certainly would not have been beyond my dream. But on the other hand, in practical reality, I knew the power and guns of Europe and America, and what I wanted to do was in the face of this power to sit down hand in hand with colored groups and across the council table to learn of each other, our condition, our aspirations, our chances for concerted thought and action. Out of this there might come, not race war and opposition, but broader co-operation with the white rulers of the world, and a chance for peaceful and accelerated development of black folk. With this in mind I started to organize and hold a Pan-African Congress in 1921 which would be better attended and more carefully organized than that in 1919.

I found the board of directors of the NAACP not particularly interested. The older liberalism among the white people did not envisage Africa and the colored peoples of the world. They were interested in America and securing American citizens of all and any color, their rights. They had no schemes for internationalism in race problems and to many of them, it seemed quixotic to undertake anything of the sort. Then too, there were colored members who had inherited the fierce repugnance toward anything African, which was the natural result of the older colonization schemes, where efforts at assisted and even forcible expatriation of American Negroes had always included Africa. Negroes were bitterly opposed because such schemes were at bottom an effort to make slavery in the United States more secure and to get rid of the free Negroes. Beyond this they felt themselves Americans, not Africans. They resented and feared any coupling with Africa.

My scheme then for the Pan-African movement had to depend upon voluntary organization largely outside the NAACP. This to some degree I secured and planned a congress to sit successively in three capitals of Europe: London, Brussels, and Paris, from August 29 to September 6, 1921. This congress really deserved to be called Pan-African and it attracted world-wide attention. There were one hundred thirteen accredited delegates from twenty-six different groups, including thirty-five persons from the United States, thirty-nine from Africa and the rest from the West Indies and Europe.

Among the speakers were Sir Sidney, now Lord Olivier, and Norman Leys of England; Paul Otlet, often called the "father of the League of Nations"; and Senator La Fontaine of Belgium; Dr. Vitellian, former physician of Menelik of Abyssinia; General Sorelas of Spain; Blaise Diagne of France; and Florence Kelly and Bishop Hurst of America. The attention which the Congress attracted all over Europe was astonishing. It was discussed in the London *Times,* the *Observer* and *Daily Graphic;* in the Paris *Petit Parisien, Matin* and *Temps;* in the *Manchester Guardian* and in practically all the daily papers of Belgium. It led to heated debate in Brussels touching the rights of these delegates to discuss at all the relation of colonies, and it emphasized in the minds of all of us the importance of such discussions. Two of us visited the League of Nations and the International Labor Office with petitions and suggestions.

On the other hand the Pan-African movement ran into two fatal difficulties: first of all, it was much too early to assume, as I had assumed, that in 1921 the war was over.

In fact the whole tremendous drama which followed the war, political and social revolution, economic upheaval and depression, national and racial hatred, all these things made a setting in which any such movement as I envisaged was probably at the time impossible. I sensed this in the bitter and deep opposition which our resolutions invoked in Belgium. Both the Belgian and French governments were aroused and disturbed and the English opposition hovered in the background.

There came, too, a second difficulty which had elements of comedy and curious social frustration, but nevertheless was real and in a sense tragic. Marcus Garvey walked into the scene. I had heard of Garvey when in 1915 I took a short vacation trip to Jamaica, where I was surprisingly well-received by colored people and white, because of the wide publicity given me from my participation in the Races Congress of London in 1911. Garvey and his associates, "The United Improvement and Conservation Association," joined in the welcome.

After the war he came to America, launched a widely advertised plan for commerce between Negro groups and eventually of Negro domination of Africa. It was a grandiose and bombastic scheme, utterly impracticable as a whole, but it was sincere and had some practical features; and Garvey proved not only an astonishing popular leader, but a master of propaganda. Within a few years, news of his movement, of his promises and plans, reached Europe and Asia, and penetrated every corner of Africa. He actually bought two small boats, summoned huge conventions to New York, and paraded the streets of Harlem with uniformed troops and "Black Cross" nurses. News of his astonishing plans reached Europe and the various colonial offices, even before my much more modest proposals. Often the Pan-African Congress was confounded with the Garvey movement with consequent suspicion and attack.

My first effort was to explain away the Garvey movement and ignore it; but it was a mass movement that could not be ignored. I noted this movement from time to time in the *Crisis* and said in 1920 that Garvey was "an extraordinary leader of men" and declared that he had "with singular success capitalized and made vocal the great and long-suffering grievances and spirit of protest among the West Indian peasantry." Later when he began to collect money for his steamship line, I characterized him as a hard-working idealist, but called his methods bombastic, wasteful, illogical, and almost illegal. I begged his friends not to allow him foolishly to overwhelm with bankruptcy and disaster "one of the most interesting spiritual movements of the modern world." But he went ahead, wasted his money, got in trouble with the authorities and was deported from the United States. He made a few abortive efforts later, but finally died in London in 1940, poor and neglected.

The unfortunate debacle of his over-advertised schemes naturally hurt and made difficult further effective development of the Pan-African Congress idea. Nevertheless, a third Pan-African Congress was attempted in 1923. It was less broadly representative than the second, but of some importance, and was held in London, Paris and Lisbon. Thence I went to Africa and for the first time saw the homeland of the black race.

At the London meeting of the third Pan-African Congress, Harold Laski, H. G. Wells, and Lord Olivier spoke, and Ramsay MacDonald had promised to speak to us but was hindered by the sudden opening of the campaign which made him prime minister of England. Among other things we held conferences with members of the Labor Party of England at which Mrs. Sidney Webb, Mr. Clynes and others were present. We emphasized the importance of labor solidarity between white and black labor in England, America, and elsewhere. In Portugal our meeting was attended by cabinet ministers and deputies and though small, was of exceeding interest.

In my ensuing trip to Africa, of which I have spoken elsewhere, and which in a way was a culmination of this Congress, I was further encouraged in my belief in the soundness of its underlying idea. I met in Sierra Leone members and promoters of the Congress of West Africa. Starting after the war, this organization made such cogent and persistent representations to the British colonial office in 1920 and later, that they secured for the first time in British West Africa, popular representation in the governors' councils. Their movement resembled our National Association in the United States and I was convinced that acquaintance and correspondence between colored persons promoting such movements all over the world would be a great and wise step from many points of view.

A fourth Pan-African Congress was held in New York in 1927, chiefly as a rather empty gesture to keep the idea alive. Dantès Bellegarde and Georges Sylvain of Haiti and other speakers took part. A fifth Pan-African Congress was proposed for Tunis, Africa, in 1929, but the French government vetoed the project. Then we tried to charter a boat and hold the congress in the West Indies. There was no boat available. No further efforts have been made, yet the idea is not entirely dead.

My third effort after the war was toward the economic stabilization and rehabilitation of the Negro, and was, as I see it now, more fundamental and prophetic than any of these three lines of endeavor. It started with an effort to establish consumers' co-operation among American Negroes. On August 26, 1918, there met in the *Crisis* office, twelve colored men from seven different states, to establish the Negro Co-operative Guild. This was in response to a series of editorials and explanations in the *Crisis,* advocating consumers' co-operation for Negroes. The meeting determined to induce individuals and groups to study consumers' co-operation, to hold an annual meeting for encouraging co-operative stores and to form a central committee.

Several co-operative stores were established. The most ambitious came in Memphis where the Citizens Co-operative Stores opened five places of business in 1919 and carried on a good trade. Then the manager conceived the idea of turning this co-operative effort into a stock company. The result was that eventually he was driven out of business by competition of the chain stores. An excellent effort in the colored state school at Bluefield, West Virginia, planned to teach the students the basic theories of co-operation in a school co-operative store. From the Harvard University Graduate School of Education came a comment to the manager, W. C. Matney: "I am convinced that you are doing a splendid piece of work with this

enterprise." It was successful for many years, but the state
of West Virginia eventually forbade its continuance.
There were four or five other attempts. My trip to Europe,
the disasters of the year 1919, my concentration of interest
in Pan Africa and the depression left this, perhaps the
most promising of my projected movements, without
further encouragement. The whole movement needed
more careful preliminary spade work, with popular education both of consumers and managers; and for lack of
this, it temporarily failed. It must and will be revived.

In general, the decade from 1918 to 1928 was one of
infinite effort and discouraging turmoil as I suppose it had
to be. The economic boom and depression in the United
States were necessarily for all Americans a time of heart
searching and intellectual stock-taking. I was nervous and
restless; in addition to all my activities, I ranged the country from North to South and from the Atlantic to the
Pacific in series of lectures, conferences, and expositions.
I do not doubt but the directors of the Association and
my friends would like to have seen me settle down to
fewer lines of effort; but at the time this was impossible.
I had to be a part of the revolution through which the
world was going and to feel in my own soul the scars of
its battle.

Still racial injustice prevailed. At the time of the Mississippi flood, the Red Cross allowed the Negroes to be
treated like slaves and peons; and in Okolona, Mississippi,
a national organization of the Episcopal Church refused
to prosecute a white murderer who killed a black professor in cold blood on his own school ground. There came
disquieting situations among Negro students: a strike at

Hampton, disturbed conditions at Wilberforce, turmoil at Howard and an uprising at Fisk.

Into this last battle I had to throw myself; to resurrect and re-publish the *Fisk Herald* and to fight until Fisk deposed its dictatorial president. The struggle here was epoch-making. How far can a Negro college, dominated by white trustees and a white president and supported by white wealth, carry on in defiance of the wishes and best interests of its colored constituency? There was room at first for argument as to whether the Fisk of 1924 was inimical to our best interests. This matter, by tongue and pen, I helped to settle. The proof was unanswerable. The effort cost me friends and influence, even though eventually the righteousness of the fight was acknowledged by the most reactionary.

Gradually, however, even in the midst of my activities and distractions I began to pause and take stock; I began to look back critically at the twenty years of my life which had passed since I gave up my work at Atlanta University, joined the National Association for the Advancement of Colored People and founded and edited the *Crisis*. My basic theory had been that race prejudice was primarily a matter of ignorance on the part of the mass of men, giving the evil and anti-social a chance to work their way; that when the truth was properly presented, the monstrous wrong of race hate must melt and melt quickly before it. All human action to me in those days was conscious and rational. There was no twilight zone.

To some extent I saw in two decades of work a justification of this theory. Much of the statement, assertion and habit of thought characteristic of the latter part of the nineteenth century regarding the Negro had passed away. Wild Tillmans had stopped talking of the growing "degeneracy of American Negroes." Tom Watsons were ceasing to assert that the Negro race had always been and would always be barbarians. Even the basic excuse for lynching, the rape of white women, had been successfully countered and denied with statistical proof. And from a day when the legality of the Fifteenth Amendment had been openly denied and that denial in some cases supported by judicial decision, we had come to the recognition of full citizenship rights by the Supreme Court. All this was gratifying to the leaders of the National Association for the Advancement of Colored People and to me. In a sense it was an epoch-making achievement. No longer was it possible or thinkable anywhere in the United States to study and discuss the Negro without letting him speak for himself and without having that speaking done by a well-equipped person, if such person was wanted.

On the other hand, I began to be deeply and disturbingly aware that with all the success of our agitation and propaganda, with the wide circulation, reading and attention which the *Crisis* enjoyed, with the appearance of Negroes on the lecture platform everywhere, and the emergence of a distinct and creditable Negro literature, nevertheless the barriers of race prejudice were certainly as strong in 1930 as in 1910 the world over, and in certain aspects, from certain points of view, even stronger.

Or, in other words, beyond my conception of ignorance and deliberate ill-will as causes of race prejudice, there must be other and stronger and more threatening forces, forming the founding stones of race antagonisms, which we had only begun to attack or perhaps in reality had not attacked at all. Moreover, the attack upon these hidden and partially concealed causes of race hate, must be led by Negroes in a program which was not merely negative in the sense of calling on white folk to desist from certain practices and give up certain beliefs; but direct in the sense that Negroes must proceed constructively in new and comprehensive plans of their own.

I think it was the Russian Revolution which first illuminated and made clear this change in my basic thought. It was not that I at any time conceived of Bolshevik Russia as ushering in any present millennium. I was painfully sensitive to all its failures, to all the difficulties which it faced; but the clear and basic thing which appeared to me in unquestioned brightness, was that in the year 1917 and then, after a struggle with the world and famine ten years later, one of the largest nations of the world made up its mind frankly to face a set of problems which no nation was at the time willing to face, and which many nations including our own are unwilling fully to face even to this day.

Those questions involved the problem of the poverty of the mass of men in an age when an abundance of goods and technical efficiency of work seemed able to provide a sufficiency for all men, so that the mass of men could be fed and clothed and sheltered, live in health and have their intellectual faculties trained. Russia was trying to accomplish this by eventually putting into the hands of those people who do the world's work the power to guide and rule the state for the best welfare of the masses. It made the assumption, long disputed, that out of the downtrodden mass of people, ability and character, sufficient to do this task effectively, could and would be found. I believed this dictum passionately. It was, in fact, the foundation stone of my fight for black folk; it explained me.

I had been brought up with the democratic idea that this general welfare was the object of democratic action in the state, of allowing the governed a voice in government. But through the crimson illumination of war, I realized and, afterward by travel around the world, saw even more clearly that so-called democracy today was allowing the mass of people to have only limited voice in government; that democratic control of what are at present the most important functions of men: work and earning a living and distributing goods and services; that here we did not have democracy; we had oligarchy, and oligarchy based on monopoly and income; and this oligarchy was as determined to deny democracy in industry as it had once been determined to deny democracy in legislation and choice of officials.

My thoughts in this line were made more firm by a visit to Russia. Sometime in 1927, I met three Russian visitors to the United States. They were probably clandestine agents of the communist dictatorship. They sought me out, probably because they recognized that I had been for some time a leader of what was called the liberal if not the radical wing among Negroes; and Russia was conceiving the distinct idea that the revolution in the United States might be promoted certainly in some degree by stirring up discontent among the most oppressed tenth of the American nation, namely, the American Negroes.

Two of these Russians, a man and wife, were persons

of education and culture and sought to learn my ideas and reactions rather than to press upon me their theories. The third was a blond German and an active revolutionist. He was unwilling to wait. He wanted something done and done now. After I had sought firmly to show him that no revolution in America could be started by Negroes and succeed, and even if that were possible, that after what I had seen of the effects of war, I could never regard violence as an effective, much less necessary, step to reform the American state, he gradually faded out of the picture and ceased to visit me. I do not know what became of him. I never saw him again.

From the other two Russians I learned much. We had pleasant social relations and I sat at their feet to hear what was taking place and what was planned in Russia. I asserted my inability to judge the situation fairly, because I did not know enough of the facts and stressed my continuing doubt as to whether the Russian pattern could be and should be applied in the United States. They said I ought to visit Russia and I expressed my eagerness to do so. Finally, they offered to finance a visit to Russia, which I accepted with a written proviso which I insisted upon, that this visit entail no promise on my part of action or agreement of any kind. I was to go on a journey of free inquiry to see the most momentous change in modern human history which had taken place since the French Revolution. I went to Russia in 1928, traveling by way of Germany, where passport difficulties held me for two or more weeks.

The sight of the German Republic struggling on the ruins of the empire and tottering under a load of poverty,

oppression and disorganization made upon me an unforgettable impression. But never in my life have I been so
stirred as by what I saw during two months in Russia.
I visited Leningrad and Moscow, Nijni Novgorod and
Kiev and came home by way of Odessa and Constantinople.
I was allowed, so far as I could see, every opportunity to
investigate. I saw the wild waifs of the sewers, the fifty
thousand children who marched in the Red Square on
Youth Day, the new art galleries and the new factories,
the beginnings of the new agriculture. But this was physical. Mentally I came to know Karl Marx and Lenin, their
critics and defenders. Since that trip my mental outlook
and the aspect of the world will never be the same.

My day in Russia was the day of communist beginnings;
the red weal of war-suffering and of famine still lay across
the land. Only yesterday England, France, America and
the Czechs had invaded their land without shadow of
right. The people were ragged and hungry, the cities were
half in ruins. The masses of men who crowded the streets
and fought for places on the packed street cars, were
truculent and over-assertive in manner. Moscow did not
have a half dozen automobiles. Yet, there lay an unforgettable spirit upon the land, in spite of almost insur-
mountable obstacles; in the face of contempt and chicanery
and the armed force of the civilized world, this nation was
determined to go forward and establish a government of
men, such as the world had never seen.

Since that they have reeled on; their path has been
strewn with blood and failure; but at the same time their
accomplishment today is such that they have compelled
the world to face the kind of problem which they deter-

mined to face; and no matter how much the Fascism of
Mussolini and the National Socialism of Hitler, the New
Deal of Roosevelt and the appeasement of Chamberlain
and the new World War, may assert and believe that they
have found ways of abolishing poverty, increasing the
efficiency of work, allowing the worker to earn a living
and curtailing the power of wealth by means short of
revolution, confiscation and force; nevertheless every honest observer must admit that human civilization today has
by these very efforts moved toward socialism and accepted
many of the tenets of Russian communism. We may, with
dogged persistency, declare that deliberate murder, organized destruction and brute force cannot in the end
bring and preserve human culture; but we must admit that
nothing that Russia has done in war and mass murder ex-
ceeds what has been done and is being done by the rest
of the civilized world.

Gradually it dawned upon me with increasing clarity
just what the essential change in the world has been since
the first World War and depression; and how the tactics
of those who live for the widest development of men must
change accordingly. It is not simply a matter of change in
ideals, but even more of a decisive change in the methods
by which ideals are to be approximated. As I now look
back, I see in the crusade waged by the National Association for the Advancement of Colored People from 1910
to 1930, one of the finest efforts of liberalism to achieve
human emancipation; and much was accomplished. But
the essential difficulty with the liberalism of the twentieth
century was not to realize the fundamental change brought

+ now?

about by the world-wide organization of work and trade and commerce.

During the nineteenth century the overwhelming influence of the economic activities of men upon their thought and action was, as Marx insisted, clear; but it was not until the twentieth century that the industrial situation called not only for understanding but for action. Modern business enterprise organized for private profit was throttling democratic government, choking art and literature and leading work and industry into a dangerous paradox by increasing the production of things for sale and yet decreasing even more rapidly the number of persons able to buy and the amount of money they could spend; thus throwing industry into periodic convulsions. The number of persons who see this economic impasse is becoming larger and larger until it includes today the leading thinkers of the world.

But the difficulty was to know how, without revolution, violence, and dislocation of human civilization, the wrong could be righted and human culture started again upon its upward path. One thing, at any rate, was clear to me in my particular problem, and that was that a continued agitation which had for its object simply free entrance into the present economy of the world, that looked at political rights as an end in itself rather than as a method of reorganizing the state; and that expected through civil rights and legal judgments to re-establish freedom on a broader and firmer basis, was not so much wrong as short-sighted; that the democracy which we had been asking for in political life must sooner or later replace the tyranny which now dominated industrial life.

In the organization whose leadership I shared at the time, I found few who envisaged the situation as I did. The bulk of my colleagues saw no essential change in the world. It was the same world with the problems to be attacked by the same methods as before the war. All we needed to do was to continue to attack lynching, to bring more cases before the courts and to insist upon our full citizenship rights. They recoiled from any consideration of the economic plight of the world or any change in the organization of industry.

My colored colleagues especially were deeply American, with the old theory of individualism, with a desire to be rich or at least well-to-do, with suspicion of organized labor and labor programs; with a horror of racial segregation. My white colleagues were still liberals and philanthropists. They wanted to help the Negroes, as they wanted to help the weak and disadvantaged of all classes in America. They realized poignantly the dislocation of industry, the present economic problems; but most of them still believed in the basic rightness of industry as at present organized and few—perhaps only one, Oswald Garrison Villard—moved from this undisturbed belief in the capitalist system toward the left, toward a conception of a new democratic control of industry.

My nearest white friend, who was executive head of the organization, Joel Spingarn, was skeptical of democracy either in industry, politics or art. He was the natural anarchist of the spirit. His interest was aroused in the Negro because of discrimination, and not in the interest of ideal methods of conducting the state. Given certain rights and opportunities, it was more than wrong, in his mind, to discriminate against certain individuals because of their race and color. He wanted for me and my people freedom to live and act; but he did not believe that voting or revolution in industry was going to bring the millennium. He was afraid that I was turning radical and dogmatic and even communistic, and he proceeded to use his power and influence in order to curb my acts and forestall any change of program of the Association on my part.

Students of sociology have not yet studied widely one method of human government used in modern times and that is the carrying out of social reform of various sorts by means of the secretary-board of directors organization. A group of intelligent men of good will come together for the purpose of studying a certain problem and improving conditions. They may elect the conventional officers, but eventually they put effective power in the hands of a secretary. There ensues a peculiarly effective unity: the members of the committee consult and discuss, arrive at conclusions which the secretary carries out. In the end, the secretary, to all essential purposes, becomes the organization and his effective consultants are his office staff whom he appoints and pays. All this goes smoothly until changes in the policy, ideals, and objects are indicated. Logically these changes should come by decision of the board of directors; but the board by this time has probably become a co-opting body, whose members are suggested by the secretary, so that they are, in fact, his creatures. Moreover, the secretary is naturally tempted to fill his board with "window-dressing"; with persons who are in general agreement with his policies, but who take no active part either in attendance or discussion; and whose names, on the other hand, lend high prestige to the organization. These persons are not apt to know that changes in object are necessary or to care much, so long as the organization remains respectable.

In part the NAACP followed this development but not entirely. In any such united effort for social betterment as ours, there is bound to be some cultural gap between white and black workers. The wider the gap, the easier the collaboration which resolves itself into the standard pattern of white leaders and black followers. If the cultural gap is narrow it calls for some degree of submission of white to Negro leadership. This in the United States is so unusual a pattern that it must be handled carefully.

Our original constituents upon the board of directors were intensely and vividly interested in finding some practical solution to the Negro problems. They were not for the most part rich men, and it was necessary to secure funds. The original idea was that rich philanthropists would gladly contribute, but this assumption was to no large extent realized. On the contrary, large numbers of colored people and many white people of small means contributed through membership and donations. The major support of the organization during its effective years came from the colored people themselves, as was natural and logical.

The secretary at first was little more than an office executive. Then we hired a trained white man at a high salary, who knew methods of modern publicity and propaganda. He came at a critical time, 1917, and did a fine job, especially in increasing membership and funds. In 1920 he resigned, and was replaced by James Weldon Johnson, whose power as executive was shared with the chairman of the board. The chairman represented the board and gave considerable time as real executive. The executive power was also shared in another and rather unusual way, and that was with the editor and publisher of the *Crisis*.

The National Association for the Advancement of Colored People never accepted financial responsibility for the *Crisis*. When they first allowed me to publish it in November, 1910, it was on condition that the Association would be willing to meet any deficit which did not exceed fifty dollars a month. It was for a long time a source of great pride to me that it was never called upon to pay any deficit. On the other hand, the Association paid my salary and a part of the office expense up until January 1, 1916. From that time until 1933, the *Crisis* was self-supporting, and received and disbursed over a half million dollars and distributed seven and a half million copies. The *Crisis* came thus to form a distinct department of the NAACP, with its own office and clerical force and its own funds kept separate from those of the organization.

There soon came the delicate matter of policy; of how far I should express my own ideas and reactions in the *Crisis*, or the studied judgment of the organization. From the first to last, I thought strongly on this point and as I still think, rightly; I determined to make the opinion expressed in the *Crisis* a personal opinion; because, as I argued, no organization can express definite and clear-cut opinions; so far as this organization as such came to conclusions, it would state them in its annual resolutions; but the *Crisis* would state openly the opinion of its editor, so long, of course, as that opinion was in general agreement with that of the organization. This was a dangerous and delicate matter, bound eventually to break down, in case there arose any considerable divergence of opinion between the organization and editor. It was perhaps rather unusual that for two decades, the two lines of thinking ran so largely in agreement.

If, on the other hand, the *Crisis* had not been in a sense a personal organ and the expression of myself, it could not possibly have attained its popularity and effectiveness. It would have been the dry kind of organ that so many societies support for purposes of reference and not for reading. The editor was thus allowed wide latitude for his expression of opinion, chiefly because that freedom cost the Association nothing, gave it free publicity which otherwise would have cost thousands of dollars, and was backed by readers and subscribers who increased more rapidly than the direct membership of the Association, and became in time a body of perhaps a quarter of a million persons. The first real although tacit decision as to my power over the policy of the *Crisis* led to a change in the chairmanship of the board, which Joel Spingarn then assumed.

The next question arose over the matter of political advice in the first Wilson election. No action was taken, but some members of the board doubted the wisdom of our support of the Democratic Party. The question of a segregated camp for Negro officers again split the board; but as the chairman and the editor were in agreement, the power of the Association was used for the establishment of the camp and later the board agreed that this had been the proper procedure. After I had gone to Europe

and held the first Pan-African Congress and began to
advocate Pan Africanism, the board quite decidedly refused to accept this new activity as part of its program;
but it did not for a moment object to my further advocacy
of Pan Africanism so long as I was responsible for any
costs.

Then came the depression. The revenue of the *Crisis*
began to fall off as early as 1924 and 1925. Our circulation
dropped steadily until by 1933 it was scarcely more than
ten thousand paid subscriptions. If the magazine was to
be carried on, evidently the Association would have to
share its cost, and if it did so, it would have a right to a
larger voice in its conduct and policy.

If the *Crisis* had continued self-supporting during the
depression, I would have felt myself free gradually to force
upon the thinking Negro world and the NAACP a new
economic program. But the *Crisis* was no longer self-supporting. The mass of Negroes, even the intelligent and
educated, progressively being thrown out of work, did not
have money for food, much less for magazines. I found
myself, therefore, seeking support from an organization
for a program in which they did not wholeheartedly believe; and particularly this disbelief and growing suspicion
centered around the new conception which I had for mass
action on the part of the Negro.

By 1930, I had become convinced that the basic policies
and ideals of the Association must be modified and
changed; that in a world where economic dislocation had
become so great as in ours, a mere appeal based on the
old liberalism, a mere appeal to justice and further effort
at legal decision, was missing the essential need; that the

essential need was to guard and better the chances of Negroes, educated and ignorant, to earn a living, safeguard their income, and raise the level of their employment. I did not believe that a further prolongation of looking for salvation from the whites was feasible. So far as they were ignorant of the results of race prejudice, we had taught them; but so far as their race prejudice was built and increasingly built on the basis of the income which they enjoyed and their anti-Negro bias consciously or unconsciously formulated in order to protect their wealth and power, in so far our whole program must be changed, and we must seek to increase the power and particularly the economic organization among Negroes to meet this new situation. It was this change of emphasis that I proposed to discuss and promote through the columns of the *Crisis*.

In addition to this, the meaning and implications of the new psychology had begun slowly to penetrate my thought. My own study of psychology under William James had pre-dated the Freudian era, but it had prepared me for it. I now began to realize that in the fight against race prejudice, we were not facing simply the rational, conscious determination of white folk to oppress us; we were facing age-long complexes sunk now largely to unconscious habit and irrational urge, which demanded on our part not only the patience to wait, but the power to entrench ourselves for a long siege against the strongholds of color caste. It was this long-term program, which called first of all for economic stability on the part of the Negro; for such economic foundations as would enable the colored people of America to earn a living, provide for their own social uplift, so far as this was neglected by the state and

nation, and at the same time carry out even more systematically and with greater and better-planned determination, the fight that the NAACP had inaugurated in
1910.

Meantime, the Association itself was receiving less of
its income from colored supporters and more from white
charity. It was illogical to expect that white philanthropy
would be willing to support the economic program which
I had in mind. Moreover, the colored group did not
wholly agree with me. I realized that too much in later
years the Association had attracted the higher income
group of colored people, who regarded it as a weapon to
attack the sort of social discrimination which especially
irked them; rather than as an organization to improve the
status and power of the whole Negro group. If now the
Association was willing to allow me the same freedom of
expression in the crippled *Crisis* that I had had when the
Crisis was economically independent, I was willing to try
to set forth my new point of view while giving anyone else
who had an idea, full opportunity to express it. I wanted,
not dogmatically but inquiringly, to find out the function
of a minority group like ours, in the impending social
change. I thought that this was the highest service that
any real periodical of opinion could do for its constituents.
If we had had at this time leisure for thought and argument, my program could have been carried out; but unfortunately it happened that here dogma entered and
dogma from a source that made my new point of view
easily misinterpreted and suspected and this was the dogma
of the American Communist Party applied first and most
unfortunately to the Scottsboro cases, in which our organ-

ization was deeply interested and involved. Had it not been for their senseless interference, these poor victims of Southern injustice would today be free. To insure their freedom, we had followed a tried and successful pattern: we had secured the services of Clarence Darrow and with him a respectable firm of local white lawyers. With quiet and careful methods, the Scottsboro victims would have been freed in a couple of years without fanfare or much publicity.

But in the case of the Communists the actual fate of these victims was a minor matter. The leaders of Russian communism thought that they saw here a chance to foment revolution in the United States. This crass instance of cruelty and injustice; where ignorant colored boys, stealing a ride on a freight train, were faced with the ridiculous charge of attacking two white prostitutes on the same train, who were amply protected, if they needed protection, by white hoodlums, seemed to Russia an unusual opportunity to expose American race prejudice and to arouse the Negroes and the working classes of America and the world. All this was based on abysmal ignorance of the pattern of race prejudice in the United States. About the last thing calculated to arouse the white workers of America would be the defense of a Negro accused of attacking a white woman, even though the Negro was probably innocent and the woman a prostitute. This fact the Communists either did not know or ignored. They seized the occasion for agitation in order to forward "the Revolution." They scared respectable lawyers out of the case; they repudiated Clarence Darrow; they made the whole issue turn on property rights and race, and spread this propaganda all over the world. Right as they undoubtedly were on the merits of the case, they were tragically wrong in their methods if they were seeking to free these victims.

This, of course, exasperated our office, the *Crisis* as well as the executive office. But while in the case of the *Crisis,* it left me still determined to work for economic reform as the immediate method of attacking the Negro problem, in the case of the executive office it had the opposite effect of making both Spingarn and others determined to avoid this discussion and any drastic change in the object of the Association.

For this reason the Second Amenia Conference was called, seventeen years after the first. The first Amenia Conference in 1916 met at a strategic time. Our essential agreement on a program of advance was gratifying and epoch-making; but as I now realize, we had not only been hammered into unity by culminating oppression, but prepared for it by spade-work which had gone before, and which for ten years had been preparing the minds of Americans, black and white, for a new deal in race relations and renewed effort toward racial equality. In 1933, the situation was different. We met at the beginning rather than at the end of a period of preparatory discussion. We were still mentally whirling in a sea of inconclusive world discussion. We could not really reach agreement as a group, because of the fact that so many of us as individuals had not made up our own minds on the essentials of coming social change. The attendance was sifted—perhaps too much so; outside of four of the Elder Statesmen, the median age was thirty—persons just out of college; their life work begun but not settled. They were teachers, social workers, professional men, and two artisans.

The discussion and resolutions, while disappointing to both Spingarn and myself, as I now see them, threw a flood of light upon our situation. Four threads of thought entered into our conference: *first,* the fight against race segregation and color discrimination in any form. This was age-old among Negroes and also the bitterly felt contribution of those younger folk, who had experienced race prejudice during the war and the difficulties of getting a decent opportunity to work and live after the war. The *second* thread was Marxian economic determinism. Most of the younger trained college group were convinced that the economic pattern of any civilization determined its development along all cultural lines. In the *third* place everybody present, old and young, was seized with a new concern for the welfare of the great mass of Negro laboring people. They felt that too much in the past we had been thinking of the exceptional folk, the Talented Tenth, the well-to-do; that we must now turn our attention toward the welfare and social uplift of the masses. *Finally,* the old liberalism, resurgent in the leadership of the NAACP officials, wished to reiterate and strengthen everything that we had done in the past, as the only program for the future.

Out of these trends of thought, one can imagine the turmoil and contradiction of our discussion. Our argument was indeterminate and our resolutions contradictory. It was agreed that the primary problem before us was economic, but it was equally certain that this economic problem could not be approached from the point of view of race. The only approach to it must be through the white labor masses who were supposed to accept without great reluctance the new scientific argument that there was no such thing as "race"; and in the midst of this, nearly all the older men and some of the younger men were still trying to insist that the uplift of the Negro in the past and in the future could only take place through the development of superimposed economic and cultural classes; and that we needed in the future to reinforce the liberal program which we had been carrying out in the past.

I was disappointed. I had hoped for such insistence upon the compelling importance of the economic factor that this would lead to a project for a planned program for using the racial segregation, which was at present inevitable, in order that the laboring masses might be able to have built beneath them a strong foundation for self-support and social uplift; and while this fundamental economic process was going on, we could, from a haven of economic security, continue even more effectively than ever to agitate for the utter erasure of the color line.

I stood, as it seemed to me, between paths diverging to extreme communism and violence on the one hand, and extreme reaction toward plutocracy on the other. I saw disaster for American Negroes in following a set determination to ignore race hate and nearing instead a creed of eventual violence and revolution; simply because a single great nation, having perhaps no other alternative, had started this way, this path was for American Negroes, to my mind, nonsense. The nonsense did not end here; it was just as nonsensical for us to assume that the program which we had espoused in 1910 was going to work in 1950. We had got to prepare ourselves for a reorganization of society especially and fundamentally in industry. And for that reason we had got to work as a group toward the socialization of our own wealth and the establishment of such social objects in the nation and in the world.

Spingarn was disappointed and in some degree impatient. I remember one amusing incident: there was a young man in attendance (we will call him Jones), well-educated and in some ways brilliant, but on the other hand, a communist and also irresponsible and unreliable. The members of the conference had been invited up one day to the Spingarn home, a beautiful spacious country mansion with pools and gardens in the English style. Jones stood in the parlor and grinned; and said aloud to the visitors: "Comes the revolution, and Commissar Jones will live here!" Spingarn did not appreciate the joke.

The end of it all was inconclusive resolutions and no agreement; and greater conviction on the part of the executive office that discussion of economic change and organization among colored people to effect a stronger economic position, was not in the line of the policy of the NAACP; and that neither the *Crisis* nor anyone else ought to discuss these matters nor agitate them. I began to see that for a second time in my life my occupation was gone, unless I made a very complete surrender of my convictions. I was not and am not a communist. I do not believe in the dogma of inevitable revolution in order to right economic wrong. I think war is worse than hell, and that it seldom or never forwards the advance of the world.

On the other hand, I believed and still believe that Karl

Marx was one of the greatest men of modern times and that he put his finger squarely upon our difficulties when he said that economic foundations, the way in which men earn their living, are the determining factors in the development of civilization, in literature, religion, and the basic pattern of culture. And this conviction I had to express or spiritually die.

My leadership was a leadership solely of ideas. I never was, nor ever will be, personally popular. This was not simply because of my idiosyncrasies but because I despise the essential demagoguery of personal leadership; of that hypnotic ascendancy over men which carries out objectives regardless of their value or validity, simply by personal loyalty and admiration. In my case I withdrew sometimes ostentatiously from the personal nexus, but I sought all the more determinedly to force home essential ideas.

I think I may say without boasting that in the period from 1910 to 1930 I was a main factor in revolutionizing the attitude of the American Negro toward caste. My stinging hammer blows made Negroes aware of themselves, confident of their possibilities and determined in self-assertion. So much so that today common slogans among the Negro people are taken bodily from the words of my mouth.

But of course, no idea is perfect and forever valid. Always to be living and apposite and timely, it must be modified and adapted to changing facts. What I began to realize was that the heights and fastnesses which we black folk were assailing, could not in America be gained by sheer force of assault, because of our relatively small numbers. They could only be gained as the majority of Americans were persuaded of the rightness of our cause and joined with us in demanding our recognition as full citizens. This process must deal not only with conscious rational action, but with irrational and unconscious habit, long buried in folkways and custom. Intelligent propaganda, legal enactment and reasoned action must attack the conditioned reflexes of race hate and change them.

Slowly but surely I came to see that for many years, perhaps many generations, we could not count on any such majority; that the whole set of the white world in America, in Europe and in the world was too determinedly against racial equality, to give power and persuasiveness to our agitation. Therefore, I began to emphasize and restate certain implicit aspects of my former ideas. I tried to say to the American Negro: during the time of this frontal attack which you are making upon American and European prejudice, and with your unwavering statement and restatement of what is right and just, not only for us, but in the long run, for all men; during this time, there are certain things you must do for your own survival and self-preservation. You must work together and in unison; you must evolve and support your own social institutions; you must transform your attack from the foray of self-assertive individuals to the massed might of an organized body. You must put behind your demands, not simply American Negroes, but West Indians and Africans, and all the colored races of the world. These things I began to say with no lessening, or thought of lessening of my emphasis upon the essential rightness of what we had been asking for a generation in political and civic and social equality.

It was clear to me that agitation against race prejudice and a planned economy for bettering the economic condition of the American Negro were not antagonistic ideals but part of one ideal; that it did not increase segregation; the segregation was there and would remain for many years. But now I proposed that in economic lines, just as in lines of literature and religion, segregation should be planned and organized and carefully thought through. This plan did not establish a new segregation; it did not advocate segregation as the final solution of the race problem; exactly the contrary; but it did face the facts and faced them with thoughtfully mapped effort.

Of course I soon realized that in this matter of segregation I was touching an old and bleeding sore in Negro thought. From the eighteenth century down the Negro intelligentsia has regarded segregation as the visible badge of their servitude and as the object of their unceasing attack. The upper class Negro has almost never been nationalistic. He has never planned or thought of a Negro state or a Negro church or a Negro school. This solution has always been a thought up-surging from the mass, because of pressure which they could not withstand and which compelled a racial institution or chaos. Continually such institutions were founded and developed, but this took place against the advice and best thought of the intelligentsia.

American Negroes have always feared with perfect fear their eventual expulsion from America. They have been willing to submit to caste rather than face this. The reasons have varied but today they are clear: Negroes have no Zion. There is no place where they can go today and not be subject to worse caste and greater disabilities from the dominant white imperialistic world than they suffer here today. On the other hand there is no likelihood just now of their being forcibly expelled. So far as that is concerned, there was no likelihood ten years ago of the Jews being expelled from Germany. The cases are far from parallel. There is a good deal more profit in cheap Negro labor than in Jewish fellow citizens, which brings together strange bed-fellows for the protection of the Negro. On the other hand one must remember that this is a day of astonishing change, injustice and cruelty; and that many Americans of stature have favored the transportation of Negroes and they were not all of the mental caliber of the present junior senator from Mississippi. As the Negro develops from an easily exploitable, profit-furnishing laborer to an intelligent independent self-supporting citizen, the possibility of his being pushed out of his American fatherland may easily be increased rather than diminished. We may be expelled from the United States as the Jew is being expelled from Germany.

At any rate it is the duty of American Negroes today to examine this situation not with hysteria and anger but with calm forethought. Whether self-segregation for his protection, for inner development and growth in intelligence and social efficiency, will increase his acceptability to white Americans or not, that growth must go on. And whatever the event may bring, it must be faced as men face crises and not with surprise and helpless amazement. It was astonishing and disconcerting, and yet for the philosopher perfectly natural, that this change of my emphasis was crassly and stupidly misinterpreted by the Negroes. Appropriating as their own (and indeed now it was their own) my long insistence on self-respect and self-assertion and the demand for every equality on the part of the Negro, they seemed determined to insist that my newer emphasis was a repudiation of the older; that now I wanted segregation; that now I did not want equality; that now I was asking for black people to act as black people and forcibly overthrow the dominance of the white.

I can see an assembly in Philadelphia, when I went down to say to the colored people that the demand of Leslie Hill to make the Cheyney school a college supported by the state of Pennsylvania, was wise and inevitable. "It will be a Negro college!" shouted the audience, as though such a thing had never been heard of. "It will be Segregation," said a woman, who had given much of her life to furthering the fight for Negro equality. I can see her now, brown, tense, bitter, as she lashed me with the accusation of advocating the very segregation that I had been fighting. It was in vain that I pointed out that Cheyney was already segregated; that without the help of the state, the school would die; that with the help of the state it could be a great school, regardless of the fact that its teachers and students were Negroes. And moreover, there was no reason in the world why some of the teachers and some of its students could not eventually be white.

Another incident occurred during these years, which shows the increasing paradox of race segregation in the United States. The Rosenwald Fund proposed in 1931 to start a crusade for better hospitalization for Negroes.

Negro health needed to be safeguarded and improved and one of the main reasons for the Negro sickness and death rate was the fact that Negroes were not furnished hospital facilities; and that their physicians were very often not admitted to medical schools for study nor to hospitals for practice. They proposed therefore to help in the building and equipment of Negro hospitals and in the education of Negro physicians.

Just how far they proposed to go, they did not make clear because before they had thoroughly matured their plans they were bitterly attacked by Dr. Louis Wright of New York and others. Louis Wright was a special favorite of mine. The stepfather who brought him up was my own family physician for years. I had followed Wright's career as he fought his way through Harvard and made a fine record. He began practice in New York and then at the time of the World War went to France as a captain in a colored medical unit of the AEF and there had a distinguished career. He came back and fought his way into prominence in the Harlem Hospital of New York, which up to his time had admitted no Negro physicians, although nearly all the patients were Negroes. In time Louis Wright became an authority in many branches of surgery and medicine; he was with reluctance admitted to the American College of Surgeons and was appointed one of the seven members of the Board of Surgeons of the Police Department of New York. He is an outstanding man; gifted and thoroughly unselfish, and the one thing that he fought with unceasing energy was discrimination against Negroes in hospitals, whether as medical practitioners or patients. He violently attacked the Rosenwald board saying that the method of segregated hospitals and segregated training for Negro physicians was not the way to go at the matter; that what ought to be done was to insist in season and out that Negroes be admitted to medical schools and hospital practice without regard to color.

I saw and saw clearly the argument on both sides to this controversy. I was heart and soul with Louis Wright in his fight against segregation and yet I knew that for a hundred years in this America of ours it was going to be at least partially in vain. I was heart and soul with the Rosenwald Fund; what Negroes need is hospital treatment now; and what Negro physicians need is hospital practice; and to meet their present need, poor hospitals are better than none; segregated hospitals are better than those where the Negro patients are neglected or relegated to the cellar.

Yet in this case I was unable to decide or take part. I wrote a rather perfunctory editorial in general upholding Dr. Wright, but I was sorry to see the larger plan of the Rosenwald Fund curtailed and cut down to a mere ghost of its first self. Whatever the merits of this particular controversy were, I am certain that for many generations American Negroes in the United States have got to accept separate medical institutions. They may dislike it; they may and ought to protest against it; nevertheless it will remain for a long time their only path to health, to education, to economic survival.

The NAACP from the beginning faced this bogey. It was not, never had been, and never could be an organization that took an absolute stand against race segregation of any sort under all circumstances. This would be a stupid stand in the face of clear and incontrovertible facts. When the NAACP was formed, the great mass of Negro children were being trained in Negro schools; the great mass of Negro churchgoers were members of Negro churches; the great mass of Negro citizens lived in Negro neighborhoods; the great mass of Negro voters voted with the same political party; and the mass of Negroes joined with Negroes and co-operated with Negroes in order to fight the extension of this segregation and to move toward better conditions. What was true in 1910 was still true in 1940 and will be true in 1970. But with this vast difference: that the segregated Negro institutions are better organized, more intelligently planned and more efficiently conducted, and today form in themselves the best and most compelling argument for the ultimate abolition of the color line.

To have started out in this organization with a slogan "no segregation," would have been impossible. What we did say was no increase in segregation; but even that stand we were unable to maintain. Whenever we found that an increase of segregation was in the interest of the Negro race, naturally we had to advocate it. We had to advocate better teachers for Negro schools and larger appropriation of funds. We had to advocate a segregated camp for the training of Negro officers in the World War. We had to advocate group action of Negro voters in elections. We had to advocate all sorts of organized movement among Negroes to fight oppression and in the long run end segregation.

On the other side, white friends and enemies were rather gleeful in having so apt a club fashioned to their hands. "Chauvinism!" they said, when I urged Pan African solidarity for the accomplishment of universal democracy. "Race prejudice," they intimated, was just as reprehensible when shown by black toward white as when shown by white toward black. Here again it was nearly useless to reiterate. So long as we were fighting a color line, we must strive by color organization. We have no choice. If in time, the fight for Negro equality degenerates into organized murder for the suppression of whites, then our last case is no better than our first; but this need not be, if we are level-headed and clear-sighted, and work for the emancipation of all men from caste through the organization and determination of the present victims of caste.

All this is bound to right itself logically in the minds of American Negroes and Africans, and West Indians, once it has been thoroughly digested and thought through. But the domination of ideas always has this disadvantage in the presence of active, living, personal dictatorship. It is slow, painfully slow. It works with the vast deliberation or perhaps that lack of rational thought which is characteristic of the human mind; but its ultimate triumph is inevitable and complete, so long as the ideas are kept clear and before the minds of men. I shall not live to see entirely the triumph of this, my newer emphasis; but it will triumph just as much and just as completely as did my advocacy of agitation and self-assertion. It is indeed a part of that same original program; it is its natural and inevitable fulfillment.

No sooner had I come to this conclusion than I soon saw that I was out of touch with my organization and that the question of leaving it was only a matter of time. This was not an easy decision; to give up the *Crisis* was like giving up a child; to leave the National Association was leaving the friends of a quarter of a century. But on the other hand, staying meant silence, a repudiation of what I was thinking and planning. Under such circumstances, what could I do? I had seen the modern world as few of my fellow workers had: West African villages, Jamaican homes, Russian communism, German disaster, Italian fascism, Portuguese and Spanish life, France and England repeatedly, and every state in the United States. I knew something of the seething world. I could seek through my editorship of the *Crisis* slowly but certainly to change the ideology of the NAACP and of the Negro race into a racial program for economic salvation along the paths of peace and organization.

There were two alternatives: to change the board of directors of the NAACP so as to substitute a group which agreed with this program, or to leave the Association. If the first could be done without a prolonged fight, I was willing to undertake it. I was appointed a member of the next nominating committee; five new members were proposed who would have begun the reorganization. When, however, the committee gave its report the majority had changed from the persons agreed upon and substituted two or three excellent persons who unfortunately were either absolutely reactionary in their social and economic outlook or basically ignorant.

The Association seemed to me not only unwilling to move toward the left in its program but even stepped decidedly toward the right. And what astonished me most was that this economic reaction was voiced even more by the colored members of the Board of Directors than the white. One could realize why a rich white liberal should suspect fundamental economic change, but it was most difficult for me to understand that the younger and more prosperous Negro professional men, merchants, and investors were clinging to the older ideas of property, ownership and profits even more firmly than the whites. The liberal white world saw the change that was coming despite their wish. The upper class colored world did not anticipate nor understand it.

When now I came advocating new, deliberate and purposeful segregation for economic defense in precisely the lines of business and industry whither the NAACP was not prepared to follow it was not an absolute difference of principle, but it was a grave difference as to further procedure. When I criticized the Secretary for his unsound explanation of the historic stand of the NAACP on segregation, the Board of Directors voted May 21, 1934, "that the *Crisis* is the organ of the Association and no salaried officer of the Association shall criticize the policy, work or officers of the Association in the pages of the *Crisis*." Thereupon I forthwith gave up my connection with the Association saying:

"In thirty-five years of public service my contribution to the settlement of the Negro problems has been mainly candid criticism based on a careful effort to know the facts. I have not always been right, but I have been sincere, and I am unwilling at this late day to be limited in the expression of my honest opinions in the way in which the Board proposes. . . . I am, therefore, resigning, . . . this resignation to take effect immediately." The board refused to accept this resignation and asked me to reconsider. I did so, but finally wrote, June 26, "I appreciate the good will and genuine desire to bridge an awkward break which your action indicated, and yet it is clear to me, and I think to the majority of the Board, that under the circumstances my resignation must stand."

In finally accepting my resignation the Board was kind enough to say in part: "He founded the *Crisis* without a cent of capital, and for many years made it completely self-supporting, reaching a maximum monthly circulation at the end of the World War of 100,000. This is an unprecedented achievement in American journalism, and in itself worthy of a distinguished tribute. But the ideas which he propounded in it and in his books and essays transformed the Negro world as well as a large portion of the liberal white world, so that the whole problem of the relation of black and white races has ever since had a completely new orientation. He created, what never existed before, a Negro intelligentsia, and many who have never read a word of his writings are his spiritual disciples and descendants. Without him the Association could never have been what it was and is.

"The Board has not always seen eye to eye with him in regard to various matters, and cannot subscribe to some of his criticism of the Association and its officials. But such differences in the past have in no way interfered with his usefulness, but rather on the contrary. For he had been selected because of his independence of judgment, his fearlessness in expressing his convictions, and his acute and wide-reaching intelligence. A mere yes-man could not have attracted the attention of the world, could not even have stimulated the Board itself to further study of various important problems. We shall be the poorer for his loss, in intellectual stimulus, and in searching analysis of the vital problems of the American Negro; no one in the Association can fill his place with the same intellectual grasp. We therefore offer him our sincere thanks for the services he has rendered, and we wish him all happiness in all that he may now undertake."

I had already for some years begun to canvass the possibility of a change of work. This, of course, is not easy when a person is over sixty years of age. If he has not had the grace to die before this, he ought, in accordance with prevalent public opinion, at least to be willing to stop acting and thinking. I did not agree with that. I thought of many possibilities, but at last determined to accept an offer that had been made to me quietly in 1929, and periodically repeated from time to time when John Hope of Atlanta came to town. We had been close friends since 1897. We taught together until 1910. Hope had joined the Niagara Movement and the NAACP. We met in France in 1918 while he was a YMCA secretary, and I promoting Pan Africa. Always when he came to New York, we did a theater and a dinner, and discussed the reformation of the world. When he became President of the newly organized Atlanta University, he invited me to join him.

Of course, this change of work had certain unpleasant necessities. It would not only involve giving up the *Crisis* and my connection with the Association. It also involved the cold douche of a return to life in the South. I knew the South. In part I had been educated there. I had spent thirteen years teaching in Georgia and during my connection with the NAACP nearly every year I traveled in the

South to keep myself closely acquainted with its problems. The South of 1933 was not the South of 1897. In many respects it had improved and the relations between the races were better. Nevertheless the South is not a place where a man of Negro descent would voluntarily and without good reason choose to live. Its civilization is decidedly lower than that of the North. Its state and local governments are poor and full of incompetency and graft, and its whole polity is menaced by mass hysteria and mob-law. Its police system is wretched and the low grade white policeman full of crude race hate is the ruler who comes closest and in most immediate contact with black folk of all classes. There is a caste system based on color, fortified in law and even more deeply entrenched in custom, which meets and coerces the dark man at nearly every step: in trains, in street cars, in elevators, in offices, in education, in recreation, in religion and in graveyards. The economic organization is still in the nineteenth century with ruthless exploitation, low wages, child labor, debt peonage, and profit in crime. The better classes, with gracious manners and liberal outlook, exist and slowly grow; but with these I would have little contact and fear of the mob would restrain their meeting me or listening to me.

All this I faced, but I saw too the compensations. After all, the place to study a social problem is where it centers and not elsewhere. The Negro problem in the United States centers in the southern South. There in the place of its greatest concentration, forces are working for its solution and the greatest of these forces are institutions like Atlanta University. The university throws around its professors and students a certain protective coloration.

It is an inner community surrounded by beauty with unusual chances for intellectual and social contact. To a
degree it furnishes recreation and avenues to culture. Our
library without doubt is the best in Atlanta; our music
is unsurpassed and the chances here for quiet contemplation and the intellectual life are considerable.

Then too, I could not forget that even in New York,
with all its opportunity for human contact, with its un-
rivaled facilities for a center of world thought and culture,
it was nevertheless no heaven for black folk. Negroes were
not welcome to its hotels and restaurants nor to most of its
clubs and organizations. Contact with human beings despite color is far wider than in Georgia; but yet, it is not
wide. Theaters and great music center in New York as
nowhere else in America. But they are very costly; a
theater once a month and opera once a year was as much
as I could afford. By careful choice and delicate prevision
I may in New York foot a path of broad cultural contact
and wide physical freedom; it would be difficult to find a
quiet, clean place to live; but if I can earn a living, I can
be fairly content. I should certainly have there no such
dread of the white mob and the police as Negroes must
have in the southern South. Weighing and balancing all
these considerations, I came back to Atlanta. In a sense
I returned to my ivory tower, not so much for new scientific research, as for interpretation and reflection; and for
making a record of what I had seen and experienced.

The situation to which I returned was new. Back as
early as 1905, I had proposed to the seven colored colleges
of Atlanta the beginning of efforts toward uniting these
various institutions into one university. We actually once

had a meeting at Spelman, but the dean was definitely opposed. She said crisply that if her head was going to be taken off, she would prefer to bite it off herself. I turned then in 1909 to John Hope, the president of Morehouse, and we worked out an interchange of lectures between Morehouse and Atlanta University. He wrote me in 1910: "I hope and believe this is the beginning of new and larger things in an educational way among our colored institutions. . . . I feel down-right enthusiasm over the beginning that our two schools made this year and hope that, now that we have made a start and have some slight idea of what can be accomplished, the two schools may next year do larger things." Hope was then president of Morehouse College, but in 1929, he realized our dream in the affiliation of three Negro colleges of Atlanta in the new Atlanta University, with himself as first president.

Far back in 1910 before leaving Atlanta University I had read before the American Historical Association a paper on "Reconstruction and Its Benefits," which greatly exercised Ulrich Phillips, protagonist of the slave South, but brought praise from Dunning of Columbia, Hart of Harvard and others. I was convinced then, and am more certain since, that the reason for certain adjectives applied to Reconstruction is purely racial. Reconstruction was "tragic," "terrible," a "great mistake," and a "humiliation," not because of what actually happened: people suffered after the Civil War, but people suffer after all wars; and the suffering in the South was no greater than in dozens of other centers of murder and destruction. No, the "tragedy" of Reconstruction was because here an attempt was initiated to make American democracy and the tenets of the Declaration of Independence apply not only to white men, but to black men. While still in the *Crisis* office, through a grant from the Rosenwald Fund I had begun a history of the black man's part in Reconstruction. This was my thesis. Two years' work at Atlanta University finished my "Black Reconstruction" and it was published in 1935.

Next I naturally turned my thought toward putting into permanent form that economic program of the Negro which I believed should succeed, and implement the long fight for political and civil rights and social equality which it was my privilege for a quarter of a century to champion. I tried to do this in a preliminary way, through a little study of the "Negro and the New Deal" which I was asked to undertake in 1936 by the colored "Associates in Negro Folk Education," working under the American Association for Adult Education. The editor of this series, Alain Locke, pressed me for the manuscript and by working hard I finished it and was paid for it just before my trip abroad in 1936. I think I made a fair and pretty exhaustive study of the experience of the Negro from 1933 to 1936 and by way of summing up I appended a statement and credo which I had worked out through correspondence with a number of the younger Negro scholars. It was this:

1. We American Negroes are threatened today with lack of opportunity to work according to gifts and training and lack of income sufficient to support healthy families according to standards demanded by modern culture.

2. In industry, we are a labor reservoir, fitfully employed and paid a wage below subsistence; in agriculture, we are largely disfranchised peons; in public education, we tend to be dis-

inherited illiterates; in higher education, we are the parasites of reluctant and hesitant philanthropy.

3. In the current reorganization of industry, there is no adequate effort to secure us a place in industry, to open opportunity for Negro ability, or to give us security in age or unemployment.

4. Not by the development of upper classes anxious to exploit the workers, nor by the escape of individual genius into the white world, can we effect the salvation of our group in America. And the salvation of this group carries with it the emancipation not only of the darker races of men who make the vast majority of mankind, but of all men of all races. We, therefore, propose this:

BASIC AMERICAN NEGRO CREED

A. As American Negroes, we believe in unity of racial effort, so far as this is necessary for self-defense and self-expression, leading ultimately to the goal of a united humanity and the abolition of all racial distinctions.

B. We repudiate all artificial and hate-engendering deification of race separation as such; but just as sternly, we repudiate an ennervating philosophy of Negro escape into an artificially privileged white race which has long sought to enslave, exploit and tyrannize over all mankind.

C. We believe that the Talented Tenth among American Negroes, fitted by education and character to think and do, should find primary employment in determining by study and measurement the present field and demand for racial action and the method by which the masses may be guided along this path.

D. We believe that the problems which now call for such racial planning are Employment, Education and Health; these three: but the greatest of these is Employment.

E. We believe that the labor force and intelligence of twelve million people is more than sufficient to supply their own wants and make their advancement secure. Therefore, we believe that, if carefully and intelligently planned, a co-operative Negro industrial system in America can be established in the midst of and in conjunction with the surrounding national industrial organization and in intelligent accord with that reconstruction of the economic basis of the nation which must sooner or later be accomplished.

F. We believe that Negro workers should join the labor movement and affiliate with such trade unions as welcome them and treat them fairly. We believe that Workers' Councils organized by Negroes for interracial understanding should strive to fight race prejudice in the working class.

G. We believe in the ultimate triumph of some form of Socialism the world over; that is, common ownership and control of the means of production and equality of income.

H. We do not believe in lynching as a cure for crime; nor in war as a necessary defense of culture; nor in violence as the only path to economic revolution. Whatever may have been true in other times and places, we believe that today in America we can abolish poverty by reason and the intelligent use of the ballot, and above all by that dynamic discipline of soul and sacrifice of comfort which, revolution or no revolution, must ever be the only real path to economic justice and world peace.

I. We conceive this matter of work and equality of adequate income as not the end of our effort, but the beginning of the rise of the Negro race in this land and the world over, in power, learning and accomplishment.

J. We believe in the use of our vote for equalizing wealth through taxation, for vesting the ultimate power of the state in the hands of the workers; and as an integral part of the working class, we demand our proportionate share in administration and public expenditure.

K. This is and is designed to be a program of racial effort and this narrowed goal is forced upon us today by the unyielding determination of the mass of the white race to enslave, exploit and insult Negroes; but to this vision of work, organization and service, we welcome all men of all colors so long as their subscription to this basic creed is sincere and is proven by their deeds.

This creed proved unacceptable both to the Adult Education Association and to its colored affiliates. Consequently when I returned from abroad the manuscript, although ordered and already paid for, was returned to me as rejected for publication. Just who pronounced the veto I do not know.

I had next two other projects: first, that large mass of material relating to the Negro in the World War, which the NAACP had never made an effort to use or publish. I had been working at that off and on since 1919, and one year had a grant from the Social Science Council. But I had not yet got it in shape for publication. Another project in which I had long been interested was an Encyclopaedia of the Negro. As early as 1909, I had planned an Encyclopaedia Africana and secured on my board of advisers Sir Flinders Petrie, Sir Harry Johnston, Giuseppe Sergi, Dr. J. Deniker, William James, and Franz Boas; and on my proposed board of editors I had practically all the leading Negroes of the United States who were then inclined toward research. My change to New York and the work of starting the *Crisis,* and finally the World War, put this quite out of my mind.

In 1931, the Phelps-Stokes Fund called together a committee to consider a plan of arranging for the preparation and publication of an Encyclopaedia of the Negro. To this first meeting I was not invited as my relations to some of the executives of the Fund during the past had not been cordial. But those who met insisted upon myself and others being invited to the second meeting. Overcoming a natural hesitation I went. Eventually and to me quite unexpectedly I was designated as future chairman of the editorial board, in case the funds for the enterprise should ever be found.

Since the incorporation of the Encyclopaedia in 1932, by the help of a small appropriation from the Phelps-Stokes Fund, I have been planning and working on preliminary arrangements for such an undertaking. We found the great Funds, from bitter experience, encyclopaedia-shy. But, in addition to that, I fear that no money sufficient for the publication of such an encyclopaedia under the leadership of colored scholars and the collaboration of white men can be soon found. I doubt if men would formulate their objection to such a procedure, but after all it would seem to them natural that any such work should be under the domination of white men. At any rate, we have gotten together a definite and completely worked-out plan, even to the subjects and many of the proposed writers, which can in the future be used for an Encyclopaedia of the Negro, a publication sure to come in time.

In 1936, my application to the Oberlaender Trust for a chance to restudy Germany was granted. I spent five months in Germany, and some time in England, France, and Austria, interviewing scholars on the encyclopaedia

project. I then took a two months' trip around the world.
I was not allowed to stop as long in Russia as I would have
liked; but I traversed it in a swift week from Moscow to
Otpur. Then I spent a week in Manchoukuo, ten days in
China, and two weeks in Japan. I seemed confirmed in the
wisdom of my life choice by the panorama of the world
which swept before me in London and Paris; Berlin and
Vienna; Moscow and Mukden; Peiping and Shanghai;
Kyoto and Tokyo; and heavenly Hawaii. Singularly
enough in that journey I was most impressed with the
poignant beauty of the world in the midst of its distress.

For several years I had been importuning my publishers
to get out a new edition of the little book called "The
Negro" published first in 1915 in the Home University
Series. Finally in 1938 they consented by suggesting an
entirely new book. This entailed a good deal of work of
the highest interest and in which I took much satisfaction.
The resulting volume, "Black Folk: Then and Now,"
was published in 1939. Since then I have been interested
in the book I am now writing, a further essay into fiction,
and a university review of race and culture, *Phylon*, born
this year.

In February, 1938, I reached the arresting age of seventy
and despite some effort on my part to escape the immediate consequences of this indiscretion, two of my younger
colleagues, Ira Reid and Rayford Logan, initiated and
carried through a University celebration, with a convoca-
tion, a bust by Portnoff, a dinner and a talk. In that talk
I was called upon to set forth something of my philosophy
of life after traversing so many years. The essence of what
I said can be summed up in these words:

I have been favored among the majority of men in never being compelled to earn my bread and butter by doing work that was uninteresting or which I did not enjoy or of the sort in which I did not find my greatest life interest. This rendered me so content in my vocation that I seldom thought about salary or haggled over it. My first job paid me eight hundred dollars a year and to take it I refused one which offered ten hundred and fifty. I served over a year at the University of Pennsylvania for the munificent sum of six hundred dollars and never railed at fate. I taught and worked at Atlanta University for twelve hundred a year during thirteen effective and happy years. I never once asked for an increase. I went to New York for the salary offered and only asked for an increase there when an efficient new white secretary was hired at a wage above mine. I then asked equal salary. I did not want the shadow of racial discrimination to creep into our salary schedule. I realize now that this rather specious monetary independence may in the end cost me dearly, and land me in time upon some convenient street corner with a tin cup. For I have saved nearly nothing and lost my life insurance in the depression. Nevertheless, I insist that regardless of income, work worth while which one wants to do as compared with highly paid drudgery is exactly the difference between heaven and hell.

I am especially glad of the divine gift of laughter; it has made the world human and lovable, despite all its pain and wrong. I am glad that the partial Puritanism of my upbringing has never made me afraid of life. I have lived completely, testing every normal appetite, feasting on sunset, sea and hill, and enjoying wine, women, and song.

I have seen the face of beauty from the Grand Canyon to the great Wall of China; from the Alps to Lake Baikal; from the African bush to the Venus of Milo.

Perhaps above all I am proud of a straightforward clearness of reason, in part a gift of the gods, but also to no little degree due to scientific training and inner discipline. By means of this I have met life face to face, I have loved a fight and I have realized that Love is God and Work is His prophet; that His ministers are Age and Death.

This makes it the more incomprehensible for me to see persons quite panic-stricken at the approach of their thirtieth birthday and prepared for dissolution at forty. Few of my friends have openly celebrated their fiftieth birthdays, and near none their sixtieth. Of course, one sees some reasons: the disappointment at meager accomplishment which all of us to some extent share; the haunting shadow of possible decline; the fear of death. I have been fortunate in having health and wise in keeping it. I have never shared what seems to me the essentially childish desire to live forever. Life has its pain and evil—its bitter disappointments; but I like a good novel and in healthful length of days, there is infinite joy in seeing the World, the most interesting of continued stories, unfold, even though one misses THE END.

INDEX